Re-Forming Capitalism

Re-Forming Capitalism

Institutional Change in the German Political Economy

Wolfgang Streeck

OXFORD
UNIVERSITY PRESS

OXFORD
UNIVERSITY PRESS

Great Clarendon Street, Oxford OX2 6DP

Oxford University Press is a department of the University of Oxford.
It furthers the University's objective of excellence in research, scholarship,
and education by publishing worldwide in

Oxford New York

Auckland Cape Town Dar es Salaam Hong Kong Karachi
Kuala Lumpur Madrid Melbourne Mexico City Nairobi
New Delhi Shanghai Taipei Toronto

With offices in

Argentina Austria Brazil Chile Czech Republic France Greece
Guatemala Hungary Italy Japan Poland Portugal Singapore
South Korea Switzerland Thailand Turkey Ukraine Vietnam

Oxford is a registered trade mark of Oxford University Press
in the UK and in certain other countries

Published in the United States
by Oxford University Press Inc., New York

© Oxford University Press 2009

The moral rights of the author have been asserted
Database right Oxford University Press (maker)

First published 2009

British Library Cataloguing in Publication Data

Data available

Library of Congress Cataloging in Publication Data

Data available

Typeset by SPI Publisher Services, Pondicherry, India
Printed in Great Britain
on acid-free paper by
the MPG Books Group

ISBN 978-0-19-955677-9

10 9 8 7 6 5 4 3 2 1

Preface

In writing this book I benefited from the support of two truly outstanding institutions. When I started, in February 2007, I had just begun a half-year term as a Visiting Scholar at the Russell Sage Foundation in New York. When I finished a year later, I had been back at the Max Planck Institute for the Study of Societies in Cologne, also known as the MPIfG, for several months. Nobody in the world of social science knows better than Eric Wanner at Russell Sage how important it is for scholars to be given time, not just to do research, but also to reflect in quiet and solitude on their findings. And nowhere else in the world could I have found a more congenial and exciting environment than at the MPIfG, where new ideas come up all the time in projects, seminars, conferences, and discussions and may be explored in a scholarly community that includes everyone, from famous leaders in their fields to graduate students, until they can finally be written up, sometimes at a place like the Russell Sage Foundation on the East Side of Manhattan.

The present book had a long period of gestation, going back to the mid-1990s. It was then that I became more convinced than ever that what was going on in Germany's political economy might offer important general insights. A research group then began to emerge at the MPIfG that came to include scholars, mostly at an early stage of their career, like Anke Hassel, Jürgen Beyer, and Bernhard Ebbinghaus; Martin Höpner and Britta Rehder; and Christine Trampusch and Armin Schäfer. Over time, the group also included several graduate students, among them were Gregory Jackson and, of course, Martin and Britta, who later joined the institute as full-time researchers. In addition there were my colleagues as directors, Renate Mayntz and Fritz Scharpf, both now retired but still very involved in research, and later Jens Beckert, who joined the institute in early 2005. Renate and Fritz are a source of continuing inspiration, the former because of her unflinching conviction that social science can be methodologically sound without having to become scientistic or irrelevant to the real world, and the latter because of his profound insights into German politics and the politics and economics of the modern welfare state. As to Jens Beckert, he has been reminding all of us about the significant contribution theoretical sociology can make to the study of political economy—an insight that has become fundamental for the further development of our research.

One of the inestimable benefits of an institution like the MPIfG is that it makes it possible to build and maintain extensive working relations with scholars in other countries. So many colleagues outside the institute have contributed directly and indirectly to the ideas developed in this book—without, of course, being in any way responsible for what is still unfinished or, worse, unfounded—that I cannot mention them all. To name just a few, the MPIfG is lucky to have Kathleen Thelen and Colin Crouch as External Members, just as we enjoy the support of our Scientific Advisory Board, chaired by Peter Hall, who knows that without vigorous debate there can be no progress in scholarship. I was also inspired by several sessions of the "Complementarity Project," run jointly in Paris and Cologne by Bruno Amable, Robert Boyer, and me, which included David Marsden and Peter Hall among the participants. And there is also SASE, the Society for the Advancement of Socio-Economics, and its journal, the *Socio-Economic Review*, both of which are great meeting places for ideas and the people that produce and work with them.

As to this book in particular, while it draws extensively on a decade of research at the MPIfG and beyond, trying to pull together the results of a great number of projects, I am especially indebted to Kathleen Thelen, Marius Busemeyer, Martin Höpner, Britta Rehder, Armin Schäfer, and Christine Trampusch, who read the manuscript as it was being written and provided excellent comments and criticism. Above all, Kathy Thelen, cherished colleague and friend for decades now, not only made extremely helpful suggestions but also offered essential encouragement at an early stage, when I sent her the first sketch of what I then expected to become my argument. I am also grateful to faculty and students at the NYU Sociology Department and the Columbia Political Science Department, where I had the opportunity to present my work when it was still in what I hope was progress. Heartfelt thanks must go to my fellow members of the Russell Sage "Class of 2007" who patiently listened to my "European" story during a session of the RSF internal seminar in May 2007, and to my students at Cologne who read the full manuscript and commented on it. Others who did so include Martin Hellwig and David Stark. Here as everywhere, the usual disclaimer applies, according to which nobody but the author can be taken to account for the many imperfections that remain in spite of all the help received.

A book that has come such a long way should not go without a proper dedication. I dedicate this book to my wife, Sylvia, in memory of our time in New York, when she listened patiently to my ideas—at the park and the Public Library, in the subway, and during regular visits to the Metropolitan and, of course, the Brio—and for making me aware that every book must come to an end, because there is only one thing in life that is worth working on forever, and this is not a book.

Wolfgang Streeck

Contents

Contents

List of Figures

List of Tables

Introduction: institutional change, capitalist development

At the end of this book the reader will, I hope, have learned something about the "German model" of political economy and its current transformation—something, however, that will not be reassuring to those who have come to believe in capitalism being and remaining neatly divided in two or more "varieties." In fact one of the main intentions of the book is to convince readers that the time has come to think, again, about the *commonalities* of capitalism. Along the way, readers will also be advised that the institutions of a political economy cannot really be understood one by one, in isolation from one another, but only as elements of the larger social system to which they belong—which in addition must be conceived not as a static *structure*, but as a dynamic *process*. This implies that *institutional change*, while rightly popular in research and theory today, should be regarded not as a subject of its own, but as a constitutive feature of any social formation, which requires social systems of all sorts to be conceived in a way that avoids creating the illusion of static equilibrium as an empirical or ideal condition.

Those who suspect that the agenda of this book is impossibly broad and excessively ambitious are probably right. Reconstructing the evolution over a quarter-century of five institutional complexes, or sectors, of a leading national example of what has been referred to as "nonliberal capitalism" (Streeck and Yamamura 2001), the inquiry proceeds in a quasi-inductive manner, following up on and drawing out the manifold theoretical implications and questions raised by its empirical observations. "Institutional change in the German political economy," to cite the book's subtitle, is shown to have been and to continue to be gradual but nevertheless fundamental and, indeed, historical. Later, as the argument follows the evidence, rather than beginning and sticking with

1

a theoretical problem for which evidence is then selectively adduced, it arrives at propositions that become increasingly daring. For example, "variable sociology," based on the idea of a static property space and with its pretensions at prediction, is suggested to be a systemically flawed approach to social science, constructing reality in a far too mechanistic manner to be able to deal with some of the central issues of contemporary political economy. Systematic attention to history and, in particular, periodicity is urged as a correction to what is suspected to be a static bias in much of today's social theory. Even more fundamentally, the language of institutional analysis, while extensively employed in the construction of the empirical accounts on which theoretical reflection draws, is suggested to be of limited value when it comes to explaining institutional change and identifying its driving causes. This can only be achieved, it is claimed, if institutional analysis is systemically specified with respect to time and place, shifting from a formal to a substantive perspective, and from a concern with institutions in general to one with the unique features of historical social orders—in the present case, of modern capitalism during the period of the dissolution of its postwar institutional form.

As the argument unfolds, a series of far-ranging conclusions are offered based on the empirical material, first on institutional change in general and how to analyze it, and then on the nature and dynamics of contemporary capitalism. I suggest that gradual change in a given institution—or in part of a social order—can be identified and assessed only in the context of other institutions, or in systemic context. I define parallel change following the same pattern in different sectors of the same practical economy as systemic change. As it turns out, in the system under observation, the German political economy after the end of the "Golden Age," parallel, or equidirectional, change in different sectors was continuous. Interdependence between sectors, caused by a multitude of external effects of sectors on one another, first stabilized and then destabilized sectoral institutions and the social order as a whole. Positive externalities, or complementarities, sometimes arose by accident and sometimes by political design, when contingent opportunities offered themselves for purposeful intervention, but they did not last. Indeed "systems," I will argue, are merely moments in continuous processes of change. While stability is a temporary product of social and political construction, change is endemic and in fact may be largely endogenous, external shocks notwithstanding. An especially interesting sort of endogenous change, as observed in my research, is the "dialectical" self-undermining of institutions and social orders in the course of their normal operation. The notion of dialectical change, in turn, raises the issue of time and age as, perhaps, essential properties of social structures. It also draws attention to the possibility of a limited lifetime of institutional configurations, due to positive externalities turning negative and institutional complementarity giving way to mutual undermining of institutions over time.

Ultimately, however, the subject of this book is *not institutions but capitalism.* Continuous, systemic, endemic, and dialectical change, gradual disorganization of institutional structures, slowly decaying institutional complementarity, the emergence of tipping points in historical processes where images of stability and stasis no longer serve constructive purposes etc. are useful concepts for describing and summarizing important formal properties, static and dynamic, of an institutionalized social order. Even the most lucid account of institutional conditions and their change, however, says nothing about the forces by which these were produced; why specific institutions in a specific place and time happen to be structured the way they are and evolve the way they do; and what has kept them from assuming different properties or changing in different ways and directions. Indeed there is nothing in the conceptual apparatus of institutional analysis that would or could by itself preclude specific institutional structures becoming more rather than less centralized, or sectors becoming more rather than less complementary to each other. What institutional forms emerge and how they evolve is *not a matter of form but of substance.* Why institutional change in today's capitalist political economies proceeds the way it does rather than some other way cannot, I suggest, be explained in terms of an institutional theory *as such* but only in terms of a theory *of capitalism* as a substantive, that is, historical social order. It is in this intersection between social form and historical substance that the current book has the, undoubtedly highly immodest, ambition to contribute to theoretical progress.

Considering capitalism as an institutionalized social order, as I will try to show, opens up a perspective in which capitalism is much more than a combination of private property rights and free markets, and indeed more than just an economy. Conceiving of capitalism as a social order draws attention to the micro-dynamics of its enactment and reenactment within a specific context of instituted constraints and opportunities. I claim that a micro-perspective describing the reproduction of capitalism as a process of institutional compliance and noncompliance adds importantly to the macro- and meso-level analyses that predominate in historical-institutionalist political economy. In particular, it helps avoid the fallacies of economistic functionalism and political voluntarism and the tendency to import equilibrium models from economics or systems theory. Providing institutional analysis with a micro-foundation in the form of a theory of institutional action—of what might be referred to as action-centered or action-based institutionalism—makes it possible to offer an account of capitalist development in terms of characteristic conflicts between expected and actual behavior, or between rule-makers and rule-takers. Recognition of the open dynamic of institutional enactment and reproduction at the micro level highlights the inherent insufficiency of static and efficiency-theoretical concepts of social systems. Historical specification of actor models pushes the analysis beyond the empty generalities of "rational choice" and recognizes, for example, the Schumpeterian unruliness of capitalist entrepreneurs as an important source of the entropic tendencies in capitalism that, in turn, elicit continuous efforts at social reconstruction. In other words, an institutional action perspective on capitalism makes it possible to reconstruct capitalist development as a conflictual interplay between the individual pursuit of economic advantage and collective political efforts at restoring and protecting social stability, rather than as a negotiated rearrangement of meso-level institutions in pursuit of national competitiveness. Historically it seems that "political moments" when new institutional forms can or must be forged, like in the years after the Second World War, tend to be followed by periods of entropic erosion of institutions, in capitalism under the impact of the slow grinding force of continuous efforts at the micro level to replace politically imposed social obligations with economically expedient contractual arrangements supporting the expansion of markets, and thereby opening up new opportunities for the accumulation of capital.

The present book uses institutional analysis, and the fine-grained, action-based accounts of structure and process that it makes possible, to learn something about capitalism, *rather than the other way around*. While it is of course far from offering anything like a comprehensive theory of capitalism as an institutional order, I believe it does raise vital issues of political economy that urgently need to be put on the agenda of a discipline that has for some time now contented itself with the reassuring functionalist statics of efficiency-theoretical accounts of "varieties of capitalism." These issues include the following:

(1) *The inherent dynamism and instability of capitalism as a social order.* My research shows that functionalist constructions that view capitalist systems as seeking and remaining in static equilibrium are wishful thinking at best. In an institutional perspective, capitalist actors are most realistically stylized as endowed with an ethos of unruliness that makes

them routinely subvert extant social order in rational-egoistic pursuit of economic gain. Conceiving of the capitalist economy as an impersonal machine for the creation of wealth overlooks the anarchism of the Schumpeterian entrepreneur and the animal spirits of the Keynesian capitalist predator. The modern capitalist ethos of maximization, prohibiting actors from ever being content with their present level of profit or need satisfaction, is reinforced, if necessary, by the institutionally protected possibility of competition—of rival advantage-seekers entering the field and upsetting the established distribution of market share. From an action-theoretical point of view, rather than seeking social integration, capitalist actors are constantly eager to seize new opportunities or defend their existing ones. In the process, collective institutions imposing social obligations on individual actors to restrain themselves are continually undermined, and wherever possible and necessary they are replaced with economically expedient contractual arrangements that are voluntary rather than obligatory.

(2) *The contradictory and conflictual logic of capitalist development.* My account of institutional change in the German political economy suggests that capitalist development is fundamentally misconstrued as a collective and consensual quest for ever higher levels of efficiency—as historical progress, or a contingent lack of such, in a collective effort at "economizing" on transaction costs. Instead I propose that institutional development and institutional change under capitalism are the outcome of a struggle between pressures for an expansion of markets and increasing commodification of social relations on the one hand, with the uncertainty and social instability these entail, and with social demands for political stabilization of relative prices and extant social structures on the other. Pressures for capitalist progress compete for the attention of political government with demands for a stable lifeworld, the latter representing a no less legitimate and in principle no less urgent concern for politics and society than the former. Similarly, national politics cannot be reduced to a pursuit of international competitiveness, but is at least equally concerned with social order and political stability, often to be achieved at the price of allocative efficiency. Reducing politics to economic–technocratic coordination for the purpose of competitive performance in a specific corner of the world market misses both the conflicted nature of capitalism and the limited contribution of allocative efficiency to private profit-making and capital accumulation. The way the conflict between market expansion and protection is, always temporarily, adjudicated—as it was for a while in the "postwar settlement" between capital and labor—depends on

contingent political, economic, technological, and other conditions that are bound to change with time, thereby upsetting the historical balance between capitalist rationalization and social stability and calling for new efforts at social reconstruction.

(3) *The functional complexity of the social-institutional embeddedness of capitalism.* Exploration of the postwar order of democratic capitalism and its current transformation suggests that the institutions that govern economic transactions under capitalism, and the social relations that underlie them, cannot be explained in a functionalist way as devices for the promotion of allocative efficiency or the reduction of transaction costs. While some of the institutions of capitalism support commodification, others contain or prohibit it. Some sort of obligatory limitation of commodification and control of rational egoism may dialectically be needed for markets to work, but it is unlikely to be instituted, nor will rational egoists respect it, *for that purpose.* Countermovements to capitalism may be needed for capitalism to survive, but the survival of capitalism will not usually be their objective. Moreover, the progress of capitalist development may consume noncapitalist social relations essential for efficient capitalist exchange. In a dynamic perspective, the boundaries between market and nonmarket transactions are likely to be continually contested, with what appears to be a historical bias under capitalist institutions and dispositions for markets to expand at the expense of nonmarkets. At the same time, even the strongest pressure to rationalize social institutions is not likely to give rise to a social order entirely subservient to the accumulation of capital. In fact it seems that the pursuit of economic advantage typically occurs, and is bound to occur, in the form of improvised circumvention or experimental reutilization of institutions and institutionalized constraints not originally conceived to support capitalist expansion.

(4) *Capitalism as culture.* Social countermovements to marketization take different forms and pursue different objectives in different stages of capitalist development. To a certain extent, the form and content of social demands for protection from the uncertainties of markets are the product of contingent economic conditions, political mobilization, and cultural evolution. A comparison of the capitalist social formation today with that of postwar "Fordism," for example, suggests that the willingness to live with the uncertainties of markets has greatly increased, not only as a result of economic pressure and, for a broad new lower class, a lack of an alternative, but also because of a decay of the organizational resources required for countermobilization, as well as for cultural reasons, such as changing forms of family life and social integration in general. Even basic

human needs for social integration and stability are shaped by history and vary historically. The evolution of cultural definitions of a good life and of the proper place of markets in it make countermovements against marketization historically specific and give conflicts over market expansion historically different forms of expression. Still, while capitalism can be conceived as a culture, and probably must be so conceived today more than ever, also with respect to dominant patterns of consumption, work performance, and the market-accommodating organization of everyday life, it can be expected that the basic conflict between capitalist markets and the social lifeworld will not disappear even though it is likely to assume new forms and crystallize around new and ever-changing issues.

(5) *The state as a precarious underwriter of capitalist relations of production.* Class conflict between capital and labor may be conceived as one expression among others of an endemic tension between the volatility of self-regulating markets and historically changing needs for some degree and form of stability and security in social life. Empirically, the postwar democratic welfare state was committed to reconciling free markets with a stable social order, by a variety of forms of economic, political, and social intervention. Public interest came to be identified with a combination of *social integration*—to be achieved by way of protection and stabilization of social relations against unpredictably fluctuating relative prices—and *system integration* providing for stable cooperation between capital and labor at the point of production, in spite of their different levels of exposure to risk and uncertainty. However, while state authority under the postwar settlement was drawn into the role of organizer and guarantor of capitalist relations of production, especially by ensuring that political demands for social protection did not go unheeded, its "function" cannot be reduced to "coordination" in an economistic or structural-Marxist sense. Paradoxically, this was partly because protecting the viability of free markets required opposing their further expansion, with uncertain success. Nor was it ever guaranteed that the enforcement of political limitations on markets as a condition for the compatibility of capitalism with social peace, essential as it once might have been for both economic performance and social stability, would continue to be possible or necessary. In fact empirical observation, in contradiction of functionalist and structural-Marxist theories, suggests that the role of the state in capitalism has fundamentally, albeit gradually, changed over time. Apparently this was a consequence of two parallel developments. One was a specific historical dynamic of the democratic state as a political institution leading to accumulating problems of governability. The other

7

was the discovery by capital of newly arisen opportunities to get by without political protection, stop paying for it, and extricate itself from social obligations accepted at a time when free markets were not otherwise to be had. As capitalism became less and less dependent on social stabilization by political means in the course of economic, political, and cultural change, states finally gave up on trying to mobilize the resources needed to exempt social relations from commodification. Instead they began to rely on markets as a means to control organized social interests and generally to relieve themselves of tasks they found increasingly impossible to perform.

(6) *The possible secular exhaustion of the governing capacities of the postwar welfare state.* Social protection and decommodification of social relations require conversion of private resources into public ones, often in the face of resistance from owners of capital and a powerful citizenry. A tempting way out is to draw resources from the future, which may however cumulatively foreclose political options and generally cannot be continued forever. Moreover, mobilizing public resources in a private economy presupposes effective institutions of social control. These, however, are difficult to maintain for states increasingly located in international markets and confronted with owners of private property exposed to exogenous competitive pressures and capable of moving their assets outside the reach of national governments and collective obligations. In fact my historical narrative suggests that the growing demand for resources for social pacification and the subsidization of cooperation in the sphere of production over time became a crippling Achilles' heel of postwar politics. This raises the possibility of the postwar interventionist state having been no more than a temporary stopgap whose capacity to underwrite the expansion of markets by containing that same expansion was historically limited and perishable. Eventually this would force the state to redefine itself under the auspices of a turn to fiscal austerity, by shedding previously public responsibilities to individuals and markets, in the hope that the resulting increase in uncertainty would be absorbed by society without a critical loss of political stability.

(7) *The nature of liberalization.* The German experience suggests the possibility of a secular fiscal crisis of the interventionist welfare state forcing it to turn over broad areas of what used to be public policy to private providers in free markets. In this context, privatization of publicly owned assets would seem to be another, albeit temporary recourse for a state whose fiscal means have increasingly fallen short of what would be needed to perform traditional postwar political functions associated with

the protection of society from market uncertainties. Efficiency-theoretical accounts of liberalization as an effort to increase national competitiveness would be misleading, as would be theories that consider the long-term increase in citizen inequality that liberalization entails as its principal objective, rather than a more or less welcome side effect. Instead liberalization would appear as a last line of defense for an overburdened and exhausted democratic welfare state having reached the limits of its governing capacities, with recourse to the market being part of government's attempt to relieve itself of tasks it can no longer perform, and thereby protect or recover its authority. Moreover, historically, liberalization coincided with "globalization," or internationalization, of market relations. While globalization tends to be represented as both an intensification of competition and a contingent new opportunity for profit, it may also be described as an escape for capital from the increasingly burdensome obligations imposed on it under the neo-corporatist amendments to the postwar settlement in the 1970s. There are also indications that the expansion of markets beyond national borders was sometimes actively promoted by national governments striving to extricate themselves from domestic pressures for social and economic protection and redefine their responsibilities, if at all, in terms of preparing their citizens as well as possible for intensified competition in free markets beyond the reach of national political intervention.

(8) *The relationship between convergence and divergence of national capitalist systems.* Much of the current debate on the potential convergence or non-convergence between national systems of capitalism is phrased in a language of international competition, with national governments presumably acting in a mercantilist fashion as agents on behalf of integrated national societies striving to survive in a hostile environment. My research suggests that this is an overly simplified perspective. First, it overestimates not only the governing capacity of national states but also the extent to which individual interests in private capital accumulation are linked to collective-national interests in "competitive" institutions, or are shared among firms based in the same country. Just as national institutional development is far from being engineered by circumspect governments devoted to competitive efficiency as a public interest, the significance of national institutions for the market fortunes of firms is anything but certain or invariant in time and place. My observations suggest that convergence and divergence must be conceived as multi- rather than mono-dimensional, among other things, because political and economic pressures may affect the differences between economic

systems differently. In particular, divergence in institutions used to coordinate market relations may evolve or persist as a matter of economic expediency alongside politically generated convergence toward a more contractual and less obligatory type of order. Moreover, current ideas of efficiency-driven institutional convergence suggest a choice between two alternative conditions of static equilibrium with no historical time required for change from one to another. If time and history are considered, lasting divergence between two systems may go hand in hand with parallel change in the same direction, and growing convergence in the course of such change may be hidden by one system having started its transformation earlier than the other.

(9) *The relationship between trends and events in capitalist development.* Empirical observation suggests a specific directionality in the development of capitalist social relations, in the form of a more or less steady expansion of markets driven by pressures "from within" against whatever institutional containments may be devised to keep them in check. In this perspective, "globalization" is not an accident, but just another stage in a long, more or less continuous process of capitalist progress, one that is not in any way derailed by single political-historical events, even if they are as major as, for example in our case, national unification. There is little in the toolkit of social science and indeed of history that would enable us convincingly to account for the phenomenon of different stages of development following one another under a common logic. Social science is agnostic with respect to historical direction, having taken refuge in a post-Hegelian constant property space where, in principle, anything can move anywhere if the respective "independent variables" happen to assume the right values. Modern historiography, in turn, insists on the uniqueness and, as it were, the dignity of individual events and is suspicious of any general "logic," or "force," suggested to underlie or control historical development. It is true that economic historians and rational choice institutionalists sometimes try to reconstruct history—in the manner, for example, of modernization theory, which is much discredited in today's social science—as long-term progress to ever higher levels of efficiency. But this is not easy to reconcile empirically with the contested nature of market expansion and the complexity of collective objectives—including those reflecting the traditionalism of social life as such—that struggle with each other in social contexts, and with the social limits on rational choice necessary for rational choice to be possible in the first place.

Even mentioning the possibility of historical directionality seems passé at a time when modernization theory has lost its charm and what used to be philosophy of history is considered to be no more than metaphysical speculation. Still, somehow the studied historical agnosticism of contemporary social science leaves too many questions unaddressed that impose themselves even and precisely when one deals with the empirical reality of the changing political economy of contemporary capitalism. Perhaps some new sort of action-based institutionalism may be able conceptually to embed the voluntaristic creativity of social action under uncertainty and in the horizon of an open future in a nondeterministic historical logic of progressive capital accumulation and market expansion. A properly elaborated micro-perspective on the tension between institutions and their enactment, historically specified in terms of a particular nature and distribution of resources and actor dispositions, may make it possible to understand how the necessarily imperfect reproduction of a social order in the course of its necessarily creative enactment may be so "biased" that its results add up to an identifiable historical trend. In my analysis I briefly touch on the possibility of the theory of biological evolution as natural history, stripped of its naturalistic and social-Darwinist distortions, serving as a model for a theory of social history that can recognize a pattern of development without assuming intelligent design by all-powerful governance, one that would be capable of conceiving of under-determined, "random" events as fitting in and indeed constituting a long-term, intelligible but non-teleological logic of change. Be this as it may, the historical nature of the renewed dynamism of capitalist development forces us to return to very old questions and reconsider very old attempts to come to terms with them.

Political Economy: Static and Dynamic

Classical social science examined how the modern way of life had evolved out of the past, and what this might imply for the future. Both early sociology and early economics explored in one the *functioning* and the *evolution* of the emerging political-economic institutions of capitalist society. In the writings of Marx, Durkheim, and Weber, even of Adam Smith and certainly of Schumpeter, static and dynamic analyses of modern society were inseparable: how institutions worked was explained by their place in a historical process, and how that process would continue was assumed to be driven by institutions' present functions and dysfunctions.

Today, most of social science has adopted a much more static perspective. Where the aim is "theory," empirical observations are preferably organized into abstract concepts and property spaces supposedly accommodating all human societies at all times, without allowing for historical or geographic location to make a difference in principle.[1] Political-economic institutional analysis in particular tends to believe that it is at its best if it succeeds in uncovering relations between institutions, or logics of institutional functioning, that can account equally well for observations in the US of today, the Mediterranean of early modernity or, for that matter, the Roman Empire. Clearly, the search by much of current social science for historically universal, invariant principles governing social organization reflects the model of the physical sciences, which feel most comfortable assuming that they are dealing with ahistorical, invariant nature. Another explanation may be identification with that powerful disciplinary aggressor, modern economics, which in mimicking nineteenth-century mechanics[2] has long ceased to add indices of time and place to the supposedly universal principles it claims to be able to discover. Afraid of being accused of atheoretical "story-telling," many of today's social scientists have resorted in effect to ahistorical theory-building.

The tendency to organize empirical observations in historically invariant and in this sense static property spaces prevails also in the study of comparative politics, and sometimes even among those who pursue an approach they refer to as "historical institutionalism." While this is deplorable, it is not difficult to understand. Today's historical institutionalism, in political science and elsewhere, developed out of comparative politics, which in turn may be seen as a critical response to two mainstreams of social science in the 1960s, "pluralist industrialism" and orthodox Marxism.[3] Each of them offered a grand historical narrative. The former told of impending worldwide convergence somewhere between the political-economic models of the US and the then USSR, implying an end to ideological politics as one knew it at the time and predicting its replacement with rational technocratic administration of the constraints and opportunities of industrial modernity (Kerr et al. 1960). Marxism, by contrast, foresaw a gradual but irreversible decline of capitalism as a result of its own success, with an ever-growing organic composition of capital being both the destiny and the fate of capitalism as an accumulation regime (Grossmann 1929). Comparative politics, including the neo-corporatist literature that developed in its tradition during the 1970s,[4] was rightly skeptical of both. Against pluralist industrialism, it insisted on the continuing significance of politics as collective agency and as a source of diversity in social organization, including the social organization of capitalism (Crouch and Streeck 1997*a*). Against orthodox Marxism, it emphasized the capacity of the diverse social institutions into which modern capitalism is nationally organized, including the national state, to modify substantially and even suspend some of the alleged "laws of motion" of the capitalist accumulation regime.

In the process, however, as comparative politics and comparative political economy turned into comparative institutionalism, they seem to have lost sight of both capitalism and historical change, the two core subjects of modern social science in the nineteenth century. What had begun as an exploration of the underlying social and economic forces driving the development of the contemporary world turned into a comparative statics of selected institutions represented in increasingly abstract models and analyzed outside of their social and historical context. Indeed, more often than not, comparative institutionalism transformed into pseudo-universalistic *variable sociology*:[5] if you have centralized collective bargaining and an independent central bank, you can expect an inflation rate different from countries whose institutional *ameublement* differs from yours. The fact that most of the cases studied were taken from a very narrow universe of time and space was conveniently forgotten. "Historical" institutionalism meritoriously added policy legacies and institutional pasts to the set of variables routinely considered when trying to account for structures and outcomes of political-economic institutions. In fact, however, it was not really history that was brought into play but, at best, chronological time and, in the study of "path dependence" (Pierson 2000), the costs of change in comparison to its expected returns.

Small wonder, then, that the principal finding of historical-institutionalist research on political-economic institutions seems to be simply that different institutional arrangements are likely to remain different and will in particular not converge on a universal model. Institutions matter, their *Eigenlogik* rules supreme, but capitalism does not matter, and its *Eigenlogik* does not exist. Institutions may be constrained and shaped by their past or by other institutions, but not by their location in an unfolding historical process or by their association with a historical mode of production and social order. Moreover, by implication, their evolution follows no particular direction; anything within the property space circumscribed by the value range of the relevant variables— which may include institutions' historical trajectories—is possible if the necessary causes somehow happen to be present. Alas, the self-imposed agnosticism of comparative institutionalism with respect to the big questions that were at the origin of modern social science did not really pay off as its capacity to predict remains hampered by the low number of cases available for testing, as well as by high volatility over time of the coefficients in its equations.[6] In fact, while the scientistic self-definition of comparative politics and its insistence that it is ultimately aimed at "theory" promise "scientific" predictions, very few such predictions are ever offered—apart perhaps from a general *basso continuo* that observed changes must not be overestimated and that most things will basically remain the way they are.[7]

In a context like this, studying institutional change amounts almost to a subversive program. Before change began to be taken seriously as a subject of inquiry, in particular empirical inquiry, cutting-edge institutionalist theory conceived of the dynamics of socioeconomic institutions, if at all, in terms of a "punctuated equilibrium" model which divided history into long periods of static reproduction and short, formative moments of exogenous shock causing institutions to be profoundly rearranged for another long period of stability.[8] While recognizing the "stickiness" of institutions, the model made change dependent on momentous external events forcing those in control of institutional design to work out a new settlement, of which they were usually considered to be capable. The problem, of course, was that such dramatic disruptions of continuity occur only rarely, implying stasis as the normal condition of social institutions short of catastrophe, with social order almost as a matter of definition being capable of reproduction as long as exogenous shocks fail to materialize or remain too weak to overcome the—strong—forces of self-enforced stability.

To those studying the postwar political economy of Western countries empirically, this image of social order was bound to appear increasingly counterintuitive, and the more so the longer they looked at their subject. The first effective attack on the "punctuated equilibrium" concept was launched in the work of Kathleen Thelen (1999, 2002). Thelen suggested two ideal-typical, stylized accounts of processes of institutional change, "conversion" and "layering," drawn from empirical observation rather than derived deductively from general theoretical premises, that may proceed slowly and do not need exogenous shocks to get started.[9] In principle, both conversion and layering may take place in response to endemic conflicts and contradictions, or to a gradually evolving mismatch with a gradually changing external environment. Although advancing in small steps, however, conversion and layering need by no means be inconsequential; indeed a most important implication of Thelen's conceptualization of institutional change is that it opens a perspective on a

14

type of change that is *slow and transformative at the same time,* allowing for a much more dynamic view of social order than implied by the long stability–short rupture punctuated equilibrium model.

Further drawing out this line of thought, and identifying the development of a better grasp on gradual but nonetheless transformative change as the main challenge for institutional theory today, Thelen and I later tried to add essentially three things (Streeck and Thelen 2005). First, we suggested a few more types of slow change, in particular "displacement," "drift," and "exhaustion." Time will tell which of these will survive, and whether they were more than elaborations on the two original Thelen models. With hindsight, they may be regarded as an attempt to describe in empirically grounded institutionalist language "dialectical" tendencies in social institutions undermining themselves in the course of their normal operation—the opposite of path-dependent reproduction. Second, and I believe more important, we conceived really existing socioeconomic institutions as the product of conflicts and agreements, not just over their *design* between the elites that control them, but also over their *enactment* between "rule-makers" and "rule-takers." The latter we imagined as differently willing and contingently able to comply with institutionalized rules, with some actors normatively socialized, others rationally calculating, and yet others resisting. In this way we included agency, not just at the top, but also at the bottom of social institutions, opening a space for their gradual transformation during their inevitably less than perfect and more or less subtly contested functioning.[10]

Third, we identified the present period of liberalization of the postwar order of democratic capitalism as one of, indeed, gradual transformative change, *suggesting that theoretical analysis of the latter be grounded in an empirical-historical exploration of the former.* This was not because we believe that change that is both slow and profound could not take place in circumstances other than today's political economy, or that in contemporary capitalism disruptive–catastrophic change can be precluded once and for all. What we do believe, however, is that the current phase of capitalist development is characterized by deep changes that mostly and typically are moving forward gradually and often almost imperceptibly. It follows from this that institutional analysis must equip itself with a conceptual apparatus that does not oblige it to suppress empirical observations and historical intuitions that take note of this. In fact, by conceiving of the current liberalization of the postwar political-economic order as of a period of slow but fundamental institutional transformation, we more or less implicitly undertook to revive the ambitions of the classics and reconnect institutional analysis with its traditional theme of the historical evolution of capitalism.

Institutional Change, Systemic Transformation, Capitalist Development

How, then, does capitalist development manifest itself as institutional change, and how do the proper dynamics—the *Eigendynamik*—of institutional change inform the development of modern capitalism? As already noted, looking back at the decades since the end of the "Golden Age" (Glyn 2006)—the two decades of uninterrupted growth after the Second World War—one has the puzzling impression that profound transformations of the socioeconomic order have occurred and are occurring in the absence of dramatic disruptions of continuity. The challenge, then, is to understand how slow and gradual change may accumulate over time to become fundamental and transformative, as well as how ongoing changes in individual institutions or institutional sectors may aggregate into something like systemic change. One problem is that slow change is easily overlooked, regarded as immaterial and insignificant, or mistaken as a stabilizing response to external shocks restoring a system's past equilibrium. This is far from new:

Another hidden source of error in historical writing is the ignoring of the transformations that occur in the condition of epochs and peoples with the passage of time and the changes of periods. Such changes occur in such an unnoticeable way and take so long to make themselves felt, that they are very difficult to discern and are observed only by a small number of men.   (Ibn Khaldûn 1950 [1377], 29–30)

Among the reasons why slow but transformative change is so difficult to recognize is that without a historical rupture, it is hard to determine the threshold beyond which observations are better interpreted as manifestations of an emerging new order rather than, still, fluctuations within an old one—in other words, where flexible reproduction through adaptation ends and the replacement of one social order with another begins. That problem seems to arise in particular where, as is now normally the case in the social sciences, institutions are studied one by one, in sectoral isolation. Students observing and describing slow change in, say, regimes of collective bargaining or corporate governance often find it impossible to decide whether what they see is flexible stability or a transition to something new (Streeck and Rehder 2005). Thus fruitless debates may arise, and often do, of the sort of whether the glass, whatever it may be, is still half full or already half empty. Incidentally, such debates are not settled by cross-national comparison, which can do no more than establish whether a given process has proceeded farther in one country than in another, and what the causes of this may be.

In this book I follow the intuition, and intend to demonstrate, that *only in a panoramic view can one truly recognize the details*. By this I mean that in order to know what slow change in a given institution may indicate for its stability and continuity, the institution must be placed in the context of the development of neighboring institutions in the same society over a longer period. As a rule, that society will be a national one, as nation-states still generate strong interdependencies between the sectoral institutions that regulate their political-economic life. In other words, whether slow change is transformative or not may best be discovered by exploring whether it is involved in general, systemic change. As a side effect, the need to understand gradual change may rehabilitate holistic-monographic country studies that opt for historical depth at the expense of cross-sectional breadth, taking seriously the uniqueness of a country's institutional order and treating it, in a Weberian sense, as a "historical individual" (Roth 1976). Unfortunately, an approach like this tends to be discounted by today's scholarly mainstream in favor of quantitative comparisons, which not only appear technically more elegant but also greatly economize on the information one needs to collect and digest. Among other things, this makes for shorter, more, and more easily readable journal articles.

Much, of course, depends on how the national context is conceptualized within which sectoral change is interpreted. A heuristic framework that has become popular in contemporary political economy is the "varieties of capitalism" approach (Amable 2003; Crouch and Streeck 1997*b*; Hall and Soskice 2001*b*). Among its numerous merits are its adherence to an institutionalist perspective, its recognition of the lasting significance of national contexts even in a period of "globalization," and its steadfast rejection of a neo-liberal convergence-on-best-practice model of political economy. At the same time, the "varieties" literature has met with extensive criticism, for example, where and to the extent that it reduces the diversity of national capitalisms, or "market economies," to only two alternative models, a "liberal" and a "coordinated" one (Hall and Soskice 2001*a*). Moreover, it has been argued that with two models constructed on efficiency-theoretical, functionalist premises, the theory is ill-suited to account for change,[11] let alone slow change. As each of the two types is defined as commanding distinctive competitive advantages which actors have rational reasons and the political capacities to protect, stability seems to take precedence conceptually over change, as it generally does in functionalist theorizing. This is because, since economic institutions in each of the two versions of capitalism are conceived as complementing each other in support of a specific type of economic performance, change in any one institution, exogenous or endogenous, can be expected to be followed by balancing changes in others, restoring the system's typical performance equilibrium. Basically this limits change to flexible adaptation securing continuous reproduction of the system as it is. Or, as Hall and Soskice put it, "institutional complementarities generate disincentives to radical change" (Hall and Soskice 2001a, 64).

In fact, following the seminal work of Hall and Soskice in particular, "varieties of capitalism" seems to allow for only one exceptional case of "radical," system-transforming rather than just equilibrium-restoring change. Surprisingly, the causal mechanism that is to be responsible for this is, again, functional complementarity. Now, however, instead of preserving an existing type of competitive advantage, complementarity is to promote systemic change by seeing to it "that institutional reform in one sphere of the economy could snowball into changes in other spheres as well" (Hall and Soskice 2001a, 63f.):

If the financial markets of a coordinated market economy are deregulated, for instance, it may become more difficult for firms to offer long-term employment. That could make it harder for them to recruit skilled labor or sustain worker loyalty, ultimately inspiring major changes in production regimes... *Financial deregulation could be the string that unravels coordinated market economies*

(Hall and Soskice 2001a, 64; italics are mine, WS).

One reason why the introduction of systemic change driven by finance as a dominant *master sector* looks suspiciously like an ad hoc addition basically incompatible with what remains a functionalist equilibrium model[12] is that it is envisaged only for the "coordinated" type of a "market economy." Indeed, Hall and Soskice explicitly suggest that it may be easier to liberalize coordinated market economies than to coordinate liberal market economies. This time the causal mechanism invoked is neither complementarity nor the primacy of financial markets but "the importance of common knowledge to successful strategic interaction":

Because they have little experience of... coordination to underpin the requisite common knowledge, LMEs [liberal market economies] will find it difficult to develop non-market coordination of the sort common in CMEs [coordinated markets economies], even when the relevant institutions can be put into place. Because market relations do not demand the same levels of common knowledge, however, there is no such constraint on CMEs deregulating to become more like LMEs. (Hall and Soskice 2001a, 63)

If this is to mean that institutional change in "coordinated market economies" moving toward liberalization is a critically important subject for the study of contemporary political economy, I can only agree. I intend to show, however, that the dynamics of such change cannot be understood on functionalist premises, even if these are extended to cover radical change caused by pressures for complementarity from a hegemonic lead sector like finance. In fact, I hope to demonstrate that if the realities of institutional change as observed in the real world are taken seriously, major amendments need to be made in the way political science and sociology deal with issues of political economy. These amendments include the rediscovery of a *systemic* as opposed to a sectoral perspective on institutions and the social order, one that is, furthermore, *historical* rather than *functionalist,* as well as *dynamic* and *processual* instead of *static.* Moreover, and just as importantly, I will argue that abandoning the economistic-functionalist conceptual framework now dominant in the study of "varieties of capitalism" allows for a new appreciation of the importance, not just of *time,* but also of *history,* far beyond the narrow and abstract recognition afforded both in contemporary treatments of "path dependence." And, finally, I want to show that appreciation of institutional change as it really happens militates toward "the economy" being replaced as the subject of study with capitalism as a specific historical formation, rephrasing current debates on liberalization, convergence, competition, internationalization, and the like in terms of an *institutionalist theory of capitalist development.*

While I will return to the "varieties of capitalism" conceptual framework several times in the course of this book, especially as developed in the representative essay by Hall and Soskice, it is not my intention to engage the complex subtleties of the debate that has taken place since that essay first appeared. That debate has produced a vast list of amendments, qualifications, additions, extensions, and exceptions to the original formulation of the approach, through constructive criticism and reconstructive response. Trying to do justice to it by pursuing its many ramifications would not only fill a book of its own but would also leave no space for what is my main purpose: presenting and analyzing strategically important empirical evidence. Moreover, amendments made to concepts and theories in order to accommodate uncomfortable observations, while perfectly legitimate, sometimes obscure the underlying fundamental assumptions that make for a theory's paradigmatic identity. It is exactly some of these fundamentals, however, that I have become convinced must be challenged if the theory of political economy is to move forward. Among them I include, in line with the popular reception of "varieties of capitalism," although perhaps not always and entirely with its revised and compromised later versions, that social systems are politically structured to compete with each other economically; that competitive institutional arrangements tend to move and settle into a self-stabilizing equilibrium; that politics is about designing institutions that enable an efficient deployment of economic resources; that today there exist basically two variants of capitalism that are in principle equally competitive and therefore unlikely to "converge"; that especially employers and their firms, interested as they are in their own competitiveness, can and do instruct states and governments on how optimally to organize a society as an efficient production regime; and that social systems are kept together by pressures for institutional complementarity in the service of competitive production.

Much of the debate that accompanied and followed the evolution of the "varieties of capitalism" paradigm, it seems to me, was concerned with saving it from its critics, if need be by ad hoc concessions to smoothe over its hard edges. However, such modifications are of interest mainly if one shares the basic assumptions of the paradigm as such. That I do not share these means that I do not have to do justice to the many subtle afterthoughts which adherents especially to the bipolar version of "varieties" have devised to defend their leading intuitions. Instead, I can cut right to the bone and concentrate on the identifying essentials, if not of the original formulation, then of what the still booming "varieties of capitalism" industry understood them to be, leaving it open to what extent they were already present in the industry's foundational document (Hall and Soskice 2001a) or were read into it. It is these essentials— the baselines of theoretical interpretations on which all exceptions and modifications rest and which should be amenable to being put clearly and simply—that I want to confront with empirical evidence, expecting that they will fail to correspond to it, in a way fundamental enough that efforts toward reconciliation by exception or complexification would be unacceptably awkward. As a consequence, I will suggest that to make progress in the theory of political economy, we must go back from conceptual subtleties to underlying principles, placing and reflecting on what was and is phrased as a discussion of the "institutional foundations of comparative advantage" in the context of more general controversies on the nature of social order and of modern capitalism as its currently dominant historical emanation.

To make my case I will draw extensively on evidence from one country, Germany. Rather than in cross-national comparison, I have invested my empirical efforts in the construction of a longer-term diachronic narrative of institutional change in five core dimensions, or sectors, of a single but theoretically and practically central political economy, that of Germany, a narrative that covers roughly three decades. Selecting Germany for a longitudinal case study offered itself not just because I happen to know this country best—from my own work, beginning with studies on German trade unions and collective bargaining in the early 1970s, as well as more recently from a decade of collaborative research at the Max Planck Institute for the Study of Societies in Cologne. More importantly, Germany has always been the literature's most prominent example of what one may call, with a somewhat neutral term, "nonliberal" capitalism,[13] and with good reasons. Being by far the largest economy in Europe and still—or again—the world's leading export nation, Germany has long been considered a "model" for countries unwilling to subject themselves to the rule of the market in the same way and to the same extent as Anglo-American countries. Also, whether there will be a "European model" of a socially embedded and politically domesticated capitalism, and what it will look like, will depend in large part on how the German political economy will evolve. To any theory of alternative variants of a capitalist political economy, it must therefore be of central importance whether or not the German case conforms to its intuitions and expectations, if only because of the country's size and the strong external effects it has on others, especially in Europe.[14] My claim is, in short, that if a theory of advanced capitalism cannot account for the German experience, it is hard to treat that experience as an exception to a rule that remains generally true.

The Course of the Argument

The present book proceeds, as it were, bottom-up: it moves from the specific to the general, from the empirical to the theoretical, and from a morphology of institutional change in one country to a historical perspective on capitalist development as a whole. While adding successive

layers of interpretative reflection, the discussion keeps reconnecting to
the empirical evidence for instruction and guidance. Thus detailed doc-
umentation of, for example, the changing form and extent of sectoral-
level wage setting in Germany leads, after several intermediary steps, to
an exploration of the role of pressures for efficiency in institutional development, which in turn brings up the subject of the historicity of social
organization in general and its implications for social theory. Readers are
invited to work through the different layers, beginning at the bottom
with the empirics; while they may stop any time, for example when the
treatment has finally become too speculative or far-fetched for their taste,
it is not suggested that they start reading somewhere in the middle or
limit their efforts to the final chapters only. This is because the argument
is not linear but resembles a scale: every new step rests on top of the
steps that precede it. An additional peculiarity, incidentally, is that as the
argument moves upward, theoretical abstraction is at some point traded
in again for historical concreteness, in an effort to get a better grip on
the empirical evidence. Specifically, "institutions" and "the economy"
are gradually replaced as the subjects of inquiry by the historical social
order of capitalism, which I believe needs to be urgently rediscovered as a
subject of institutionalist research and political economy.[15]

As indicated, the book initially was conceived as an investigation into
institutional change in contemporary political economies, one that was
to avoid dealing with individual institutions in isolation from others and
from their social contexts. Thus, Part I presents five parallel narratives,
by necessity highly condensed, of trajectories of gradual change over
three decades in crucial sectors of the German political economy: wage
setting; the intermediary organization of producer interests; social policy;
the fiscal policy of the state; and corporate governance and the structure
of the German company network. The intention is to demonstrate how
sectoral changes, which taken by themselves might seem inconsequential
or merely adaptive, may be recognized as part of a broad stream of
transformative *systemic change* if considered together with simultaneous
changes in other sectors. Empirically it appears that, rather than change in
one sector being balanced by change in others, maintaining "the system"
in functional equilibrium, all five sectors have evolved in the same general
direction during the period of observation. To characterize that direction
in a first, as it were, phenomenological approximation, I provisionally
employ the concept of "disorganization" as suggested some time ago by
Scott Lash and John Urry (1987). While in their book the concept has
a very broad meaning, extending, in the language of the Communist

Manifesto, to literally "all that is solid" in modern society and predicting its imminent melting "into air,"[16] I use it more specifically, to characterize a decline in centralized control and organized regulation and an increase in competition in labor markets; in the collective articulation of interests; in the promotion of class cooperation and social peace by state intervention; and in the relationship between the state and the economy, between large firms, and between them and the banking system. In Part III, after some conceptual preparations, I return to the concept of disorganization to introduce a range of distinctions and qualifications and, importantly, connect it to the theme of the liberalization of contemporary capitalism.[17]

Before I get there, however, Part II will be devoted to a *synthetic morphology* of the pattern of multi-sectoral institutional change found in the German political economy since the late 1970s. It will rely basically on the conceptual language of historical institutionalism, which deals with the origins and the regularities of the formal structures of institutions. Above all, the discussion will point out the *endogeneity* and *interdependence* of the observed sectoral changes. Among other things, it will show that the different streams of gradual change in the five sectors were not, and did not need to be, driven by one "master sector" such as, in particular, finance. Certainly in the case at hand, that of the German political economy, each of the parallel strands of sectoral change seems to have originated on its own (merging into a pattern of multiple instabilities caused by evolving internal contradictions) rather than being set in motion, directly or indirectly, by one leading sector. Independent sectoral developments did, however, become *interdependent* as manifold relations of mutual reinforcement arose between them, again all pointing in the same direction of systemic disorganization and increasingly aggregating into *systemic change*. In subsequent analytical chapters I will try to trace and disentangle these emerging interrelations as best as possible, also to establish that they cannot be accounted for in functionalist terms as products of efficiency-enhancing institutional complementarity. In fact, it will transpire that an important role in driving institutional change toward disorganization was played, not by economic or "market forces," but by a distinctive evolutionary dynamic of the democratic state. As indicated, the role of economic efficiency in the evolution of institutions and the social order will be a major theme in the final part of the book.

Obviously, particular attention will be paid in Part II to the *mechanisms* of institutional change at work in and across the five sectors. Some of them seem to involve historical *tipping points* where self-stabilization or mutual stabilization turns into self-undermining or mutual undermining. In my reading of the empirical evidence, this suggests the possibility of a tendency for the type of political-economic institutions under study to be exhausted or to exhaust themselves *over time*. Especially important in the German case seems to be the progressive erosion since the 1970s of the capacity of the state to compensate for or contain various self-destructive tendencies inherent in its own operation as well as in that of other political-economic institutions. To the extent that this sort of erosion would be observable in other countries as well, it might imply that state interventionism of the postwar sort may be, or may have been, a historically finite phenomenon. This is one of many findings that raise the issue of the historicity of social institutions *in general*, that is, of their inherent instability and perishability; of time and age affecting the way they operate; and of the existence of something like an institutional life cycle. In fact, my analysis suggests that a full understanding of this might require a general heuristic that regards *social systems as historical processes*, and their observed conditions as no more than provisional and subject, not just to preemption by changing external circumstances, but also to strong inherent forces of self-consumption.

Structural analysis of institutional arrangements and institutional change, however, gets us only so far. Historical institutionalism provides us with a rich vocabulary with which to capture intricate morphological details and develop sophisticated taxonomies of social institutions in a wide variety of contexts. It also help us identify complex phenomena such as institutional conversion and path dependence, the role of agency and *bricolage* in institution-building, or the impact of critical junctures and formative historical moments on social orders. Unfortunately, however, it tells us little about where the institutional dynamics that it enables us to perceive are coming from, and where they may be going. Efficiency theories, individualistic ones emphasizing "rational choice" and collectivistic ones building on a logic of institutional complementarity, at least try to give an answer to questions like these.[18] The problem with them, as we will see, is that they fail in a major way to do justice to the empirical evidence as they are far too simple in the wrong places and too abstract with respect to essential facets of reality.

What then? The answer I will suggest, based on my wrestling with the evidence from what I believe must be a crucial case for any theory of political economy, is to take the historical character of social institutions and social order seriously and ground institutional analysis more firmly in time and place, preserving its rich conceptual toolkit while bringing it to bear on a more historically grounded line of inquiry. In this vein, Part III uses the fine-grained accounts of institutional change given in Parts I and II as empirical reference for sketching out selected elements of a macro-sociological theory, which is really not much more than a research program at this point, of the development of contemporary capitalism *as a historically specific social formation*. The decisive step is where "disorganization" as a phenomenological concept is translated into "liberalization," referring to the gradual dissolution after the 1970s of postwar "organized capitalism" in a process of slow systemic institutional change. Hence the title of Part III and of the book as a whole: "Re-Forming Capitalism," meaning both *change* and *restoration*—the *re-composition*, in part through political design and in part as an emergent process, as well as the *return* of capitalism and capitalist development after its temporary, as it were: artificial, confinement in an elaborate set of market-breaking institutions after the Second World War.

How can something re-form that has never quite dissolved? The claim I make is that postwar capitalism, especially in Europe, was so deeply embedded in its social containment that it could be overlooked, or mistaken as having turned into something abstract and neutral like "industrial society" or "advanced economy." Even its re-forming—its breaking-out of its postwar social shell—was and is not easily noticed as it proceeded and is proceeding so slowly, by re-form rather than by revolution, that it could escape the attention even of those who after 1989 specialized in the study of capitalist "variety." Meanwhile, however, the re-forming of the capitalist social formation has advanced far enough for historical-institutionalist political economy to have to "bring capital-ism back in," abandoning its preoccupation with a timeless "economy" and returning to the study of really existing capitalism.[19] Attempting simultaneously to transcend the formalism of institutionalist analyses that concern themselves with the structural properties and dynamics of institutions in general and with the substantive biases they create for decisions on conflicting interests, Part III also rejects as incompatible with the empirical evidence approaches that treat the social as subordinate—as either support or obstacle—to the economic. Instead it advocates a radical departure from an economistic, efficiency-theoretical perspective on soci-ety and history, and generally from theories that construe society as an economy, toward a concept of *economy-in-society*, with economic action conflictually and indeed dialectically contained in social organization.

Part III, that is to say, seeks to link the patterns of change and the mechanisms of causation and cross-sectoral interdependence described in the sectoral narratives and specified in Part II to a broad concept of capitalist development, or a theory of capitalism as a distinctive political economy. The underlying intuition is that the mechanisms that bring about systemic institutional change in contemporary capitalism cannot be understood on strictly institutionalist terms alone, not to mention the logic of comparative economic advantage employed by much of current writing on capitalist variety. For a more credible causal account, the argument makes reference to fundamental exigencies of capitalist value creation and of the political management of the tensions between market exchange and the lifeworld. In particular, it shows that institutional change as observed in the case under study cannot be explained as convergence on a "best pattern" of economic organization. Nor can it be accounted for as a collective effort at "economizing," for example by saving on transaction costs. In order to explore the contribution of exogenous as opposed to endogenous sources of change, the impact of economic and political internationalization investigation, showing that endogenous institutional change has preceded internationalization and indeed has significantly shaped its course. Moreover, German unification is taken as a natural experiment offering a unique opportunity to explore the significance of exogenous shocks, the result being that unification had almost no lasting effects on long-established trends of endogenous change. Analysis of both internationalization in the 1990s and of unification after 1989 provokes a general discussion of the proper way of placing institutional change in historical context. At the end, a tentative and partial outline is offered of a theory of capitalism as an institutionalized order, that is, as a system of social action within and in relation to social institutions.

As the argument proceeds, it may look increasingly unorthodox to some readers. As indicated, it suggests that convergence and continued divergence of national institutional arrangements may exist side by side, the former, surprisingly, due to political and the latter to economic reasons. It also proposes a distinction between two types of institutions, "Durkheimian" and "Williamsonian," which are claimed to represent different modes of the "embeddedness" of economic action in a social order. Also, it grounds what it conceives as a specific dynamism of capitalism in a peculiar disorderliness, or unruliness, of capitalist behavior within and in relation to social institutions. Moreover, inspired above all by Karl Polanyi, capitalist institutional development is presented as inherently dialectical, driven by a fundamental conflict between market expansion and market containment, which is claimed to render static equilibrium analysis of any sort profoundly unsuitable for political economy. Furthermore, economic action, the maximization of individual utility as well as the rationalization of institutionalized practices, is firmly located conceptually in a constraining context of nonrational social institutions that fundamentally resist rationalization, with economic actors forced to pursue their objectives opportunistically and by experimentation and improvisation, working sometimes around and sometimes with social structures institutionalized for purposes other than economic ones. Above all, as has been said, the claim is made of a historical return of a capitalism that had never disappeared, in the course of gradual attrition of the institutional safeguards that had temporarily contained it—a development, it is suggested, that should make social science refocus its conceptual lenses, to look beyond the reassuring generalities suggested by or extracted from the *posthistoire* of the postwar era, at a newly and rapidly changing historical world.

Notes

1. There are of course important exceptions to this. See, for example, the work of Renate Mayntz, which offers reliable guidance and encouragement to those refusing to join the search for general social "laws" (e.g., Renate Mayntz 2004).
2. What Albert Hirschman has called the "physics envy" of present-day economics.
3. While orthodox Marxism was not present in the West due to the Cold War, it was the backdrop against which much of Western (American) social science developed, and a crucial though often unidentified partner in a continuing dialogue. Moreover, some theories current at the time, including prominently the theory of pluralist industrialism with its deep-seated technological determinism (Kerr et al. 1960), shared fundamental premises with the Marxist tradition, usually without mentioning and sometimes without knowing it.
4. On this and the following, see Streeck (2006b).
5. Leaving behind in the process a more monographic and truly historical tradition of institutional analysis, as exemplified by Barrington Moore (1966) and Theda Skocpol (1979). The more technically advanced the methods became, the less historical the perspective. This tendency was reinforced by the unfortunate influence of "rational choice" on social theory. On this whole complex see a recent essay by Peter Hall, written from the perspective of

political science, but applicable to sociology and political economy as well (Hall 2007).

6. Problems that, as we now know, are definitely not healed by using more sophisticated methods, such as pooled time series analysis (Kittel and Winner 2002).

7. As an untranslatable German phrase has it: Nichts wird so heiß gegessen wie es gekocht wird.

8. The concept was first suggested by two evolutionary biologists, Niles Eldredge and Stephen Jay Gould (Eldredge and Gould 1972). Among the first social scientists to make use of it was Stephen Krasner (1988).

9. As Martin Höpner reminds me, Durkheim was already aware of conversion. See Chapter 5 of the "Rules," where he claims that "it is a proposition true in sociology as in biology, that the organ is independent of its function, i.e. while staying the same it can serve different ends" (Durkheim 1968 [1894]). On "layering," see also Schickler (2001).

10. I will return to this subject in Chapters 9 and 17.

11. As pointed out by, among others, Blyth (2003), Hay (2005), Howell (2003), Jackson and Deeg (2006), and Pontusson (2005).

12. Unlike, incidentally, Amable (2003), who explicitly provides for hierarchy of institutions in addition to complementarity (see especially Chapter 2).

13. On the concept, see Streeck and Yamamura (2001).

14. In other words, I base the selection of my case on its position in a universe of cases considered unequal and interdependent. This is in contrast to the standard $N = 25$ format of quantitative comparison among OECD countries, in which the medium-sized city of Luxembourg, with its population of 480,000—just half the size of Cologne—is treated as one "case" in the same way and on the same plane as, say, Germany or France.

15. Another metaphoric representation of the organization of the book might be a system of concentric circles. Readers start with a small "hard" core of empirical observations, which they are subsequently led to inspect from ever-growing distances and changing directions, circling them on increasingly higher orbits.

16. But see the somewhat less sweeping enumeration on pp. 5ff. (Lash and Urry 1987).

17. Obviously the notion of "disorganization" comprises much of what Thelen in her book on training systems refers to as "segmentalism" as distinct from "collectivism" with respect to the way specific problems of political economy are resolved (Thelen 2004). I avoid the concept here because I wish to emphasize an evolutionary time perspective, rather than a choice perspective dealing with alternative problem solutions.

18. So, in a way, do "political" theories, where the ultimate explanation is the power with which different groups with conflicting interests happened to have

been endowed at a critical juncture. Power, however, cannot be measured independently, which threatens to make the argument circular: the group whose preferences have prevailed must have been the one with the most power.

19. "Bringing Capitalism Back In" was the working title of this book, referring to both the historical process of liberalization and the challenge it poses for the theory of political economy.

Part I

Gradual Change: Five Sectoral Trajectories

1

Five sectors

The following five accounts of sectoral processes of institutional change present the hard data for the sometimes far-flung theoretical explorations in later chapters. Readers exclusively interested in the German political economy may want to read Part I only and then put the book aside. They will find what I believe to be a comprehensive summary of the main results of up-to-date research on collective bargaining, the intermediary organizations of capital and labor, social policy, the evolution of the governing capacities of the state, and corporate governance and financial markets in Germany, before and after unification. Accounts concentrate on institutional structures conditioning the outcomes of public policy and of the pursuit of collective and individual interests. They are less concerned with the outcomes themselves, except where they in turn affect the future development of institutional structures. For example, the chapter on collective bargaining (Chapter 2) presents a historical account, not of wage setting, but of the institutional framework within which it took and takes place. It takes notice of the results only where there is reason to believe that they have in turn come to affect the institutions that have given rise to them.

As indicated, the structural properties of the institutional settings whose development the five narratives are to trace are described in terms of sectoral organization or disorganization. The main finding will be, to repeat, that sectors have evolved in parallel in a direction of growing disorganization, that is, of a loss of centralized control, toward decentralization, individualization, "segmentalism" (Thelen 2004), competitive pluralism, and the like, with market forces slowly taking the place of political decisions. What exactly the dimensions of institutional disorganization are is not decided a priori by definition but is left open, to be empirically discovered and conceptually integrated in the course of the investigation.

The institutional settings, or sectors, that are examined in this study are demarcated pragmatically rather than ontologically, following established distinctions in policymaking and scholarly writing. In fact, one important result of my empirical research is that the five lines of institutional change for which narrative accounts were constructed hang closely together in many, sometimes quite surprising ways. In the end, they turn out to be no more than different aspects of one broad stream of systemic change—an observation whose far-reaching implications will be considered in depth in subsequent parts of the book.

Turning to the details of the research, collective bargaining and social policy are usually considered to be separate domains as a matter of course. I have followed this convention, although important connections have been shown to exist even between them that must be taken into account in the study of either of the two settings (see the introduction by the editors and the contributions in Ebbinghaus and Manow 2001). Also, corporate governance, financial markets, banking systems, and structures of corporate ownership are normally treated as a social field distinct from both collective bargaining and social policy—one that could either be regarded as a whole or divided in several subfields—even though here, too, one can, as we will note, discover a wide range of interrelations. Intermediary organization of capital and labor is included as a fourth domain, reflecting its crucial importance for the operation of a corporatist or, as the case may be, postcorporatist political economy as a whole, and due to the fact that its causal repercussions extend far beyond any one sector, such as collective bargaining.

Finally, I have decided to include the postwar tax state, or better: tax-and-spend state, as another institutional domain in its own right. This is probably my least conventional decision in this respect, especially since I focus mainly on the relationship between capitalist–corporatist democracy and public finance. Public finance is, surprisingly, an underdeveloped subject of political science and political economy, especially in a diachronic perspective, regardless of Schumpeter's largely unheeded call from almost a century ago for a "fiscal sociology":

The public finances are one of the best starting points for an investigation of society, especially but not exclusively of its political life. The full fruitfulness of this approach is seen particularly at those turning points, or epochs, during which existing forms begin to die off and to change into something new. This is true both of the causal significance of fiscal policy (insofar as fiscal events are important elements in the causation of all change) and of the symptomatic significance (insofar as everything that happens has its fiscal reflection).

(Schumpeter 1991 [1918], 101)

Encouraged by Schumpeter, I take the fiscal situation of the state both as a reliable proxy for its general political capacities and as a powerful explanatory factor with respect to a wide variety of political phenomena that might otherwise remain difficult to understand. This I find validated by the fact that my account of the evolution of social policy in Germany leads directly to the overall financial condition of the state, via the rising subsidies to the social security system from the federal budget, so all that was needed in this respect was to follow the guidance provided by the empirical evidence. Tracking the development of the German state's fiscal crisis in the first decade of the twenty-first century, in turn, opened the way toward a plausible interpretation of the active contribution of state policy to the disorganization of social policy and intermediary organization, in the wake of the gradually emerging refusal of the state to continue to serve as banker of last resort for the corporatist political trading between organized capital and labor. The same holds for the role of public policy in the disorganization of collective bargaining, via the privatization of public enterprises, as well as its contribution to the dissolution of the institutional complex of German corporate governance and the German company network.

Clearly there are more than five sectors, or institutional settings, in the German political economy whose story could have been told in the present study. Trying to offer a complete inventory of sectors would, however, not only go beyond the capacities of any author, but would also neglect the fact that sectoral subdivisions and demarcations will always remain arbitrary to an important extent. For example, I have refrained from including the institutional structure of German federalism or the German party system, although their development might also have been fruitfully investigated in terms of change from organization to disorganization. Where that heuristic clearly *could* have been applied, and I am convinced with the same result as in the five existing accounts, is the field of vocational training, which is of course another core institutional setting of the German political economy. Detailed up-to-date research on this has been lacking until recently, or has not yet been sufficiently synthesized and theorized. As deeper analyses become available,[1] however, it is becoming obvious that the same dynamics have been and continue to be operative in this field as in the five others, so that its inclusion as a sixth case, had it already been possible, would only have added to and reinforced the picture of institutional change drawn in this book.

My presentation begins with the bread-and-butter institutional domains for much of historical–institutional analysis in political economy, collective bargaining, intermediary organization, and social policy. From there it moves on to less familiar terrain, first to fiscal policy, and from there to corporate governance and corporate networks. As the story progresses, parallels as well as interdependencies become increasingly visible, and while their detailed inspection will begin only in Part II, there is no way the individual narratives can leave them aside. As a result, the stories become longer the later they appear in the succession of chapters, as they have to reflect back on a growing number of preceding accounts to take note of at least some of the many causal linkages that emerge (others will be pointed out further down in the analytical chapters of the book). The slow accumulation of cross-references, or back-references, also testifies to the systemic character of the institutional change under way, as well as to the fact that what is presented as separate institutional sectors are in fact nothing more than dimensions of one encompassing and highly interactive institutional system.

As readers move through the five narratives they will discover many remarkable parallels, apart from and in addition to the general trend toward disorganization. Processes of change start earlier in historical time than one may have thought; they move slowly and continuously, at least at first; they are mainly driven endogenously; and each of them is better understood when placed in the context of the others. In addition to morphological parallelism, or homology, there is also and equally impressively a high degree of interdependence. Homology and interdependence are far from the same, which is of the highest importance. If sectoral processes did not move in parallel and in the same direction, their interdependence could conceivably allow for mutual correction, with negative feedback stabilizing or reestablishing a previous systemic equilibrium. As it is, however, sectoral changes, all toward disorganization, reinforce each other. It is this observation above all that needs to be understood and fully appreciated in its theoretical significance.

Note

1. For instance in ongoing work by Marius Busemeyer at the Max Planck Institute for the Study of Societies.

2

Industry-wide collective bargaining: shrinking core, expanding fringes

Comparative assessments of the centralization of collective bargaining in Germany waver between high and intermediate (Kenworthy 2001; Soskice 1990). Unlike Sweden, there is not and never was intersectoral collective bargaining at the national level. Wages are, or used to be, typically negotiated by industry, and often regionally rather than nationally. However, regional wage variation has tended to be low due to high centralization of national unions, at least until unification. There also was, and continues to be, some sort of intersectoral coordination of wage bargaining, as sectoral unions normally follow a pilot agreement negotiated by a designated wage leader. In the past this was almost always the metalworkers' union, *IG Metall*, bargaining with its counterpart employer association, *Gesamtmetall*. Most importantly, coverage of workers and workplaces by collectively bargained industrial agreements used to be high and in fact almost universal, and observance of agreements was effectively enforced by a quasi-statutory system of elected workplace representatives, called works councils *(Betriebsräte)*, which extended well into the small-firm sector of the economy.

In any case, however, one may choose to rate the centralization of postwar German wage setting; it used to generate remarkably low wage dispersion for a large country. An account of the "German model" written in 1995 found that between the early 1980s and the early 1990s, the D1:D5 wage ratio[1] in Germany, which was already among the highest in the OECD, *increased* from 61 to 64 percent while it declined almost everywhere else, for example, in the United States from 45 to 40 percent (Streeck 1997b, Table 2). Intersectoral wage dispersion in particular was low by a variety of measures, and so was, importantly, the wage

Percent

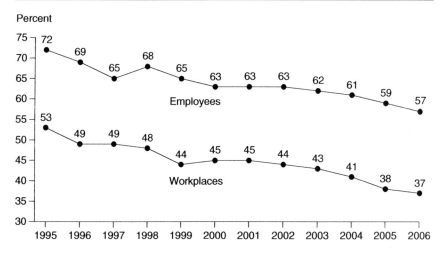

Figure 2.1. Employees and workplaces covered by industry-wide collective bargaining, in percent of all employees and workplaces, West Germany (1995–2006)

differential between small and large firms, at least in manufacturing (Streeck 1997*b*, Table 3).

Recently, coverage by industry-wide collective agreements has fallen and continues to do so (Artus 2001; Streeck and Rehder 2005). The main mechanism bringing this about is firms resigning from employer associations, or new firms never joining (Schröder and Ruppert 1996). Between 1995 and 2004, according to the *Betriebspanel*—a yearly panel study of 16,000 establishments conducted by IAB, the research bureau of the Federal Employment Agency—the share of West German workplaces bound by industry-wide collective agreements declined continuously from 53 to 41 percent; these workplaces employed 72 and 61 percent of the West German workforce, respectively (Figure 2.1).[2] The decline did not spare the industrial core sector of the German economy and stronghold of its traditional industrial relations regime, metal manufacturing. As reported by *Gesamtmetall*, workforce coverage in West Germany, which had still been at 67 percent in 1995, was down to 59 percent in 2003; in East Germany, coverage fell from 44 to 21 percent in the same period (Streeck and Rehder 2005, see especially Diagrams 3 and 4). Unions may try to negotiate company agreements (*Haustarife*) with firms outside the industrial agreement (*Flächentarif*), which is legally possible but organizationally difficult. However, the percentage of workplaces with company agreements seems also to have declined—in the West from 5 percent in

39

1998 to 2 percent in 2004[3]—whereas the share of the workforce covered has remained roughly constant, at about 7 percent in West Germany in 2004.[4] Company agreements, while they help keep the nonunion sector smaller, fragment the collective bargaining regime as a whole and make it less comprehensive and more diversified.

In addition, there appears to be a significant long-term decline in the number of workplaces with works councils and in the workforce represented by them. Since works councils have a legal mandate to supervise the enforcement of applicable collective agreements, their decline detracts from the efficacy of the collective bargaining regime. Until the mid-1990s, statistics on the works council system were provided by the national union confederation, the DGB, based on reports from affiliated unions on the results of the regular works council elections held by law every three and, later, every four years.[5] According to this data, the share of private sector workers represented by an elected works council fell continuously from roughly 50 percent in 1981 to a little above 45 percent in 1990; in the following four years, it declined to less than 40 percent (Hassel 1999, 7). Union data on the subsequent elections in 1998, 2002, and 2006 are not available, due perhaps to the increasing disorganization of the unions' national federation (see below), a potentially embarrassing further decline in coverage, or both. Interestingly, the first wave of the IAB *Betriebspanel* in 1996 found a higher level of representation than the unions, with 50 percent of private sector workers in the West and 41 percent in the East being covered. The difference might reflect a weakening presence of unions at the workplace, which is also indicated by a slow but steady increase in the number of nonunion works council members.[6] Apart from this, the panel, too, shows a decline, albeit slow, in works council representation, to 46 and 39 percent in 2005, respectively (Ellguth 2007, 157).

Even where works councils continue to exist, a steep increase in the number of firms that fail to honor the industrial agreements to which they are formally subject began in the mid-1990s. How widespread this phenomenon was and is can only be guessed. Looking exclusively at firms with works councils and more than 20 employees, the trade union research institute WSI found that in 1997–98 no less than 18 percent "occasionally" or "repeatedly" breached their industrial agreement, mostly on wages and working time (Bispinck 2001, 128).[7] Moreover, works councils were increasingly drawn into supplementary concession bargaining in the context of so-called "workplace alliances for employment" (*betriebliche Bündnisse für Arbeit*), urged on them by employers seeking legitimation for breaching the industrial agreement.[8] Again

Table 2.1. Controlled decentralization: workplaces covered by industry-wide collective agreements making use of provisions for locally negotiated modification of employment conditions (*Öffnungsklauseln*)

	1999/2000	2002	2004/2005
Workplaces using *Öffnungsklauseln* (in percent)	22	35	75
Subjects			
Extension of working hours	44	41	68
Shorter hours	25	24	20
Reduction of bonus	14	15	22
Reduction of holiday pay	6	9	9
Suspension of wage increase	12	10	17
Reduction of base pay	6	6	10

Source: 1999/2000: Bispinck (2001, 130); 2002: Bispinck and Schulten (2003, 160); Bispinck (2005, 304).

according to WSI, no fewer than 30 percent of the firms surveyed in 1999 had "alliances" of this sort, mostly on working time and work organization (Massa-Wirth and Seifert 2004). Ultimately unions had no choice but to make space for local deviations in industry-level collective agreements, through so-called "opening clauses." In effect, these clauses delegated major bargaining rights to the works councils, which are formally nonunion bodies and legally prohibited from negotiating wages and working hours. Between 1999 and 2004, the percentage of firms in the WSI sample making use of opening clauses in industrial agreements increased dramatically from 22 to no less than 75 percent (Table 2.1)[9] while illegal deviations (Bispinck 2001) and "workplace alliances" (Massa-Wirth and Seifert 2004) receded.

As one might expect, the German wage structure has become significantly less egalitarian in line with the transformation of the collective bargaining regime, changing in the same direction as wage structures in most countries at the time.[10] Gernandt and Pfeiffer (2007) surveyed 11 studies on wage dispersion published between 1998 and 2007.[11] They find that authors using very different sources and techniques agree that the German wage structure remained largely unchanged until the early or mid-1990s, after which inequality started to increase on a broad range of parameters. Increases in inequality were particularly pronounced below the median, in both West and East Germany. (There are conflicting views as to whether the relative decline of the wages of low-wage workers already started in the 1980s.) Gernandt and Pfeiffer themselves, drawing on the highly reliable Socio-Economic Panel (SOEP), find a marked relative decline of wages at the 10th percentile level beginning in 1997, at a time when median and high wages (at the 90th percentile) continued to increase. The divergence was especially pronounced among prime-age male workers.[12] Overall, Gernandt and Pfeiffer locate the beginning of the increase in wage dispersion around 1994. The impression that there was a break in the continuity of the traditionally flat German wage structure somewhere in the middle of the 1990s is confirmed by Schettkat (2006), who also summarizes the results of several empirical studies (see especially his Table 3.2).

Other recent studies point in the same direction. Kohn, looking mainly at the D8:D2 differential from 1992 to 2001, confirms that "wage inequality has in fact been rising in many dimensions over this period" (Kohn 2006, 18). Möller (2005), using a representative data set with about 50,000 cases, finds an increasing wage spread between 1992 and 2001. The strongest increase turned out to have taken place among low-skilled workers, where the group-specific D5:D1 ratio was found to have risen from 1.43 to 1.65 for male employees in the West. In fact, Möller claims that wage dispersion among the low-skilled in East Germany is now higher than in the United States. While this may be affected by different skill definitions, a study by Batt and Nohara on call centers in eight countries reports wage disparities in the German call center industry to be "much closer to the United States" than to other Continental-European countries, noting that "the German case represents a serious departure from previous research" (Batt and Nohara 2007, 25). Like Bosch and Weinkopf (2008), the authors relate the increase in wage spread to the parallel decline in bargaining coverage—a connection that is also suggested by Dustmann et al. (2007). Using a two-percent sample of social security records, the authors show that wage inequality has increased in the 1980s, but only at the top of the distribution. In the early 1990s, wage inequality started to rise also at the bottom (Dustmann et al. 2007, 1).

Moreover, given that there is "strong evidence," according to the authors, "that unions compress the wage structure in Germany, and more so at the lower end of the wage distribution" (Dustmann et al. 2007, 27), the authors devote part of their analysis to exploring the link between rising wage inequality and the concurrent decline in unionization. They conclude:

The results indicate that the decline in union recognition in the 90s had a profound impact on the wage structure predominantly, but not only, at the lower end of the distribution ... It is important to note that, other than in the US, workers are only entitled to a minimum wage if their employer is unionized.

(Dustmann et al. 2007, 29)

Summing up, institutional change in the German collective bargaining regime over roughly two decades involved a continuous shrinking of its traditional core of industry-wide, encompassing industrial agreements. Moreover, declining reach of the regime was accompanied by progressive internal "softening," in the sense of agreements becoming less binding on individual firms and, subsequently, less uniform. Today, in fact, a majority of firms in the system make use of a wide range of newly created possibilities to amend the terms of the industrial agreement to make them fit better with their specific circumstances. Moreover, surrounding the shrinking core are several fringes, some of which have been vigorously expanding in recent years. Fringes consist of firms with company agreements; firms covered by but not complying with industrial agreements; and firms not covered by collective bargaining at all. Among the latter, according to the IAB Betriebspanel of 2006, a substantial percentage—all in all no less than 23 percent of all firms in the West employing 16 percent of the workforce—"orient themselves" toward the industrial agreement, whatever that means in practice.[13] Overall the system is now far more fragmented and "pluralist" than 20 years ago.

What does this tell us about institutional stability and change? More specifically, is the German wage-setting system of the first decade of the twenty-first century an updated and reinforced version of the "German model" of the 1970s and 1980, or is it something new? Is the change that is obviously under way a process of—potentially successful—adaptation of the existing regime to altered circumstances, perhaps with temporary losses that may, however, be recovered? Or does it signify a historical demise of the encompassing corporatist industrial relations system of the postwar era and its replacement with a more liberal and less "organized" system? Both cases, for functional adjustment as well as for historical transformation, can be and have been made. Those who would like to see centralized wage setting and its egalitarian consequences preserved have gone to great lengths to argue that the system is still stable in its core (Streeck and Rehder 2003) or may yet be salvageable, if proper measures are taken (Schnabel 2005). Indeed large, export-oriented German firms continue to be strongly committed to industry-level wage bargaining, if only to secure industrial peace along their domestic supply chain (Thelen 2000). Opening clauses and workplace "alliances for employment," while they do de-standardize working conditions, render them more flexible and thereby make it unnecessary for firms to defect from industry-wide bargaining (Streeck and Rehder 2005). *Haustarife* are usually modeled after the *Flächentarif,* and the same applies more often than not to workplaces that are no longer, or not yet, formally covered by collective bargaining (Streeck and Rehder 2005). East Germany may simply need more time to catch up, or if it fails to do so may become an economically insignificant and institutionally encapsulated special case. And union-friendly legislation under more favorable political conditions might once again shore up the works council system by improving its fit with the changed structures of workplaces and firms.[14]

As indicated, I suggest that the true significance of the evolution of the German system of wage setting during the past three decades may be understood only in the context of the simultaneous development of other institutions in the German political economy. In a neo-corporatist social order, of which postwar Germany is or was a prime example, the institutional complex that is most closely related to wage setting is the large intermediary organizations of capital and labor that perform a variety of quasi-public governance functions. Our next subject, therefore, must be the changing political status and organizational structures of German trade unions and business associations.

Notes

1. The relationship in the wage distribution between the first decentile (from below) and the fifth decentile, which is the median.
2. In East Germany, only 28% of workplaces and 56% of workers were covered when the study was first conducted there in 1996. By 2004, these figures had declined to 19 and 41%, respectively, as continuously as in the western part of the country (IAB Betriebspanel, consecutive years).
3. In East Germany the decline was from 8 to 4%. All figures are from the IAB Betriebspanel.
4. The corresponding figure for East Germany is 12%. Responses are probably not very reliable, however, as respondents may not always fully understand the distinction between company agreements and industrial agreements.
5. Works councils are quasi-statutory bodies as they come into existence only on demand by workers. The threshold is, however, low, and in principle an election must be held if just one employee asks for it. Rights and obligations of established works councils are legally regulated, and while trade union members can be and are in fact elected, works councils are formally not union bodies (Müller-Jentsch 1995).
6. Exact figures depend on the source. Union representation on works councils may be estimated to have declined from roughly four-fifths to two-thirds over the past 25 years.

7. Figures for East Germany are about twice the German average (Bispinck 2001). Since survey respondents were leaders of the works councils responsible for enforcing the collective agreement, the level of contract delinquency is likely to be understated.

8. The leading source on this practice, and how it came about and developed, is Rehder (2003). See also Seifert (2002) and Massa-Wirth (2007).

9. Widespread use of opening clauses is confirmed by the 2005 IAB Betriebspanel, although it reports somewhat different numbers. According to it, 53% of the workplaces in the West that knew about opening clauses in relevant agreements made use of them East: 50% (East: 50%, Kohaut 2007). See also Kohaut and Schnabel (2006).

10. I am grateful to Sebastian Lippold for providing me with a selection of the most recent and most important research results on the subject.

11. For a useful survey of the older literature, with essentially the same result, see Bosch and Weinkopf (2008, especially Chapter 1).

12. For all workers (prime-age male employed workers), Gernandt and Pfeiffer (2007) find a slight decline in the 90:10 ratio between 1984 and 1994 from 2.69 (2.14) to 2.47 (2.11), and a marked increase between 1994 and 2005 to 3.08 (2.51).

13. The respective figures for East Germany are 31 and 23%.

14. On the presumable effects of legislation of this kind in 1999, see Rudolph and Wassermann (2007).

3

Intermediary organization: declining membership, rising tensions

The gradual transformation of the German collective bargaining regime was accompanied by a slow decline of the main pillars of German neo-corporatism, organized labor and capital (Streeck and Hassel 2004). In Germany, collective bargaining and union membership are not linked directly. Coverage always significantly exceeded membership, the latter being formally voluntary even in firms subject to a collective agreement. In fact, union membership was never high in postwar Germany compared to Scandinavia or, for that matter, Italy. Still, the 1990s saw a steep decline in union density. According to Ebbinghaus (2002), union members, excluding pensioners, accounted for 35.4 percent of the West German workforce in 1950, 33.8 percent in 1960, and 31.1 percent in 1970. During a brief intermission in the "roaring seventies," the postwar decline was reversed and membership went up, to 32.9 percent in 1980. In the following decade, however, it began falling again, to 29.3 percent in 1990 (West Germany). Then, after a short sharp increase in the wake of unification, the decline accelerated. By 2003, according to estimates based on Ebbinghaus (2002), another 10 percentage points had been lost (Streeck and Rehder 2005), pushing trade union membership down to below one-fifth of the workforce, including the public sector, for the first time after the war (Figure 3.1).[1]

Membership in employer and business associations declined, too, but figures are generally not published. Some data are available on *Gesamtmetall*, the employer association of metal manufacturing, traditionally the flagship sector of the German industrial relations system. In 1985, *Gesamtmetall* still organized roughly 55 percent of the firms in its domain, employing 74 percent of the sector's workforce (Table 3.1). In 1993, density among firms had fallen to 42.8 percent for Germany as a whole, and

46

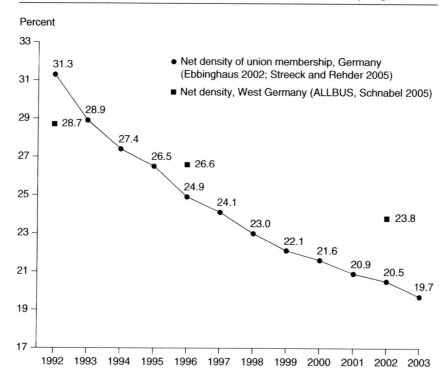

Figure 3.1. Net union membership density, Germany (1992–2003)

among employees to 63.1 percent. By 2003, the last year for which exact information is available, firm membership was down to 25.5 percent in the West and no more than 7.6 percent in East Germany, and member firms employed only 55.1 percent of the—shrinking—sectoral workforce.

Unlike unions, membership in employer associations directly affects coverage by collective agreements since only member firms are formally bound by sectoral negotiations (Haipeter and Schilling 2005). Comparing the two columns of density figures in Table 3.1, one notes that it was above all small firms that defected, pointing to particularly strong dissatisfaction among this group (Schröder and Ruppert 1996). The trend, which is widespread among employer associations although it is rarely publicly documented, is in fact understated in the *Gesamtmetall* figures. This is because in the early 1990s, *Gesamtmetall* created special regional sections for firms unwilling to be covered by the industrial agreement (the so-called *OT-Verbände*). While the 8,116 firms organized by the association in 1989 (46.5% of firms in the sector) were all covered, it is reported

Table 3.1. Membership density, metal industry employer association (*Gesamtmetall*), 1985–2003

	Companies		Employees	
	N	Density (%)	1,000	Density (%)
1985	8,374	**54.6**	2,817	**73.8**
1989	8,116	**46.5**	2,891	**70.3**
1993	8,863	**42.8**	2,663	**63.1**
West	*7,752*	*44.0*	*2,459*	*63.3*
East	*1,111*	*35.7*	*204*	*60.0*
1998	6,810	**31.8**	2,167	**62.2**
West	*6,307*	*34.1*	*2,079*	*64.8*
East	*503*	*17.1*	*88*	*32.2*
2003		**22.5**		**55.1**
West		*25.5*		*58.5*
East		*7.6*		*21.5*

Notes: In bold: directly comparable over time. In italics: West and East (after 1990).
Source: Gesamtmetall (direct communication); for 2003: Haipeter and Schilling (2005).

that in 2004, when roughly 7,000 member firms were left, about 2,000 of them (30%), employing a little less than 20 percent of the workforce of organized firms, were *OT* members (Schnabel 2005). Originally established to keep firms from leaving the association altogether, *OT* sections can also be used to put pressure on the union to moderate its demands, lest even more firms opt to exit from the industrial agreement (Haipeter and Schilling 2005, 180).

Today *OT-Verbände* has spread from metal manufacturing to most other industrial sectors. Their impact on the collective bargaining regime and the stability of the intermediary organizations operating it is complex. As Haipeter and Schilling (2005) point out, *OT* as a strategy of employers is possible only because trade unions no longer have the capacity to drive defecting firms back into the employer association and under the roof of the industry-wide collective agreement. Unlike in the past, when the opposite used to be the case, company agreements today tend to be more favorable to employers than the industrial agreement (Haipeter and Schilling 2005, 181). But while *OT* has destructive effects on collective bargaining above the level of the individual firm, and in this way weakens the unions, it saves employer associations from attrition as it enables them to continue to organize firms even when these no longer want to be represented in collective bargaining. In fact, regional employer associations of the metal manufacturing sector were able significantly to increase their staff after they had set up an *OT* section (Haipeter and Schilling 2005, 178).[2]

Tensions between small and large firms have always been a fact of life in German employer associations. Large firms need the smaller firms to hide behind their lower ability to pay. While small firms benefit from associational services and a strike fund they could not afford on their own, they also suspect large firms of being overly accommodating in wage negotiations, to avoid losses of market share through work stoppages. In the 1990s, that suspicion became overwhelming as heightened international competition made it seem even less likely that export-oriented large manufacturers would risk a strike, not to mention lock out their workers when ordered by the association to do so. Indeed after a disastrous defeat in a strike in 1995 in Bavaria,[3] the new leadership of *Gesamtmetall* publicly declared itself unable to resist whatever wage demand the union chose to make, rhetorically offering the union to decide for itself how much unemployment it was willing to inflict on its members.[4] Shortly thereafter, in the fall of 1996, *Gesamtmetall* was spectacularly deserted by its most important member, Daimler-Benz, in a conflict over sick pay in which Daimler gave in hours after its main plant had been shut down, without even consulting the association.[5]

Doubts about the solidarity to be expected from large member firms were reinforced by a new, more aggressive outsourcing policy. Many of the small and medium-sized firms in *Gesamtmetall* are part suppliers, especially to the large German automobile manufacturers. In the 1990s, it became customary for the latter to ask for deep price reductions to offset increasing labor costs resulting, among other things, from industrial wage settlements. These, of course, had been negotiated by *Gesamtmetall*, under the leadership of the very same large firms that were demanding the price reductions, and they applied to all firms in the industry, including the small suppliers that were asked to reduce their prices. The issue, which continues to be highly virulent, was deeply intertwined with economic internationalization as large firms not only justified their demands with foreign competition, but also increasingly turned to less expensive foreign suppliers if their demands for lower prices were not met.

Declining cohesion among employers came to be reflected in the 1990s in a new, unprecedented rivalry between the two national peak associations, BDA and BDI.[6] Dissatisfaction with the collective bargaining regime and the employer associations sustaining it sought and found expression through associations affiliated with the BDI, especially trade associations representing medium-sized firms of subsections of the metal industry. Although the BDI continued to be dominated by the large manufacturing concerns, its leadership in the 1990s championed the cause and vented the sentiments of small independent entrepreneurs.[7] By aggressively urging radical neo-liberal reforms and adopting highly adversarial rhetoric regarding trade unions and industrial relations, the BDI embarrassed the employer associations that had to deal directly with the unions and therefore were disposed to take a more moderate line. In 1996, the president of the BDI, Henkel, in an entirely unprecedented move, intervened publicly to prevent the election of the head of the BDA, Murmann, as president of the European business confederation, UNICE. Subsequently pressure from the BDI and its member associations gradually succeeded in making employer associations take a more conflictual stance. In 1999, one year into the first Schröder government, BDA and BDI together lobbied intensively against proposed legislation to shore up the sagging works council system. While they were ultimately unsuccessful, the legislation had to be passed outside the tripartite "Alliance for Jobs" and remained far behind what the unions had hoped for. In 2000, to assuage the growing number of opponents in its own camp, *Gesamtmetall* agreed to fund a large-scale public relations effort, *Initiative Neue Soziale Marktwirtschaft* (INSM; Initiative for a New Social Market Economy) which propagates a neo-liberal program of institutional reform (see, among others, Kindermann 2005). INSM receives about €9 million annually from *Gesamtmetall*. Four years later, under the presidency of the owner-manager of a medium-sized machine-tools firm, who had been one of the most outspoken opponents of the *Gesamtmetall* leadership, the BDI started a campaign to abolish worker co-determination on the supervisory boards of large German firms. While further aggravating relations with the unions, the project never had a chance of success since no government could be expected to spend political capital on it. Still, the BDI managed to get the BDA to support its campaign even though, or precisely because, it was never more than a symbolic exercise, mostly for the benefit of small- and medium-sized firms which, of course, are not subject to supervisory board co-determination.

Divisions also opened up among national trade unions. Beginning in the 1980s, economic change rendered the postwar demarcations between the 16 industrial unions affiliated to the DGB increasingly obsolete. In the subsequent decade, rising competition for a declining union constituency, also in the wake of unification (see Part III), resulted in mergers and various efforts at redrawing interorganizational boundaries. Preparations for organizational reform had been under way since the mid-1980s. In the end, however, mergers were not driven by sectoral but mostly by political affinities, to a large extent following the battle lines of a formative conflict in 1984 over how to use early retirement to manage industrial restructuring and rising unemployment (see the next chapter, on social policy). While the union of the leather industry, under centrist-conservative leadership, joined the chemical workers, which subsequently merged with the miners, the textile workers and the wood workers merged with *IG Metall*. Today there are only eight DGB unions left, with the two largest, *IG Metall* and the united service sector union, Verdi, together accounting for no less than 70 percent of total membership (2006). Both unions, Verdi more than *IG Metall*, incline toward the left of the SPD, with growing sympathies among their ranks for the post-Communist *Linkspartei*. On the other side, IG BCE, the former union of chemical workers, with only 11.1 percent of union members, maintains close connections to the SPD leadership and to moderates in the CDU, which makes it highly politically influential regardless of its small size. The deep divisions between the two camps on almost every major issue, from wages to social policy, together with the changed size distribution among its affiliates and the intensified competition for members following the blurring of sectoral boundaries, have effectively immobilized the national federation, the DGB, which has finally lost whatever capacity it may once have had to make its members line up behind a common position.[8]

Unlike what one would expect in a self-equilibrating "coordinated market economy," then, unions and employer associations *declined in parallel and together*, unwilling or unable to help each other maintain their organizational capacities for joint corporatist governance and coordination. Employer associations resisted legislation to bolster the works council system, which would have facilitated union membership recruitment. In fact they weakened both unions and industry-level bargaining by setting up special sections for members wanting to opt out of the centralized industrial relations system. Unions, for their part, lacked the strength to drive defecting firms back into employer associations or out of the new *OT* sections. Both camps faced a growing proclivity among nonmembers not to join, a rising tendency for members to defect, as well as declining discipline among remaining members, partly but not entirely related to a decline in organizational capacities to exercise effective control. Associations of both business and labor found themselves increasingly diminished in their ability to unify divergent interests and rein in the centrifugal tendencies of particularistic identities among their constituents. In this respect, they were and continue to be confronted with the same difficulties that confront political parties, churches, and other membership organizations today, difficulties that have become associated with the notion of a general trend toward "individualization."

Looking at the relationship between the collective bargaining regime and the organization of capital and labor, we find what might once have been a relationship of complementarity, in the sense of mutual enhancement, to have gradually given way to one of *mutual destabilization*. In the past, a variety of legal provisions and established practices, among them the settlement of workplace grievances and the enforcement of industrial agreements through works councils, helped sustain the internal cohesion and the representational monopoly of comprehensive, nationally based organizations of business and labor and enhanced their capacity to govern their members (Streeck 1979) (Streeck et al. 1981). Encompassing organization, in turn, produced relatively uniform employment standards covering a wide variety of firms and sectors. Over time, however, the very policies, above all of wage compression, that were made possible by the mutual reinforcement of encompassing organization and industry-level collective bargaining, changed the causal relation between the two by eroding the communality of interests underlying it, especially as external economic conditions also began to change.

A defining moment was when the same large firms that dominated the joint employer associations forced small- and medium-sized supplier firms to cut their prices. Roughly at this point, a formerly self-reinforcing institutional configuration became self-undermining,[9] and perhaps ultimately self-destructive. With more firms exiting from sectoral collective bargaining, thereby narrowing its coverage and adding to the diversity of industrial relations practices, unions and employer associations had to allow for decentralization of wage setting and ever more deviations from the industrial agreement, in response to growing demands mainly from small- and medium-sized firms for attention to their special interests. Still, as declining comprehensiveness of collective bargaining in turn deprived encompassing interest organizations of vital institutional supports, unions and employer associations continued to lose members: unions because their accelerating loss of control over the wage bargain made membership less attractive, and employer associations as firm-specific employment regimes became less risky and more acceptable. Finally, conflicts within declining labor market associations over policies and domains, coupled with dwindling capacities of associational leaders to bind their members, further accelerated the contraction and the softening of the traditional collective bargaining regime.

In the following chapters, we will trace in some detail how a gradual exhaustion of social policy, an evolving fiscal crisis of the state—leading among other things to a wave of privatization of public enterprises—and the dissolution of the German company network further reinforced both the transformation of the collective bargaining system and the attrition of corporatist intermediary organization. How far the two related processes have meanwhile advanced was indicated, among other things, by the defeat of *IG Metall* in its 2003 strike for a reduction of working hours in East Germany. The defeat, which resulted in a leadership crisis that almost tore the union apart, had been caused less by the fierce resistance of the employers, but by the opposition of the works councils of the large West German automobile manufacturers, who feared a loss of production and market share due to missing supplies. By watching from the sidelines how the national union ran into a disaster unprecedented in its postwar history, works council leaders established once and for all that they had acquired an effective veto over union policy, and that the union's traditional centralization and collective discipline had given way to a new pluralism and strong sectional interests. We will return to this signal event below in a different context.

The destruction of what the detractors of the corporatist industrial relations system of the postwar era had begun to call in the 1990s a *Reichseinheitstarif* has given rise to two other developments that are also indicative of a process of profound disorganization. One is the emergence of independent unions of small groups of professional or highly skilled workers aggressively representing their members outside established channels and in opposition to the industrial unions of the DGB. Prominent examples are airline pilots, hospital doctors, and locomotive engine drivers, all of whom suffered from or are averse to compression of wage differentials in the course of encompassing collective bargaining. Especially the recent strikes of hospital doctors (2006) and engine drivers (2007), organized by unions not affiliated with the DGB, and their successful achievement of separate collective agreements have shown to what extent the capacity of the traditional industrial relations system to control sectional interests has already eroded. Among the likely consequences is that other, similar groups will feel encouraged to try the same methods. As one side effect, industrial unions will have to become, if not more militant, then certainly more considerate of the special interests of their skilled members, making it much more difficult for them than in the past to engage in wage leveling. Here, as in many other respects, IG BCE, the former union of chemical workers, now merged with the mineworkers, is likely to be a model for others, although very probably without being given public credit for it.

The weakening of corporatist intermediary organization results in widening wage differentials, not just at the upper end of the labor market, but also, and even more so, at its lower end. In the preceding chapter we documented how the bottom fell out of the German wage distribution in the 1990s, a development that has in the meantime opened up a broad political space for the introduction of a legal minimum wage—an issue that came to dominate the domestic political agenda at the end of 2007. A suitable institutional toolkit for this is available in the form of the German legislation implementing the so-called Posted Workers Directive of the European Union (Eichhorst 2000). Legal minimum wages have long been anathema to German trade unions, who considered them incompatible with free collective bargaining and eschewed them as an admission of union weakness. In recent years, however, unions have had to convince themselves that there are now vast sectors of the German economy where they have lost, probably forever, any influence on wage setting and the wage structure. Not surprisingly, the first to recognize this was the union of the service sector, Verdi, which in 2006 went on record calling for a nationwide legal minimum wage of €7.50 per hour. In the meantime, the DGB and other unions, including *IG Metall*, have raised the same or similar demands. It is worth noting that both sectional unionism among narrow groups of highly skilled workers and the use of legislation to prevent low wages from falling below the poverty line are characteristic, not of organized or corporatist, but of liberal and pluralist political economies.

Up to here, our treatment of change in the intermediary organization of the German political economy has focused mainly on the relationship between interest organizations and their members. However, intermediary organizations in corporatist political economies are subject, not just to a "logic of membership," but also to a "logic of influence" (Schmitter and Streeck 1999): their structure and behavior is determined, in addition to their members, by the conditions and strategic imperatives of their interaction with other organized interests and the public power. To understand fully the tensions that have emerged inside organized business and labor, and to appreciate in its entirety their impact on the collective bargaining system, one must understand how intermediary organizations in the German system relate, or used to relate, to government policy, above all social policy, which is where the state and organized economic interests come closest to each other.

Notes

1. According to data from the ALLBUS survey, density in East Germany in 1992 was far above West German rates (39.7% compared to 28.7%). In 1996, density ratios had become about the same (26.6 and 26.7), and six years later, density in the East had fallen clearly below the Western level (to 20.4% as compared to 23.8%) (Schnabel 2005).
2. The price, of course, is the internalization in the association of the competition between the traditional and a new, union-free way of regulating the employment relationship.
3. This was the first instance of major defections of large and prosperous firms. It was this defeat that gave rise to the creation of *OT-Verbände* (Haipeter and Schilling 2005, 177).
4. The message being that while the union could win any victory it wanted, all its victories would in fact be Pyrrhic given the new conditions of "globalization."
5. The conflict was over the implementation of hard-won legislation by the Kohl government fulfilling long-standing employer demands. Its symbolic significance was huge, also because Daimler had in the past always been willing to go to battle for the collective interests of employers, among other things in various costly lock-outs in the 1960s and 1970s (see below).
6. Germany has a dual system of business associations, with employer associations federated in the BDA, and industry or trade associations in the BDI. Most firms belong to one BDA and at least one BDI association.
7. This was similar in other European countries at the time (Streeck and Visser 2005). For more on this development, see below.
8. The German development follows a pattern that can be observed in a number of other European countries as well. While trade union amalgamations were common in the 1990s, they as a rule failed to end membership decline. Instead they resulted in increased competition for organizational domains and a weakening of the relative power and the coordinating capacity of national union federations (Ebbinghaus 2003).
9. To draw on the highly pertinent terminology suggested by Greif (2006). I will make use of this figure of thought—which of course has long been present in the social sciences, not least in its Marxist tradition—in the analytical sections of the book, especially in Part II.

4

Social policy: the rise and fall of welfare corporatism

As in most Bismarckian welfare states, organized business and labor in Germany share in the governance of the social security system.[1] Over time this gave rise to complex relations of interdependence between collective bargaining, the status and structure of intermediary organizations, and government social policy.[2] As has frequently been shown, the way the three happened to be connected in Germany conditioned a "patholog- ical" (Manow 2007, Chapter 6) response to the emerging employment problems after the first oil crisis, one that used unemployment insurance, labor market policy, and the pension system for restrictive management of the labor supply (Manow and Seils 2000). While this helped main- tain the low wage spread and the downwardly rigid high wages pro- duced by the collective bargaining system, it also moved the German economy into a lasting low-employment equilibrium. After 2002, the rising costs of a "high-equality, low-activity" labor market regime (Streeck 2001a) forced deep institutional reforms that, among other things, pro- foundly diminished the political status and power of organized business and labor.

Using the welfare state to take surplus labor out of the market began long before unification. While it was after 1990 then that the practice reached its peak, it had become the policy instrument of choice to cope with economic shocks and industrial change already by the middle of the 1980s. As early as the 1960s, business and labor—the "social partners"— had managed to convince the government that it was in the public interest if the pension fund paid for early retirement of displaced workers in declining industries, such as coal mining and textiles.[3] Early retirement preserved social peace in that it enabled unions—very much in the inter- est of employers—not to oppose industrial restructuring while at the same time allowing them to avoid facing the consequences of the transition to a service economy. By taking redundant workers out of the workforce, it also protected the egalitarian German wage structure and thereby helped secure the internal cohesion of encompassing industrial unions.

Toward the end of postwar growth, two loosely related formative events came together to make using social security for stabilizing the collective bargaining regime both a political necessity and an established practice. The wave of unofficial strikes in 1969, fueled by two years of wage moderation in support of the Grand Coalition's Keynesian reflation policies, led the leadership of *IG Metall* to conclude that another round of cooperation with government wage guidelines, in whatever form, might finally cost it its control over the union and put the union itself at risk. From then on, *IG Metall* consistently refused to compromise its freedom of collective bargaining (*Tarifautonomie*) vis-à-vis the government, at least formally and in public. Five years later, partly in reaction to this, the independent German central bank, the *Bundesbank*, adopted and publicly committed itself to a monetarist policy *avant le lettre*, one that explicitly ruled out sacrificing monetary stability for employment (Scharpf 1991). In response, the unions in 1977 withdrew from what was left of the government's tripartite incomes policy.[4] As a result, the Keynesian reflation policy of 1967 and 1968 remained the only instance of its kind in postwar German economic history.

By the end of the 1970s, German firms reacted to the peculiarly German combination of a hard currency policy and a high-pay egalitarian wage regime by moving aggressively into high-quality niches in the world market, drawing on the superior skills of the German workforce and further investing in them.[5] Supported by cooperative works councils, the emerging "supply-side corporatism" (Streeck 1984*b*) made the German economy highly competitive in what came to be referred to as "diversified quality production" (Streeck 1991), which became the economic foundation of the success of the "German model" in its heyday. What was mostly overlooked at the time, however, was that the evolving new production system could absorb only part of the country's labor supply, leaving it to the state and the social security system to deal with a growing labor surplus. Squeezed between trade unions insisting on free collective bargaining and a central bank holding fast to its independent mandate to fight inflation, the social-liberal government of Helmut Schmidt initially placed its hopes for a return to full employment on fiscal expansion. When this resulted in a rapid rise of public debt, all the government could do was to make unemployment less visible and more socially acceptable by further expanding the legal opportunities for early retirement and making unemployment benefits even more generous.[6]

In subsequent years, a "de-commodifying" (Esping-Andersen 1985) social policy became the functional equivalent to Keynesian demand management for German governments (Streeck 2001c), as it was routinely used to compensate for the short-term wage rigidities and the egalitarian wage structure associated with centralized collective bargaining, securing "social peace" between business and labor and, hopefully, protecting the government in power from political discontent over unemployment. Unlike Thatcher, the government of Helmut Kohl, which entered office in 1982, found the unions too well entrenched to dislodge them. In 1984, the year in which Thatcher crushed Arthur Scargill's miners' union, *IG Metall* sought to respond to rising unemployment in the wake of the second oil crisis[7] in a way compatible with the union's traditional wage militancy and went on a six-week national strike for a reduction of weekly working time to 35 hours without loss of pay (Bosch 1986). Early in the negotiations, the government tried to defuse the upcoming conflict by making subsidies available for firms offering their workers additional opportunities for early retirement. *IG Metall*, however, stayed its course. Other unions, led by the chemical workers, followed the government and opted for "lifetime" rather than weekly working time reduction. This was the beginning of what became a lasting rift inside the DGB, ultimately setting in motion the politicized and competitive redrawing of organizational boundaries in the 1990s (see above).

The 1984 metal industry strike was the largest industrial conflict in the history of postwar Germany. In the end, the employers had to give in, but not without winning major concessions in particular on working time flexibility. It was only later that the union discovered that its victory had cost it whatever control it might still have had over productivity and the wage–effort bargain (Streeck 2001c, 2005).[8] As employers learned to use increasingly sophisticated working time regimes to mobilize productivity reserves, whatever positive employment effects shorter hours might have had withered away. In fact, working time flexibility came to be used by employers, in particular in large firms, to compensate for the real wage increases unions managed to extract in subsequent wage negotiations, resulting in successive rounds of labor shedding and a rising capital/labor ratio. Building leaner and younger workforces, employers avoided industrial conflict by using the extended early retirement provisions originally created in 1984 as an alternative rather than as a complement to shorter weekly working hours (Mares 2003, 231ff.). With early

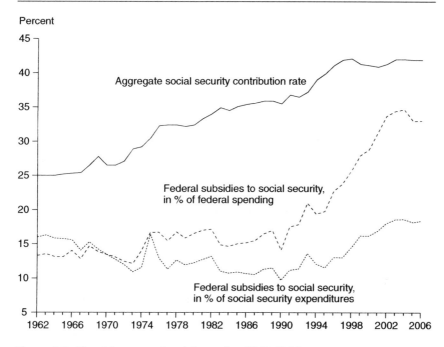

Figure 4.1. The rising cost of social security, 1962–2006

retirement, high and sometimes indefinite unemployment benefits and "active" labor market policy programs providing a safety valve, union wage demands well into the 1990s met with limited resistance from employer associations, while trade unions and works councils could afford to tolerate industry-wide workforce reduction carried out in the name of international competitiveness.[9]

Stabilization of the postwar class compromise through social policy came not without costs. From the mid-1970s, the aggregate rate of contributions to pension, health, and unemployment insurance, which had been about 25 percent of gross wages in the 1960s, rose to more than 35 percent by the end of the 1980s, and to more than 40 percent half a decade later (Figure 4.1). Since social security contributions add to the cost of labor, their increase was bound to exacerbate the German economy's employment problem (Manow 2007, Chapter 6). In particular, high non-wage labor costs stifled job growth in the service sector at a time when employment in industry was bound to decline, even in the most internationally competitive countries. As a consequence, German governments were torn between extending and retrenching early retirement and other costly measures to restrict the labor supply, such as active labor market policy. In fact, occasional attempts to restrain early retirement date back to the 1980s, but they were frustrated by employers and works councils finding ever new legal loopholes for "early exit" (Ebbinghaus 2006, 219, 227).

As Philip Manow has shown (Manow 2007, Chapter 6), German governments used the social security system not just to hide unemployment but also to balance their budgets without increasing general taxes. This was especially the case after unification when the government attempted to cover its costs, including the full extension of the West German early retirement regime to the East, mostly by higher social security contributions. However, faced with an accelerating vicious circle of increasing contributions causing rising unemployment and vice versa, the government had to commit itself publicly by the mid-1990s to keeping the aggregate rate of contributions permanently below 40 percent. Even though this goal was never achieved (Figure 4.1), it implied that federal subsidies to social security had to rise, from about 10 percent of total social security spending in the 1980s to a little under 20 percent roughly a decade later. As a consequence, the share of the federal budget going to social security increased dramatically, from roughly 17 percent of federal spending in 1989 to about 35 percent in 2004 (Figure 4.1).

With avoidance of conflict between capital and labor requiring ever higher infusions of public money, generous spending on social security ceased to facilitate compromise between divergent interests and instead gave rise to acute distributive conflicts. Small- and medium-sized firms complained that early retirement, even though it was paid for by all, benefited primarily the larger firms, compounding the advantages these were believed to have in using the more flexible working time regimes allowed by the 1984 strike settlement. Rising nonwage labor costs thus added to the discontent caused by the pincer movement of wage increases and price pressures hurting small suppliers, reinforcing the tensions described above that had been developing since the late 1980s both within employer associations and between the national federations of business, BDI and BDA.

Social policy also began to drive a wedge between organized business and labor at the national level, as well as between the government and the trade unions, undermining not just the organizational cohesion of business and labor but also the traditional pattern of corporatist cooperation between them and the government. In 1995, Chancellor Helmut Kohl sought a tripartite "Alliance for Employment" to bring down unemployment and consolidate public finances by cutting back on social security benefits and contributions. By then, however, supply-side corporatism had gradually decayed into a regime of "welfare corporatism" (Streeck 2005), in which encompassing collective bargaining and interest organization had become dependent on social policy absorbing the costs of accommodation between unions facing a demanding core membership and labor-shedding employers struggling with international competition. Although national business associations supported government efforts to put an end to early retirement and "active" labor market policy, they did so mainly to appease their small-firm constituency and widen the rift between unions and government. Unable to obtain consensus while forced to rein in growing deficits, the government legislated a series of cutbacks over passionate union protest, only to be left alone by internally divided employer associations unable to get their large member firms to implement the new laws.[10] Unions, in turn, retaliated by devoting all their political strength to unseating the government in the upcoming election in 1998.

Much to the unions' dismay, the first red-green government of Gerhard Schröder, just as its predecessor, called for a tripartite "Alliance" to increase employment by, among other things, bringing down social security contributions. Again, no compromise was found as retirement and labor market policy had become too valuable especially to the unions to be negotiable. In fact, by mid-1999 *IG Metall,* facing unexpected resistance from its membership against another reduction of weekly working hours, reversed its earlier position and demanded a further lowering of the legal age of retirement from 65 to 60 (*"Rente mit 60"*). At the end of the year this demand, which was bound to be entirely unacceptable to any government, had become so important to the union that it publicly offered, for the first time ever, to agree to a lower wage settlement in exchange. The "Alliance" collapsed for all practical purposes shortly thereafter (Streeck 2003). In the spring of 2002, with another election approaching, the government in a surprise maneuver forced a change in the leadership of one of the bastions of social partnership and social policy "self-government," the Federal Labor Agency (*Bundesagentur für Arbeit*), a para-public institution which runs the government's labor market policy programs. It also appointed a commission, with only token representation of trade unions and employer associations, to prepare major reforms in labor market policy, unemployment insurance, and social assistance.[11]

The disintegration of the Schröder "Alliance" paved the way for incisive changes in social benefits, especially those related to unemployment and the labor market. It also gave rise to an unprecedented assertion of state control over social policy, at the expense of unions and employer associations who lost their status as corporatist co-governors of the social security system. Subsequently they found themselves reduced to pluralist lobbying from the outside of a government that was determined to use its constitutional powers to legislate unilaterally. Social policy, while it had long helped organize tripartite cooperation, now turned into a source of disorganization, not just at the level of organized interests, but of the polity as a whole. In 2003 and 2004, the so-called "Hartz reforms" were passed. Among other things, they tightened the requirements for the unemployed to accept job offers, shortened the duration of unemployment benefits from 32 to 12 months, and amalgamated assistance for the long-term unemployed with social assistance into a single, flat-rate, and means-tested benefit (Streeck and Trampusch 2005). By implication, the reforms foreclosed a variety of avenues of "early exit" from employment. Mass protests organized by the unions were to no avail, although they contributed to Schröder's loss of popularity, not least in his own party, and to his decision to cut his second term one year short and call an early election in 2005, which he lost. Even this, however, could not restore the unions' political privileges. In 2006, the Social-Democratic Minister of Labor of the Grand Coalition pushed through the cabinet an extension of the legal age of retirement from 65 to 67 without even informing the unions, showing how much political time had passed since 1999, when *IG Metall* had clamored for *Rente mit 60*.

The failure of the two "Alliances" and the rise of government unilateralism in social policy were accompanied by, and greatly contributed to, a secular restructuring of interorganizational relations in the social policy field that further diminished the status of trade unions and employer associations. Among other things, this was reflected in a profound change in the composition of the Bundestag's Standing Committee for Labor and Social Policy (*Ausschuss für Arbeit und Sozialordnung*).[12] Well into the 1980s, the committee had consisted almost completely of like-minded members from the two large parties, Social Democrats and Christian Democrats, with career backgrounds in trade unions, employer associations, social services, and *Selbstverwaltung*, who between them and the Ministry of Labor in effect determined the government's social policy. In the 1990s, however, the number especially of Christian-Democratic committee members linked to the social policy establishment fell sharply, temporarily to zero, their place being taken by political generalists connected, instead, to the leadership of the party (Trampusch 2005a, 23).

At the same time, the share of SPD members with leading party positions declined (Trampusch 2005a, 23, 24). The changes reflected both a breakdown of the long-standing social policy consensus between the large parties and a growing interest taken in social policy by party leaders concerned primarily with electoral strategy and state governability.

In parallel to the fall from power of the bipartisan clan of *Sozialpolitiker* and the rising autonomy of parties, parliament, and government in the making of social policy from organized labor and business,[13] the Schröder reforms advanced the disorganization of corporatist industrial relations and intermediary organizations by accelerating the already ongoing attrition of the para-public institutions of sectoral self-government, far beyond the Federal Labor Agency where the Hartz legislation essentially abolished self-government (Trampusch 2006a). Pressures for rationalization, resulting from spending cutbacks and increasing competition from private service providers, had for some time caused a reduction in the number and size of collective representation bodies, especially in the health care system, which reduced the presence of the "social partners" in the governance of the sector. Moreover, privatization and the growing role of markets in social security provision added new players to the social policy field, in particular private firms and their associations. In addition, union failure to prevent Schröder's benefit cuts resulted in rising membership in various independent interest organizations representing beneficiaries of social security, confronting unions with a new kind of competition, one representing only the recipients of benefits and not also those paying for them. In this way, in less than a decade, the social policy field underwent a profound disorganization, with a deep transformation from a solidly corporatist to an increasingly pluralist (Trampusch 2006b) and competitive pattern of interorganizational relations and interest politics.[14]

To summarize, just as encompassing intermediary organization and centralized collective bargaining first supported and then subverted each other, and indeed strongly contributing to changing the nature of the relationship between the two, social policy originally helped sustain but later undermined peaceful relations between capital and labor, at both workplace and national level. From 1984 on at the latest, employers had to be compensated for continuing to participate in an increasingly burdensome collective bargaining regime the government did not dare to touch for fear of unmanageable industrial and political conflict. Later, however, when securing social peace by means of a de-commodifying social policy grew ever more expensive, its utility for the government declined, not least because it turned into another source of high unemployment. In addition, rising social security contributions reinforced the divisions between small and large firms, while they did nothing to heal the rift between "traditionalist" and "moderate" trade unions. What had once stabilized encompassing collective bargaining and intermediary organization began to disorganize it when its accumulated consequences had changed the external conditions on which it was premised. When in the 1990s the state's fiscal capacities were finally exhausted, public policy had no choice but to cut back on social security spending. After the failure of two attempts by successive governments of different political color to negotiate tripartite reforms of the German welfare state, organized capital and labor, unable to divorce themselves from "welfare corporatism," saw the government chip away at their political status—a loss much more painful to the unions than to the employers—and had to watch from the sidelines as deep cutbacks were unilaterally implemented by legislation.

The reorganization of the social policy field diminished the public status of the corporatist intermediary organizations of labor and capital and thereby contributed to their organizational decline, among other things by weakening their control over their members. Interest organizations that cannot rely on safe institutionalized access to political decisions and instead have to struggle for influence with competitors become more than the corporatist "private interest governments" of the past dependent on the active support of their members and clients. As the "logic of influence" ceases to sustain them organizationally, they are forced to pay more attention and orient their structures to the "logic of membership." With pluralism in their political target environment on the rise, intermediary organizations of both sides, capital and labor, must listen more than before to their members and cater more directly to their perceived immediate interests. As a result, it becomes more and more difficult for them to impose on a heterogeneous membership a common definition of interest. Internal conflicts are likely to intensify, and sectional secession, as in the case of hospital doctors and locomotive engine drivers, becomes a realistic possibility, the more so the less the established organizations succeed in monopolizing political access.

Looking back from here, the gradual decentralization of wage setting and the slow decline of the intermediary organizations of business and labor in Germany appear intertwined, not just with each other, but also with a parallel erosion of the state's fiscal capacity, caused by rising demands in the 1970s and 1980s of the postwar class compromise and its institutions for state support. Considered in isolation, the shrinking and softening of the core of German industrial relations, even in conjunction with the organizational decline of trade unions and business associations, might still appear as a temporary disturbance, to be followed sooner or later by a return to the historical equilibrium. This seems much less plausible, however, if one takes into account social policy and its latent functions (Merton 1957) for the stability of the corporatist industrial relations system of the 1980s. Here one observes *the same shift, from reinforcement to subversion,* as in the relationship between collective bargaining and intermediary organization. Like centralized wage setting used to sustain encompassing class and sectoral organizations and vice versa, until the policies this enabled the latter to pursue crossed a threshold beyond which they undermined both,[15] so corporatist social and labor market policy, as it accumulated over time, ceased to complement the traditional industrial relations system and instead became a source of intense conflict within and between intermediary organizations, as well as between them and their former sponsor, the "semi-sovereign" (Katzenstein 1987) German state. Far from being corrected by counterbalancing adjustments in intermediary organizations' "logic of influence," the decentralization of collective bargaining and the transformations in unions' and employer associations' "logic of membership" seem in fact to have been accompanied and reinforced by parallel changes in state capacities proceeding in the same direction: away from, rather than returning to, a previous institutional equilibrium.

Once again, this raises the question whether the changes we have observed might be reversible—in this case, whether there is any prospect for the supporting role of the state in relation to a corporatist collective bargaining regime and the intermediary organizations it requires being restored at some point. In order to address this, we now turn to another, related development: the slow unfolding of an endemic fiscal crisis of the postwar German state at the end of the twentieth century.

Notes

1. The German term for this is *Selbstverwaltung* ("self-government"). *Selbstverwaltung* in social security is part of a broader pattern of sharing of public authority between organized social groups and what Katzenstein, in his seminal work on the Federal Republic, called a "semi-sovereign" state (Katzenstein 1987). As Katzenstein has shown, delegation of state authority to "para-public institutions" involving organized interests is practiced in a wide variety of policy areas and is a distinguishing trait of the postwar German polity.

2. For a detailed analysis of the historical co-evolution of the three, see Manow (2007).

3. On German early retirement policies in comparative perspective, see Ebbinghaus (2006).

4. Officially this was explained as protest against the employers challenging the 1976 codetermination legislation in the Constitutional Court.

5. The changes involved in "Fordist" mass production industries, and the extent to which the restructuring of the 1970s and 1980s was in fact a return to older German traditions of manufacturing, were discussed extensively at the time (Streeck 1989a).

6. The generosity of German unemployment benefits, in turn, contributed to the high unemployment figures. The unemployment rate as calculated by German rules tended for a long time to be about 2 percentage points higher than the standardized unemployment rates under the ILO system. For example, in 1995 (2003), the German figure was 9.4% (10.5%) while the ILO figure was only 7.4 (8.7), with 745,000 (674,000) more unemployed persons according to the German than to the ILO classification (data from the website of the *Sachverständigenrat*). The reason was that to be recognized as unemployed under ILO rules, one must "have taken active steps to find work in the last four weeks" (*OECD Factbook* 2007). Some recipients of German unemployment benefit are not required to take any such steps at all, and are therefore not counted as unemployed by the ILO.

7. The German standardized unemployment rate increased from 2.6% in 1980 to 7.1% in 1984.

8. Since working time flexibility had to be negotiated at the firm level, the 1984 settlement also helped prepare the ground for the decentralization and fragmentation of collective bargaining in the 1990s. In this respect, too, it turned out to be a two-edged sword from the perspective of the unions.

9. Employment rates among males aged 55–59 (60–64) in West Germany fell continuously from 89.0% (74.0%) in 1970 to 82.1 (53.3) in 1975, 76.4 (41.5) in 1980, and 74.8 (32.9) in 1990. Five years later, the rate for Germany as a whole had fallen to 64.1% (29.6%), after which it very slowly increased to 66.0% (30.1%) in 2000 and 68.9% (33.1%) in 2003 (Ebbinghaus 2006).

10. See above on *Gesamtmetall* and Daimler-Benz in 1996.

11. On this and the following, see Streeck and Trampusch (2005, 184ff.).

12. On the following, see Trampusch (2005a).

13. Another step away from the corporatist past was the abolition of the unions' bridgehead in the federal government, the Ministry of Labor, in the second Schröder cabinet. The Ministry was combined with the Ministry of Economic Affairs, headed by a leading right-wing Social Democrat. This was, however, reversed when the Grand Coalition needed to increase the number of important Cabinet posts in 2005.

14. Bode, following the same intuition as the present author, speaks of "*disorganisierter Wohlfahrtskapitalismus*" ("disorganized welfare capitalism"), being the result of political "reorganization" of the social policy sector, in Germany as well as in France and Great Britain (Bode 2004).
15. A mechanism that Greif and Laitin call "parametric change" (Greif and Laitin 2004). See also Greif (2006).

5

Public finance: the fiscal crisis of the postwar state

The anticorporatist etatistic turn in social policy cut back self-government by means of para-public institutions, loosened the ties binding the state to organized interests, and disorganized the social policy field by opening it up for economic and political competition. Driving this were tightening resource constraints, with an ever larger share of the federal budget being consumed by subsidies to social security when further increases in contribution rates had become economically counterproductive and no longer politically viable. Corporatist sharing and, indeed, delegation of control over Germany's postwar welfare state ended when political parties and the government could no longer afford not to be in control of a social policy that had begun to crowd out all other political concerns. Disorganization by means of a strong assertion of state sovereignty was the strategy of choice of all political parties after financial constraints had caused a breakdown of the bipartisan social policy consensus and after organized business and labor, dependent on the welfare corporatism that had become dominant in the 1980s, had refused to share responsibility for reform.

The resource pressures that changed the political function and the institutional fabric of social policy were related to, and in fact were instrumental in causing, a general crisis of public finance that came to the fore and urgently demanded political attention by the end of the 1990s. Apart from the Keynesian interlude of 1967 and 1968, the German federal budget had been basically balanced until the end of the Golden Age (Figure 5.1). From then on, however, it remained solidly in deficit. High countercyclical spending in 1975 was never paid back. During the 1980s, total public debt in percent of GDP continued to rise until, at the end of Kohl's second term and shortly before unification, first effects of

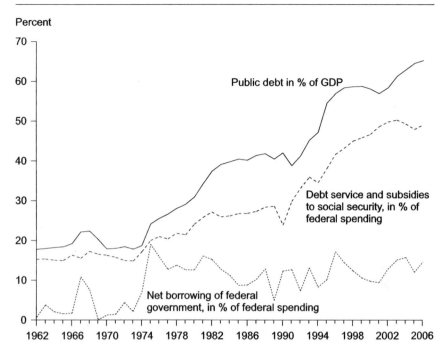

Percent

Figure 5.1. The evolving fiscal crisis of the German state

strong economic growth and intense efforts toward fiscal consolidation became visible. Unification, however, put an end to this. After the short-lived boom it caused, and especially when social security contributions had reached their economic limit, the federal budget continued to show a negative balance, of between 10 and 20 percent of total spending every year. This caused a steep increase in the accumulated public debt, which within one-and-a-half decades grew from about 40 to a little less than 70 percent of GDP (Figure 5.1).[1]

Democratic governments are expected to relieve social problems and satisfy the demands of their constituents. To do so, they require resources that they have to extract by taxation from a polity and an economy endowed with strong political and property rights and capable of placing effective limits on what the state can take from them. Demand for public policies may therefore easily outrun the supply of public resources. This makes it tempting for governments to satisfy current claims by intertemporal redistribution, mobilizing resources from future instead of present citizens. For example, governments may incur debt in capital markets to be serviced and repaid later, or they may create entitlements to pensions that, while benefiting present voters or rewarding present trade unions for wage restraint, have to be paid by future voters (Pierson 2001). Although political leaders are likely over time to become ever more adroit at moving taxation from a resistant present to a defenseless future, as debt accumulates, a point is inevitably reached when the resources borrowed today from the future *have to be used in their entirety to pay the interest on past borrowings from the present.* In Germany this happened around 2005 and 2006, when debt service and new debt both amounted to about 14 percent of federal spending (Streeck 2007).

In other words, while public borrowing increases current policy options, it at the same time forecloses future ones. If borrowing becomes routine as it did in Germany after 1974, it is not sustainable as a strategy since it gradually consumes a state's future capacity for discretionary decisions.[2] This is the case in particular if public deficits and public borrowing are incurred to cover unfunded social security entitlements (see also Pierson 2001). How this dynamic works may be seen by looking at the combined share of the German federal budget devoted to either servicing the public debt or subsidizing social security—in other words, to paying for the combined entitlements of rentiers on the one hand and *Rentner* (pensioners) on the other. In a little more than 10 years, this exploded from less than a quarter to about 50 percent of federal spending (Figure 5.1).

The political consequences of this were and continue to be nothing short of dramatic. In 2006, taking into account three other de facto fixed spending commitments—assistance for the long-term unemployed (14.7%), personnel (10.0%), and defense (9.1%)—no less than 83 percent of the federal budget were effectively frozen, leaving just a small residual of 17 percent for discretionary spending. It is remarkable that in 1970, that same figure had been still as high as 43 percent, with a rapid decline starting in the mid-1970s, followed by a short period of stabilization at the end of the 1980s, and then by another steep decline in the 1990s and 2000s (Table 5.1). Note that the apparent recovery in 1995 was not really one as it merely reflected the peace dividend at the end of the Cold War, when defense expenditures were cut sharply, by 8 percentage points in terms of federal spending, compared to 1989.

Nothing illustrates better than these figures the extent to which the political capacity of the postwar German state had withered away over time. At the end of the 1990s, its ability to absorb the costs of the corporatist class compromise by underwriting ever-rising social security entitlements was exhausted, if not forever, at least for a future long

Table 5.1. Discretionary expenditure of the Federal Government, in percent of total Federal Expenditure, 1970–2005

	Percent
1970	43.3
1975	43.0
1980	36.3
1985	30.9
1989	30.4
1995	34.1
2000	22.3
2005	18.8

Source: Bundesfinanzbericht, consecutive editions, 1975–2005, Table 4.

enough to require more than just temporary adjustments (Streeck 2007). Later than in the United States but just as definitively, the postwar era of "easy money" gave way to what Pierson calls a regime of "fiscal austerity" (Pierson 2001). In Germany, where the government had found it impossible to negotiate a consensual response to the growing costs of corporatist social peace, the new regime involved acceptance and, later, active encouragement on the part of the state of institutional disorganization, in wage setting, interest intermediation, and social policy. With insufficient resources for public provision and political coordination, government increasingly relied on privatization and private competition to compensate for its evaporating capacity to subsidize political settlements, leaving conflict adjudication more and more to pluralist pressure politics; resource allocation to markets rather than authoritative intervention; and economic efficiency to competitive pressures instead of consensual bargaining.

Privatization as a response to the fiscal crisis of the 1990s represented a fundamental break with the modus operandi of the postwar interventionist welfare state. In Germany, as elsewhere, privatization has three facets: *selling off* state property, *contracting out* state activities, and *inviting in* private competition to put existing providers of public services under competitive pressure.

(1) Facing rising deficits, German federal and *Länder* governments began in the 1990s to sell off state property, including public utilities and state holdings in private firms (for details see Beyer and Höpner 2003). At the federal level, receipts from privatization became significant in the mid-1990s (Figure 5.2), contributing a total of €73 billion to the federal budget

Million Euros

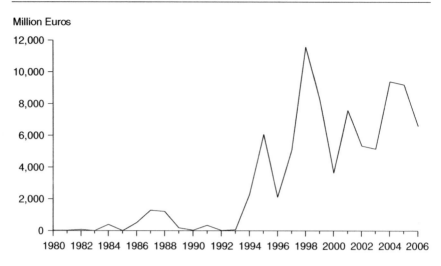

Figure 5.2. Federal receipts from privatization, in million Euros (1980–2006)

in the 11 years from 1995 to 2005. In five of these years, privatization underwrote more than 3 percent of federal spending. Over the entire period, new government debt would have had to be about 22 percent higher without the sale of public assets.[3]

Selling off state property to finance current spending is, of course, no more than a palliative, and one with a definite expiration date: when the last of the family silver is gone, the deficit will again be what it was before.[4] In other respects, however, the sale of state holdings has pervasive irreversible effects. To sell off postal services and telecommunications at favorable conditions, the German government required an efficient capital market with effective protections for small shareholders, which it created in the 1990s through extensive reform legislation. As it happened, such legislation was being demanded also by financial interests, as well as by large industrial firms eager to increase their market capitalization. Once in place, the new institutions benefited private business interests as well, especially those pushing "shareholder value" as a new guiding principle of corporate governance.

Moreover, the conversion into private firms especially of the former state monopolies in postal, telecommunication, and railway services forever disorganized the once encompassing collective bargaining system of the "public service" *(öffentlicher Dienst)*.[5] Among other things, this contributed to the extensive redrawing of the boundaries of Germany's industrial trade unions mentioned above.[6] More importantly, privatization of the formerly publicly owned utilities fundamentally changed their employment practices. In addition to deep employment cuts,[7] it completely abolished a traditional employment regime centered around the figure of the small civil servant—the *Post-* or *Bahnbeamte*—with tenured lifetime employment, effective workplace representation, and a regularly increasing if modest living wage. More often than not, what took its place, especially where private competition and stock market pressures came together, was expanding casualized low-wage employment under much more demanding working conditions.[8]

(2) As to contracting out, dwindling fiscal resources caused successive waves of ever deeper cost-cutting in public services. With their budget allocations stagnant or declining, hospitals, schools, universities, government offices, local transport authorities, and others began to purchase a growing range of nonessential services from private firms. Very often these are not covered by an industrial agreement, and perhaps cannot be if they want to win and keep their contracts. Here again, the fiscal crisis of the state contributed to the emergence of a nonunionized low-wage sector of a kind entirely unknown in postwar German industrial relations.[9] Moreover, where public service providers such as local transport agencies subcontract part of their operation to private firms with lower costs, one observes the rise of a two-tier wage system wholly incompatible with the traditional egalitarianism of industry-level collective bargaining. It is not at all by accident that pressures for a legal minimum wage are particularly strong in industries that once were public monopolies, such as postal services.

Contracting out is also used to mobilize private resources to supplement dwindling public resources, as, for example, in the partial privatization of pension insurance by the first Schröder government. In anticipation of a long-term decline of public pensions, the pension reform legislation of 2000 provided for government subsidies to individually funded private retirement accounts. While the new "fourth pillar" of German pension insurance does not add to the nonwage costs of labor, it depends on banks and insurance firms developing certifiable "products" that meet a range of legal standards making them eligible for subsidization. Like the sale of government assets, contracting out a supplementary pension system requires an active financial market and effective government capacity for regulation.[10] Private providers, once having entered pension insurance, are likely to form a powerful lobby for further expansion of market provision, in competition with the established pension insurance funds governed by the corporatist triad of state, business, and labor.

(3) Privatization furthermore includes encouragement of competition in formerly public or semi-public sectors. Examples are found in a wide variety of fields, from public banking to employment exchange, higher education, the railroads, and, again, health care and health insurance. Creating markets by bringing in private competition, often by regulatory measures that disadvantage the former state monopolies, helps governments discipline traditional service providers, some of whom are used to allying with their clients to demand higher subsidies from the public budget. Public providers have also been suspected, in a time of fiscal austerity, of harboring gross inefficiencies that supposedly can be weeded out only by competitive pressures. Once again, regulation takes the place of public provision; forces lobbying for free markets, including the sale of government assets and the contracting out of ever more public services, gain strength; and public sector jobs are being replaced with private jobs, more often than not with low pay and in nonunionized firms.

European integration offered effective support for governments intent on turning over previously public assets and responsibilities to private market forces. Privatization of the German postal, telecommunications, and railroad services would have been considerably more difficult, if not impossible, had it not been mandated by the European Union— a mandate that, in turn, would not have passed without the German government's assent. The same applies to subcontracting and to opening up public services to private competition, where the completion of the so-called Internal Market for Services required European governments to allow private firms from any country inside the Union to submit formal bids to take over the performance of all but a few public services.[11]

The transformation of public into private property, the insertion of competitive markets in the public sphere, and the substitution of private services for authoritative state provision did not always proceed smoothly. Indeed, they were politically contested at every step of the way, with the government sometimes forced, and sometimes motivated by reasons of its own, to bargain for specific protections or transition periods in European legislation for sensitive sectors and social groups. In essence, however, these were no more than modifications to a broad stream of gradual but fundamental change that redefined forever the boundary between state and market, public and private activities, and authoritative and competitive allocation, enabling governments to protect themselves from excessive demands on their resources and live with rapidly dwindling degrees of freedom in their overstrained budgets. Indeed the Maastricht guidelines themselves, which imposed rigid limits on the deficits presumably sovereign national states were allowed to incur in their spending, were instituted and welcomed by European governments as a defense against domestic pressures for additional debt that they would very likely have been unable to resist otherwise (Moravcsik 1998).

The fiscal crisis of the German state at the end of the twentieth century reflected the growing costs to the public budget of keeping a capitalist political economy nationally organized. When the exhaustion of the state's governing capacities passed a critical threshold, public policy found itself forced to switch from organizing to disorganizing interventions, causing extensive ripple effects throughout the German political economy as a whole. For instance, economic and political privatization contributed importantly to the transformation of the collective bargaining system, both to the shrinking and softening of its core and to increasing the diversity of competing modes of employment regulation. Privatization transformed public employment into private employment, expanded low-wage employment by exposing formerly protected sectors to market competition, and undermined institutionalized wage coordination. It also diminished the extent and significance of social policy *Selbstverwaltung* through para-public institutions, at the expense of organized business and labor and their political status, and added profit-seeking businesses to the variety of competing actors and interests, not just in social policy (Trampusch 2005*b*). To promote privatization so as to expose unruly domestic interests to competitive pressure, successive governments learned to take advantage of internationalization, mostly but not exclusively in the form of European integration. Lowering instead of defending the protective borders around national economies advanced the disorganization of nationally organized collective bargaining and intermediary organizations, forcing the latter to embark on a difficult and uncertain search for new bases of institutional and political power. As will be seen in the next chapter, in turning to its international environment to defend itself against domestic pressure groups, the German state joined German firms which had also discovered the advantages of border-crossing activities in their efforts to get rid of costly national social and political obligations.

Notes

1. For details on the German budget and its crisis, see Streeck (2007). A picture remarkably similar in many respects is found in the United States (Pierson 2001).

2. I am not concerned here with the potential macro-economic effects of public debt.

3. Calculations are based on Table 6 in the *Finanzbericht 2006* of the Federal Ministry of Finance (Bundesministerium der Finanzen 2006) and on Diagram 78, p. 312, of the Jahresgutachten 2006/2007 of the Sachverständigenrat (Sachverständigenrat zur Begutachtung der gesamtwirtschaftlichen Entwicklung 2006).

4. Indeed in 2005, when the Grand Coalition took over from the second Schröder government, very little was left that could still be sold, apart from the *Autobahnen* (Streeck 2007).

5. Public sector employment relations in the old Federal Republic were the most centralized of the industrial relations system. Essentially one and the same collective agreement determined the pay of municipal garbage collectors and university professors. Nowhere in German industrial relations has the regulatory regime and have the interest organizations of workers and employers been decentralized and fragmented as rapidly as in this sector, following successive waves of privatization and budget cuts in the 1990s (Keller 2006, 2007a, 2007b).

6. In particular, it led to the absorption of the solidly centrist public service union ÖTV into the Amalgamated Union of Service Workers, Verdi, which is the mainstay of the Left inside the DGB.

7. In 1989, the last year of the old Federal Republic, the public postal, telecommunications, and railway services together employed 777,000 people. In 2006, employment in their privatized successor organizations, including East Germany, amounted to 494,000, a decline by 283,000 or 36%. Further significant employment cuts are imminent (Statistisches Jahrbuch 1991, 312, 317; direct communications). Paradoxically, employment cuts at the railways and in postal services were made politically palatable by extensive early retirement programs, even more than in the private sector.

8. For a general survey of the recent spread of low-wage work in Germany, see Bosch and Weinkopf (2008, Chapter 1).

9. For the example of services in hospitals, see Jaehrling (2008).

10. As Pierson notes, fiscal austerity tends to be associated with a "shift in government activism toward regulatory policy" (Pierson 2001, 73).

11. See Barnard (2004).

6

Corporate governance: the decline of Germany Inc.

In the postwar era, large German firms formed a dense network of multiple ties, in particular cross-shareholdings of capital and interlocking directorates. Organized by a small number of leading financial institutions such as Deutsche Bank and Allianz, and closely if mostly informally related to government and the state, Germany Inc., or *Deutschland AG*, offered firms collective protection against a variety of political and economic risks, including pressure from minority shareholders and potential takeovers by foreign firms, as well as socialist and trade union demands for nationalization or economic planning. Appointed, benevolently monitored and, if necessary, nursed along by their respective *Hausbanken* (principal banks), German executives could afford to neglect their companies' share prices and content themselves with a low but steady return on investment, enabling them reliably to service the debt they owed to their banks. Firms devoted part of the rents they drew from their well-demarcated markets and their increasing international success to appeasing a workforce and a trade union movement that could not yet be entirely trusted not to opt for the socialist alternative to democratic capitalism that was being instituted in the Eastern part of the country.

The historical origins and the structure and functioning of German "organized capitalism" have been described in a number of excellent studies, some of which have become classics of the political economy literature.[1] What is important here is that the network of large German firms, in addition to the protection it offered to its members, also provided the government with an effective interlocutor, enabling it not only to speak to German business as a whole, but more often than not to extract from it collective commitments to act in line with what the government considered to be the public interest.[2] High internal solidarity, while enabling business to coordinate its actions and shielding it against a variety of risks, thus made it vulnerable at the same time to being held collectively responsible by the state. As especially Shonfield (1965) and Zysman (1983) have pointed out, it also allowed the government to delegate areas of public policy, especially industrial policy—which was not considered politically correct at the Ministry of Economics—to private actors, in particular the banks. Among other things, the banks saw to it that members of *Deutschland AG* did not excessively compete with one another in the same markets, and they ensured that firms in good standing—that is, with a record of cooperation—did not unnecessarily fall victim to the vagaries of the market.

Solidarity and discipline were also useful in relation to the unions. Having to live with them under the new democratic system, and being able to do so because of their collective system of mutual protection, large firms preferred centralized over company-level wage setting, as it shielded them from their workforces claiming a share in excess profits. It also enabled them to build amicable relations with internal workforce representatives cut off from distributive wage bargaining. At the same time, large German companies were determined to resist whatever union demands they considered inappropriate. In several cases, employer associations succeeded in calling large-scale lockouts aimed at wasting the unions' strike funds. By the 1960s, unions and employer associations had learned to appreciate each other's organizational strength, which laid the foundation for a stable "conflict partnership" (Müller-Jentsch 1993) based on high cohesion of both camps. The architect on the side of business of the corporatist industrial relations settlement was a member of the management board of Daimler-Benz, Hanns Martin Schleyer,[3] who in the 1970s advanced to become president, first of the Federation of German Employer Associations (BDA) and then also and simultaneously of the Federation of German Industry (BDI), which was to prepare the ground for an amalgamation of the two under the auspices of the former, that is, of the representation of business in its class relations with organized labor.

The disintegration of the German company network began in the mid-1980s when large German banks, led by Deutsche Bank, gradually abandoned their traditional role as providers of cheap credit and *Hausbanken* of German firms (Beyer 2006, Chapter 2.3), refusing to continue to serve as a semi-public financial infrastructure of the German economy (Beyer 2003).[4] The main motive behind this seems to have been the higher profits made by Anglo-American banks in international investment banking, tempting and perhaps also constraining German banks to move on to what was for them a new business strategy. Subsequently, they lost interest in the close internal monitoring of industrial firms that had been characteristic of German-style relational banking. Gradually they began to sever their ties with client firms, selling the shares they held in them and withdrawing from their boards[5] as investment banking is ultimately incompatible with insider relations with firms that might become targets of hostile takeovers (Beyer 2006, 102). For a while Deutsche Bank even debated in public moving its headquarters from Frankfurt to London, no doubt in part to advertise as unmistakably as possible the fundamental strategic change that had taken place.[6]

The transformation of large German banks from providers of credit for national firms into competitive players in the international financial industry in turn changed the behavior of German companies. With the banks no longer willing to protect them from takeover, German firms began to worry about their undervalued stock, even before capital market reforms increased the pressure on them to generate "shareholder value." In 2000 abolition of the capital gains tax, passed by a Social-Democratic government, provided an additional incentive for industrial firms to divest themselves of their cross-shareholdings, so as to put their capital to more profitable use. Mutual disentanglement was further advanced by the fact that during the 1990s, hostile takeovers had become not just a possibility, but a reality, again preceding legal reforms. After Thyssen-Krupp and, later, Vodafone,[7] firms could no longer, as they had in the past, rely on the banks or other firms in the network to come to their rescue, forcing them to make their own provisions against takeover, above all by driving up the price of their stock in the market for capital.[8]

The erosion of the ties between large German firms that followed the abandonment by the banks of their traditional function as organizers of *Deutschland AG* seems to have been accelerated by the completion of the European Internal Market in 1992 and by the end, shortly thereafter, of the boom caused by German unification. Höpner and Krempel (2004) show that in 1996, Deutsche Bank and Allianz, together with Dresdner Bank and Münchner Rück, were still at the center of a dense network of cross-shareholdings among the 100 largest German firms, with three sub-clusters in the energy, chemical, and electronics sectors. Only four years later, the network had thinned out considerably, as Deutsche Bank had moved out of its center. In 2002, the number of links had declined further, especially among industrial firms and between them and the banks.[9] The same development can be seen by looking at the cross-shareholdings

Table 6.1. Cross-shareholdings, 100 largest German firms, by type of firm, 1996 and 2002

	1996	2002
Percentage of capital of 100 largest firms held by . . .		
100 largest firms	15.9	9.3
Of these by . . .		
banks	5.8	1.5
insurance companies	4.7	3.3
others	5.4	4.5

Source: Beyer (2006, 127).

among the 100 largest German firms, which declined from 16 to 9 percent of total capital, mostly due to divestment by banks (Table 6.1), between 1996 and 2002. Available data show only a short segment of a process that started earlier and is still continuing. In 2002, there were only 67 capital links left between the 100 largest firms, as compared to 143 in 1996 (Beyer 2005).

As indicated, the disintegration of the German company network was related to the strategic behavior of German firms in significant ways. As Saskia Freye has found (Freye 2007), the percentage of CEOs of the 50 largest firms in Germany with previous professional experience outside the private sector—in positions linked in one way or another to government—has declined continually since the 1960s and in particular was cut roughly in half between 1975 and 2005 (Figure 6.1). Together with a steep increase in the number of CEOs with an international career (Freye 2007), this would seem to indicate a growing distance of large firms and their leaders from German public concerns, which might be interpreted as yet another facet of the ongoing disorganization and privatization of the German economy.

Strong anecdotal evidence suggests that as German private firms are becoming more private, their perception of the social responsibility is changing in the direction indicated by Milton Friedman in his famous essay, "The Social Responsibility of Business is to Increase Its Profits" (Friedman 1983 [1973]). Particularly instructive in this respect is the revolution in the 1990s in the corporate strategy and the behavior of that quintessential German industrial firm, Daimler-Benz, later Daimler-Chrysler, now Daimler (Freye 2007). For the entire postwar period, the company acted as the doyen of German big business, a national model and leader in manufacturing and marketing as well as in labor relations—the equivalent in industry to what Deutsche Bank was in finance, and

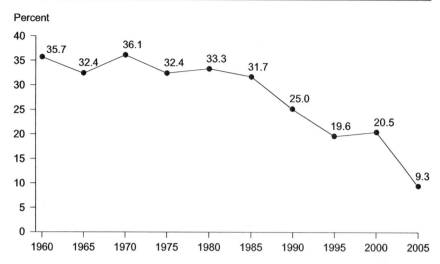

Figure 6.1. CEOs with professional experience in the public sector, in percent of all CEOs of the 50 largest firms in Germany

indeed largely owned and extensively supervised by Deutsche Bank. From the mid-1980s until 1995, the firm was led by Edzard Reuter, a card-carrying Social Democrat, whose strategy of expansion was to collect a diversity of German high-technology firms to build an "integrated technology concern," in the way of a sort of national industrial policy for Germany. In this context, for example, Daimler had picked up the ailing electronics giant AEG to protect it from failing, just as Deutsche Bank in the 1970s, urged on by Chancellor Helmut Schmidt, had bought the Flick family's Daimler shares to prevent the firm coming under the control of the Kuwaiti government. Daimler's role as the uncontested leader of the German company network came to an end when Reuter's successor, Schrempp, immediately upon taking over in 1995, sold off the firm's German aerospace and electronics interests, registered Daimler at the New York Stock Exchange, merged with Chrysler and tried to take over Mitsubishi in order to form a multinational automobile company equally at home in Europe, the United States, and Japan. Shortly after the Chrysler merger, Schrempp boasted publicly about DaimlerChrysler paying no more taxes in Germany for the rest of the century.[10, 11]

There are also other repercussions of the dissolution of the German company network on German firms and the "spirit" of German business. Again according to Freye (2007), the average tenure of the CEOs of large firms rapidly declined after 1980, from 12.4 years to 7.5 years in 2000,

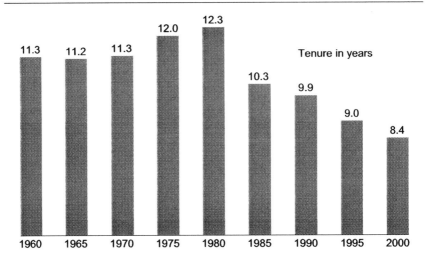

Figure 6.2. Average tenure of sitting CEOs, 50 largest companies in Germany, selected years

with a tendency to fall further (Figure 6.2). Beginning in the 1990s, in each five-year period, about 70 percent of the 50 large firms studied by Freye changed their CEOs (Figure 6.3). Moreover, to an astonishing extent, terminations are now conflictual, involving dismissal or forced resignation often accompanied by legal action. Thus, in the five-year

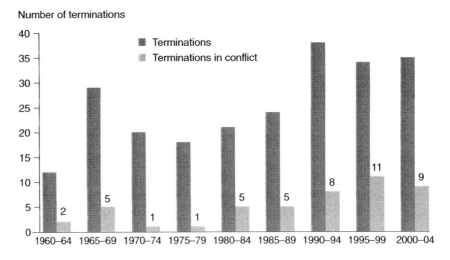

Figure 6.3. Terminations of tenure of CEO, total and conflictual, 50 largest firms in Germany, 1960–2004

82

period from 1995 to 1999, no less than 32 percent of CEOs who left office had to do so under less than peaceful circumstances. Rising turnover of corporate leadership, and in particular the increasing number of what in a different institutional sphere would be referred to as cases of "dishonorable discharge," reflect declining protection of executives and firms from business risk. It also shows growing uncertainty and insecurity in a more competitive environment in which managers are freer to make mistakes than when they were still controlled and nurtured by the solidaristic relations that prevailed in the old *Deutschland AG.*

As is often the case, more risks come with more opportunities and vice versa. The end of mutual protection meant not just a greater chance of failure, but also less external control. As in other countries, German executives' salaries have gone through the roof in recent years. For 40 large industrial companies, Höpner found an increase of no less than 66 percent in the average base pay of executive board members—not including bonuses and stock options—between 1996 and 1999 (Höpner 2004). Hickel (2004) reports an increase of 81 percent between 1997 and 2003 for the 30 firms in the DAX. During the same period, according to the internet edition of the *Frankfurter Allgemeine Zeitung,* average yearly pay for executive board members, excluding CEOs, increased from €1.16 million in 2001 to €1.71 million in 2005, that is, by 46 percent (www.faz.net, 4/28/2007; data from the Deutsche Schutzvereinigung für Wertpapierbesitz). Interestingly, several studies show increases in management compensation to be associated with a decline in monitoring by the supervisory board. For example, Beyer (2005) finds management compensation to be higher the less a firm is integrated in the company network. Similarly, Höpner (2004) reports increases in management pay to be lower where the chair of the supervisory board is a representative of a bank, and particularly high where he is a former member of the firm's own executive board, indicating a shift of control from outsiders to insiders.[12]

As indicated, the disorganization of *Deutschland AG* took place simultaneously with a series of legislative reforms of the capital market, all of which strengthened the position of shareholders.[13] Several motives came together to produce this coincidence, and there is no way of saying who the prime mover was: the government seeking to secure the international competitiveness of the national economy, striving to discipline increasingly ungovernable domestic interests, and preparing the ground for a profitable privatization of the public infrastructure; the banks demanding a new institutional framework supportive of their changed business strategies and of *Finanzplatz Deutschland* (Germany as a financial center); or large industrial firms wanting to internationalize their operations in the face of both increasing opportunities in international markets and declining capacities for and benefits of protection inside a national business community.[14] Clearly the decision of Deutsche Bank to give up its quasi-public status as guardian of German industry and turn to more profitable international capital markets was made in a political environment in which liberalization of the German economy was already a dominant theme. Strategic change at the bank may have encouraged and indeed enabled the government to move ahead faster than it would and could have otherwise, just as it may have accelerated the switch of a company such as Daimler from national technology champion proud to assume public responsibility to a large international business firm pure and simple. But then, 1992—the year of the completion of the European "Internal Market"—had been on the agenda since the mid-1980s when Jacques Delors had taken over at the European Commission. This, in turn, was preceded by the demise of the protectionist industrial policy project of a "Fortress Europe" as sponsored by the Belgian Commissioner Etienne Davignon, which disintegrated as the European Roundtable of Industrialists had come to conclude that there was no alternative to globalization (Apeldoorn 2002). By this time at the latest, the way to go for large European firms was international expansion, above all through cross-national mergers and takeovers, for which they required high market capitalization.

Regardless of whether internationalization—the breaking of firms out of national obligations and constraints in pursuit of newly arisen international opportunities—had originally been a political or an economic project, it had and continues to have profound effects on the collective action and organization of business, and especially on the pattern of interest intermediation in Germany and other countries with a corporatist heritage. In the 1980s, large firms from the European Continent, learning from their British competition (Grant 1984; Streeck and Grant 1985), began to lobby the European Commission and, subsequently, national governments directly, rather than mainly or exclusively through associations. The rise of the large firm as a political actor, with representatives of its own in Brussels and the leading national capitals, continues to stand in the way of the emergence of strong supranational, European-level business interest organizations.[15] It also detracts from the importance, and is changing the functions, of national business associations for their most powerful members. International comparison shows that in a number of countries, including Germany, the 1990s were a period in which large firms began to lose interest in national business associations as channels of collective political representation, not only since their activities by then extended far beyond their countries of origin, but because their business strategies had become increasingly different and idiosyncratic, calling for individual rather than collective political action (Streeck and Visser 2005). While typically this gave rise to pressures on associations to cut costs by rationalizing their structures, it allowed large multinational companies to let smaller entrepreneurial firms take control of national business associations and to shift the activities of the latter toward public advocacy of neo-liberal reform and entrepreneurialism. In the process, national peak associations in particular ceased to be the sort of "private interest governments" (Streeck and Schmitter 1984) that they had sometimes been during the corporatist era.[16] In Germany, this culminated in renewed pressures for the two peak associations (BDA and BDI) to merge, but this time under the leadership of the BDI, which is less contaminated by contacts with unions and therefore freer to act as a pressure group for a new, liberalized capitalism.[17]

The decline of *Deutschland AG* was accompanied by a gradual transformation of formerly corporatist into pluralist interest organizations, with public advocacy of neo-liberal reform replacing behind-the-scenes industrial diplomacy and insider deal-making between business, labor, and the state. Disorganizing effects of the dissolution of the German company network on business associations are also apparent in industrial relations, where the departure of German banks from their traditional business strategy and the internationalization of markets for capital increased the demands on small firms' return on investment and on their endowment with capital. This, in turn, seems to have contributed to the growing aversion against industry-level collective bargaining and the high labor costs associated with membership in employer associations, accounting in part for the exodus from membership in *Gesamtmetall* and, presumably, other employer associations as well (Haipeter and Schilling 2005, 174).

On the other hand, the way industrial relations are affected by the new, more market-driven corporate governance regime is shaped, in path-dependent fashion, by past legacies and experiences. Rising competitive pressures and growing uncertainty in international markets as well as the end of mutual protection against potentially aggressive shareholders and sharesellers have not made German firms seek relief in radical individualization of the employment relationship (Thelen 2000). Instead the dominant strategy was to build alliances with the elected representatives of the workforce and negotiate enough modifications to industrial agreements with them to allow for continued participation in collective bargaining at the national and sectoral levels. Firm-specific "Alliances for Employment and Competitiveness," as they are called, preserve the advantages of institutionalized cooperation between capital and labor while relying on the effects of increased market pressures to discipline worker demands and enable firms to extricate themselves from social obligations imposed on them from the outside or from above (Rehder 2003). Workplace alliances disorganize corporatist class politics, not by replacing cooperative relations between capital and labor with adversarial ones, but by reorganizing and realigning them at the firm level. The consequences may be far-reaching, as shown by the defeat of *IG Metall* in the 2003 strike in East Germany. As mentioned above, the defeat was caused by defection of the works council leaders of large West German automobile firms who were afraid of a disruption of supply and a subsequent loss of their companies' market share (Höpner 2007*a*).

Fragmented reorganization of cooperative relations between capital and labor at the level of the firm replaces an obligatory social order with voluntarily contracted, individualized arrangements responding to and controlled by competitive markets. By drawing works councils deeply into the management of economic adjustment, firms hope to build a coalition between shareholders and core employees, one in which the latter share the concern of management with raising the market value of the firm to fight off potential takeovers. Indeed, more often than not, works councils have understood in recent years that defending the integrity of the firm that employs them is in their interest as well as in that of management, leading them to support "shareholder value" business strategies even if they involve significant increases in firms' return on investment to be achieved by equally significant employment cuts (Höpner 2005*b*). Just as in the case of the corporatist version of *Konfliktpartnerschaft*, whether or not this will work in the longer term is obviously an open question (Rehder 2006), especially as opportunities for early retirement are being foreclosed under the pressure of failing government finances. What is important, however, is that the lines of conflict and the alignment of interests, the organizational substructure of coordination, the relative importance of public and private ordering—of public obligations and private voluntarism—are fundamentally different after the dissolution of the company network from what they were in the corporatist era.

Seen in context, then, the disintegration of the German company network appears as one manifestation among others, although powerful and consequential, of a general trend toward dissolution of the broad political camps and economic risk pools that were at the center of postwar German corporatism. Increasing political fragmentation and interest individualism reflect a changing balance of the costs and benefits of nationally organized solidarity, caused by rising demands on those able to pay; by new market opportunities for those able to take advantage of them; and by general exhaustion of the state's organizing capacities, especially in finance. While encompassing organization and egalitarian risk protection exacted ever more resources from the strong, rising external competition devalued the security that could be gained from mutual protection at the national level. Stronger firms in particular began to feel that they had no choice but to seek success in competition rather than rely on protection, especially as new market opportunities raised the opportunity costs of continued adherence to collective discipline and solidarity. At some point, the temptation for competitive actors to emigrate from the collective risk pool of an organized national economy and divert their resources from mutual reinsurance to investment in their own competitiveness became irresistible. As the capacity of the state declined to hold large collectivities together, by either legal force or economic subsidies, the strong began to exit from the encompassing risk pools of the postwar era in the name of individual freedom and a new liberal-voluntaristic order. With the good risks pursuing their interests on their own, the bad risks were left behind, compelled to fend for themselves. As solidaristic groups became smaller and smaller, disparities in income, competitive success, and life chances began to proliferate.[18]

Notes

1. See Gerschenkron (1968), Hilferding (1981 [1910]), Shonfield (1965), and Zysman (1983), and more recently Beyer (2003), Höpner (2005a), Höpner and Krempel (2004), Streeck and Höpner (2003), and Windolf and Beyer (1995).
2. For examples, see Höpner (2007a). The neo-corporatist literature, even where it explicitly dealt with business, focused on interest associations to the neglect of mutual shareholding, interlocking directorates or patient, "relational" credit provision as alternative or supplementary mechanisms for mobilizing collective action. It was among others Martin Höpner who rediscovered the strong connection between interfirm networks based on property rights and voluntary associations based on perceived common interests.
3. Schleyer was murdered by terrorists in 1978. He had been a Nazi student leader and later an SS economic bureaucrat serving in occupied Prague. His

main union counterpart in the 1960s was Otto Brenner, president of the metalworkers' union (*IG Metall*), a factory worker and radical socialist in the final years of the Weimar Republic, and temporarily in prison under the Nazi regime. It is emblematic of postwar German corporatism that these two men should have been able to develop an effective working relationship based on mutual respect and trust.

4. A similar story can be told about corporate networks in other countries. For a recent study on the Netherlands, see Heemskerk (2007).

5. "In 1996, 29 of the supervisory board chairmen of the 100 biggest firms were representatives of Deutsche Bank. Only two years later, this number had declined to 17. In its corporate governance principles published in 2001, Deutsche Bank announced that it would resign from supervisory board chairs altogether" (Beyer and Höpner 2003). According to Beyer (2006, 106), Deutsche Bank was represented on the supervisory boards of 40 of the 100 biggest German firms in 1980. In 1995 this number had declined to 35, in 1999 to 17, and in 2002 to 5.

6. At about the same time, Allianz, the powerful insurance corporation, began to withdraw from its unofficial postwar role as responsible investor in German industrial firms, also in pursuit of higher returns from more international and more profit-driven business engagements.

7. On the history of takeovers in Germany during the 1990s, see Höpner and Jackson (2006). On takeovers having now become an established practice in the German economy, and on the proliferation of a "market for control," see Jackson and Miyajima (2007).

8. For useful summary accounts of the changes in German corporate governance since the 1990s, see Deeg (2005), Jackson et al. (2005), and Klages (2006).

9. Diagrams depicting these networks from 1996 to 2004 can be found at http://www.mpi-fg-koeln.mpg.de/aktuelles/themen/d-ag.asp.

10. "In diesem Jahrhundert bekommt Herr Finanzminister Waigel von meinem Konzern keinen Pfennig mehr." Cited in Liebert (2004).

11. More on this in Part III, in the chapter on internationalization.

12. For the 120 largest publicly traded German firms, Schmid (1997) finds a highly significant negative effect on executive compensation of the strength of worker representation on the supervisory board. Generally, the rapid rise in managerial pay in the past one-and-a-half decades may be interpreted either as a case of highway robbery—with managers exploiting the gap in supervision caused by the decline of the company network—or as a form of compensation for the growing insecurity of top management in their positions, due to rising uncertainty in the business environment. As most of the additional pay comes from the new "shareholder value" practice of paying managers by stock options, it may also be seen as a pleasant, incentive-based form of external control by "the market" taking the place of less lucrative internal monitoring by banks and worker representatives.

13. For an overview, see Beyer and Höpner (2003) and Cioffi and Höpner (2006). See also Apeldoorn and Horn (2007).
14. A very similar configuration, with a state starved for funds and large firms seeking new opportunities in international markets, including those for capital, is reported by Mary O'Sullivan (2007) for France.
15. Again the case of Daimler-Benz, later DaimlerChrysler, is instructive. Having set up its own office in Brussels, the firm hired the general secretary of the European association of automobile makers to serve as its representative to the European Union (Streeck and Visser 2005).
16. For Germany see the example, mentioned above, of *Gesamtmetall* funding the *Initiative Neue Soziale Marktwirtschaft* (INSM).
17. Similar mergers have already taken place in other countries, like notably in Sweden (Pestoff 2006).
18. The preceding account has dealt only with the large firms that used to be part of Deutschland AG. This may seem surprising to those aware of the fact that an important strength of the German economy is its unusually large number of internationally highly competitive small-and-medium-sized firms. Indeed if this book was about German economic performance—which of course it is not—a good part of it would have to be devoted to that famous pillar of the German economy, the *Mittelstand*. Actually, small firms will be mentioned in several contexts further down. And although there is for reasons of space no specific chapter on *Mittelstand*, it would have produced essentially the same story of progressive disorganization that we have told of our five sectors. Note that the further increase in the importance of small-and-medium-sized firms in the 1990s and later, in terms of wealth creation and employment, may in itself be described as a process of disorganization, in the sense of decentralization and of market relations taking the place of corporate hierarchies. Moreover, as will be elaborated further down, the changed procurement strategies of large German companies in the course of their internationalization have made the situation of their numerous German suppliers much more uncertain and market-exposed. Third, as pointed out, the resulting conflicts between large and small firms contributed to the secular weakening of employers associations, as did the declining readiness on the part of internationalizing corporations to continue to subsidize the characteristically expensive German employer and business associations. Very importantly, the Schröder government's policies of liberalization in a variety of ways attacked the compulsory organization of small firms, especially of artisanal firms in Chambers of Artisans (Streeck 1989b). It also weakened the *Meisterprivileg* in vocational training and removed barriers to market access for unorganized and unlicensed firms in what used to be protected artisanal industries.

Part II

Systemic Change: Patterns and Causes

7

Systemic change: five parallel trajectories

Institutional change in the German political economy after the Golden Age proceeded gradually, cumulatively, and without dramatic disruptions of continuity, in a variety of institutional settings along parallel trajectories. For five sectors, independent but interrelated, we managed to construct narratives of slow change over roughly three decades. While they intersected with one another at a multitude of points, each narrative could be and has been told separately and on its own terms, although arguably all of them make sense only in the context of the others, and more generally in the changing context of the national state within which they are located and connected.

Collective bargaining and wage setting. The dominant trend was one of gradually increasing fragmentation of an encompassing, effectively centralized unified system of wage setting through industry-wide collective bargaining. Fragmentation was driven by growing tensions and conflicts among the system's constituents, caused by the slowly accumulating effects of its own routine operation, in particular wage compression and an increasingly uneven distribution of costs and benefits at the expense of smaller firms. In the process, the traditional bargaining regime ceased to be encompassing and turned into the shrinking and softening core of a new, much less unified, and much more diverse system. Within that system, it is surrounded by an expanding fringe of a variety of modes of decentralized and individualized wage setting, from company agreements to firms following industry standards voluntarily and, mostly, selectively, to a growing nonunion and antiunion sector.

Intermediary organization. Organized labor and organized capital went through a history of declining numbers and growing divisions, beginning in the 1980s and accelerating in the mid-1990s. Unionization declined while tensions between small and large firms increased. Whereas declining unionization gave rise to interunion competition and to politicized mergers that—further—weakened the national federation, small firm discontent caused defections from membership in employer associations and found political expression in unprecedented conflicts between the national federations of employer and business associations. Especially toward the end of the period of observation, one finds, as pointed out, a general weakening of the "logic of influence" of intermediary organizations in favor of the "logic of membership," meaning that leaders become more dependent on their members as they can rely less on interlocutors assisting them in the management of internal discontent. Put otherwise, this amounts to a shift from a more corporatist to a more pluralist pattern of intermediary organization.

Social policy. Here the development was dominated by growing demands emanating from the system of industrial relations for the state to absorb its externalities, to protect social peace and ensure continued cooperation between capital and labor. This resulted in gradual exhaustion of the state's and the economy's capacity to subsidize a wage setting regime that had become dependent on a restrictive management of the labor supply. Unwillingness or inability of the "social partners" to overcome that dependence ultimately forced the government to retrench social policy unilaterally. In doing so, it attacked the privileged corporatist status of the intermediary organizations of capital and labor, among other things by retrenching their position in the institutional infrastructure of the public and para-public social policy apparatus.

Public Finance. From the mid-1970s on, the postwar interventionist state of Germany was under strong and apparently irresistible pressures for fiscal overextension which emanated mainly from rapidly rising spending on social security, including active and passive labor market policy. Several attempts to preserve the state's capacity for discretionary spending failed. When in the late 1990s the gradual consumption of the degrees of freedom of public policy by unfunded liabilities had reached a critical point, the postwar fiscal regime of expansion gave way to one of austerity. This included reining in the previously semiautonomous "state within the state" of the social security system and its semi-public organized interests. Austerity as a response to the secular exhaustion of state resources also involved privatization of public assets and policy tasks, as well as reliance on markets, including international markets, to put pressure on increasingly ungovernable domestic interests. This went together with a general decline in the significance of para-public institutions and was accompanied by growing state intervention and regulation, for the purpose of protecting the state from appropriation of its resources by organized interest groups, and of introducing markets as politically neutral mechanisms of resource allocation.

Corporate governance. The story here was about the disintegration of the postwar risk pool of large German firms, with solidarity declining under the impact of growing competitive pressures and opportunities while national protection from the risks of international markets lost its effectiveness. Exit of the strong left the weak to look after themselves, especially as the state sought relief from the rising costs of national peace-making and market stabilization by opening itself and the national economy to international markets and competition. Over the years, the previously close relations between banks and industrial firms, among industrial firms, and between business and public power dissolved, with separate and individual pursuit of economic interests taking the place of the mutual risk-sharing that had been characteristic of the *Deutschland AG* of the postwar period.

7.1. Systemic Transformation

In all five settings, differences between conditions at the beginning and the end of the period, taken by themselves, might perhaps be construed as less than fundamental. In international comparison, collective bargaining in Germany is still more organized than in other large countries, in particular of course the United Kingdom and the United States. Also, while unionization in Germany is now low even by international standards, the same is not, or not yet, true for the organization of business. Social welfare spending in Germany continues to be high, and there are countries in Europe whose public debt clearly exceeds the German one. Moreover, most German companies are still controlled by large blockholders, and an institution like workforce codetermination on supervisory boards remains formally intact and, for the time being, politically untouchable. In short, separate review of the institutional spheres of the German political economy might lead one to conclude that the changes that have taken place are no more than isolated, marginal, momentary and in principle reversible fluctuations in a basically stable system that has by and large remained identical with itself. This, however, would not do justice to the fact, observable in a more encompassing perspective, that change in all five sectors proceeded in the same direction, preliminarily identified as one of increasing disorganization. If nothing else, it is these similarities between sectoral trajectories that suggest that they be considered in context, the intuition being that they are part of and add up to a broad process of comprehensive *systemic change* that must be understood as such, as a condition for understanding each of them.

Moving from a sectoral to a systemic perspective amounts to a reversal of a long-standing trend in institutional analysis. Theories of governance ("Steuerung") and governability ("Regierbarkeit") in the 1960s and 1970s referred to the national society and polity as a whole (e.g., Etzioni 1968). One obvious difficulty among others in the development of a comprehensive theory of politically produced social order was that empirically, different sectors of society seemed to be very differently amenable to political intervention, depending on their respective institutional structures. As a result the ambition was gradually dropped for a macro-level theory of governance, and system governability was redefined, if at all, as the sum, or average, of widely varying governabilities at the meso level, offering themselves to be explored empirically and comparatively, both within and between countries (Mayntz and Scharpf 1995a, 1995b). In the course of this, the notion of systemic unity was lost and replaced with the image of a more or less arbitrary collection of more or less different sectoral arrangements. The conspicuous parallels in sectoral institutional change, however, that are found in a time and process perspective as applied in the present study, are evidence of manifold lines of systemic interdependence. Taking them seriously requires that attention is shifted back from sectoral differences to the systemic context within which they originate and interact. Here, I will argue, systemic unity as produced by intersectoral interdependence is constituted by the specific historical dynamics and contradictions of the capitalist mode of accumulation. This, in turn, suggests focusing, not just on formal structures, but also on political-economic substance, in the course of a conceptual return from sector to system, which as will see must at the same time be a shift in perspective from system to process.

Disorganization, as we have used the term in the five sectoral narratives, denotes a decline in centralized control and authoritative coordination in favor of dispersed competition and spontaneous, market-like aggregation of competing preferences and individualized decisions. More specifically, as institutional settings move toward disorganization, they exhibit an increase in strategic individualism, interest diversity, competitive pluralism, and contractual voluntarism; a decline in the capacity of collective governance to impose an intentionally designed social order; and a shift toward a kind of order that emerges contractually, as it were, "from below," instead of being authoritatively instituted "from above." To the extent that disorganization is in fact the common denominator of the five sectoral trajectories, the parallel course of the change in the structure and performance of several institutional spheres of the German political economy, as documented by empirical research, raises the question of the underlying causal forces accounting for the observed equidirectionality of change in the evolution of independent though interrelated institutional settings. Ultimately, as we will see, this question can be answered only if institutional analysis takes the fact explicitly into account that the institutions whose change is to be explained were created at a particular moment in time or history, with the purpose to organize a capitalist political economy as it existed then, and embed it in a stable social and political structure.

The impression that what we have observed represents a case of comprehensive systemic transformation is reinforced by closer inspection of the interrelations between the five streams of sectoral change as they proceeded over time. Most importantly, while we found numerous causal connections across sectoral boundaries, none of them resembled the sort of counterbalancing negative feedback that one would expect in a self-stabilizing system defending its equilibrium against external or internal shocks. For example, when coverage by the traditional collective bargaining regime began to decline in the 1980s, the government failed to take corrective action to reverse the trend and restore encompassing wage setting. Later, in fact, it contributed to the disorganization of wage setting by privatizing large parts of the public sector. Similarly, declining union density, both preceding and following the transformation of collective bargaining, did not make employers or, for that matter, the government intervene. When unions pressed for legislation to facilitate the creation of works councils in small- and medium-sized firms, both to improve enforcement of industrial agreements and enhance the opportunities for themselves to recruit members at the workplace, employers objected vigorously and the government did not see fit to spend much political capital on the subject. Also, when employer associations began to lose members, this was not reversed by unions forcing defecting firms to return, if not for lack of trying then for lack of power. Employer associations themselves responded to their own organizational crisis by measures, such as the creation of *OT* membership, that came at the expense of both the encompassing nature of the collective bargaining system and the unions' capacity to recruit. Similarly, when social policy approached the limits of the state's ability to pay, trade unions and business associations jointly refused to help the government control expenditure, and when social policy was reformed for fiscal and economic reasons, it ceased to be supportive of both encompassing collective bargaining and corporatist intermediary organization. Moreover, when the exodus from the German company network became imminent, the government, for reasons of its own, further facilitated it by liberalizing capital markets and by a tax reform explicitly designed to promote divestment of cross-shareholdings. In sum, rather than providing negative feedback to the disorganization of institutional settings by restoring them to their old order or by themselves changing in a more organized direction, each of the five sectors continued on its own trajectory toward disorganization, or even responded to disorganizing changes in other sectors in ways that reinforced such changes, or took advantage of them to advance its own disorganization.

7.2. Multiple Instabilities

Again, change in each of our five institutional settings was paralleled by change in the others proceeding in the same direction, without provoking corrective responses returning the system to a previous equilibrium. Equally remarkably, examination of the manifold interactions between the five trajectories of change fails to reveal the presence of a dominant sector driving the development of the others through constraints for functional complementarity, and thereby accounting for the fact that change throughout the system proceeded in parallel. This applies in particular to corporate governance and financial markets, which, as we have noted, are regarded by some as master institutions of modern capitalism on which all others are potentially causally dependent (Hall and Soskice 2001a). Nor can we detect the guiding hand of a master architect—the usual suspect being organized business—hegemonically rebuilding the German political economy to its taste or that of its clients.

To wit, institutional change in German financial markets and corporate governance began on a modest scale in the mid-1980s with legal reforms mainly driven by a desire to strengthen *Finanzplatz Deutschland* (Lütz 2002); it took off in earnest only a decade later.[1] By then, the disorganization of the collective bargaining system had already been under way for some time. Trade union membership had been shrinking even longer, having reached its second postwar peak in the late 1970s (Ebbinghaus

2002). Also, tensions between large and small firms, crucial for the disorganization of the corporatist system of interest intermediation, had been mounting long before the internationalization of capital markets, as they had been caused mainly by rising labor costs and the unequal distribution of the costs and benefits of the 1984 settlement on shorter working hours. Similarly, social policy had become increasingly subservient to the task of absorbing a growing excess supply of labor as early as the 1970s, and public deficits had become endemic already at the end of the Golden Age, due to a widening mismatch between the demands made by the private economy on the public budget and the resources with which the same economy was willing or able to part. None of these developments can be plausibly explained as driven by pressures for complementarity with changing conditions of access to capital in international markets.

Moreover, institutional change in capital markets and corporate governance, produced by a complex interplay between government, political parties, financial and industrial firms, and European Union legislation (Beyer and Höpner 2003), was *preceded,* rather than followed, by the strategic changes in German banks and large industrial firms responding to new opportunities for profit and growing pressures for restructuring across national borders that led to the disintegration of the German company network.[2] As the disentanglement of cross-shareholdings inside *Deutschland AG* took off only in the late 1990s, it could not have caused the transformation of the wage setting system which had by then been long under way. In fact, it was not the large firms where the rising tensions over wage setting originated; while their advancing internationalization later reinforced such tensions, it had always been convenient for them under the old wage-setting regime to hide behind the small- and medium-sized firms included in joint industry-wide bargaining units (Thelen 2000). Nor could the decline of the company network have caused the disintegration of trade unions and employer associations—although, again, it later reinforced it when large firms began to go their own ways in lobbying and industrial relations and generally learned to supplement collective with individual action. Finally, the disentanglement of large German industrial firms and financial institutions neither caused the crisis of the welfare state nor was it driven by it. In fact, since some of the welfare state reforms of the early 2000s deprived large firms of a convenient instrument for cutting employment in their German operations, they were less than enthusiastic about them, although they were unable to prevent them.

Thus, in none of the five sectors whose parallel transformation we have traced over time did change have to be set in motion by an external force, such as functional pressure for complementarity, unhinging a presumably safe established stable condition. Change in all of the sectors, not just in corporate governance and finance, while proceeding in the same direction, originated *independently and endogenously,* with no need for external destabilization. Just as there was no lead sector, there was no hegemonic class, either, that would have conceived of and imposed disorganization as its political project. Much of the "varieties of capitalism" literature may be read, and usually is read, as implying that functional complementarity and structural coherence in national capitalisms are the products of purposeful collective action of organized business concerned about the international competitiveness of national firms. At least in our case, however, organized business, rather than disorganizing the German political economy, was itself disorganized in the course of institutional change, which decisively weakened its capacity for collective action in the same way and at the same time as it affected trade unions, the organizational field of social policy, and the state.

Summing up, we find that there were at all times in each of the five sectors enough internal tensions and conflicts to make for sufficient inherent instability to bring about continuous endogenous change. Even where it might pragmatically appear justified to describe a given condition of a sectoral institutional arrangement as stable, in a longer-term perspective such stability was never more than temporary, always precarious, and probably dependent on some sort of external support suspending the ever-present forces destabilizing it from the inside. For example, for German-style collective bargaining to cause discontent among small firms, nothing more was required than the regular yearly renewal of a high-average, low-dispersion wage structure forcing firms to invent ever new ways to increase productivity. Also, encompassing interest organization, in Germany as elsewhere, was at all times exposed to temptations to defect, and therefore needed to be supported by specific arrangements sustained by the state or by interlocutors with conflicting interests. Similarly, it was obvious from the beginning that absorption of a growing amount of redundant labor by the social security system could not be continued forever, and there were in fact several attempts along the way to reverse the tendency to use social security as a holding pen for redundant labor (Ebbinghaus 2006; Leibfried and Obinger 2003). The same applies to the state borrowing resources from the future, which was also unsustainable over a longer period. Finally, holding together large camps of firms or workers required leadership and discipline as well as effective means of control to contain ever-present centrifugal tendencies rooted in individual interests not being fully subsumable under collective interests. There is no guarantee that such leadership and discipline can always be secured, and in fact indications are that the capacities of established intermediary organizations to control their members and clients was as perishable a commodity in the case at hand as was the adherence of smaller firms to a wage-compressing regime of collective bargaining.

In a functionalist perspective, the cross-sectoral similarities and the structural coherence that result from equidirectional change and its intersectoral reinforcement might offer themselves to be accounted for in terms of concepts like complementarity, or systemic equilibrium based on complementarity. Complementarity, however, implying either intersectoral functional hierarchy or the presence of a hegemonic institutional designer, seems too static a concept to capture the widely distributed dynamic we have observed. Moreover, it is, as will be seen, insufficiently complex to deal with the apparent overdetermination of systemic change along but parallel sectoral trajectories, driven by a multiplicity of lines of equifinal causation.

7.3. Institutional Analysis and Political Economy

In the next three chapters, I will explore in some detail the morphology and the dynamics of gradual and systemic institutional change as gleaned from my account of the German case. In doing so, I will avail myself of the conceptual language of historical institutionalism broadly defined in order to describe the structural properties of the institutions under study, such as the extent to which they are organized or disorganized; to establish the rate and direction and the endogenous or exogenous origins of their change; to identify the general characteristics of the mechanisms through which change is produced; and to trace the interactions between the five institutional trajectories reconstructed in Part I. In doing so, I will pay particular attention to the transformative effects of gradual and, by implication, slow change. My main empirical puzzle will be the parallel, homologous, equidirectional nature of the change observed in the five sectors, as well as the way sectoral trajectories have over time reinforced each other, aggregating into a broad stream of systemic change.

Generally I will argue on the basis of my empirical observations for the superiority of a dynamic process as opposed to a static system concept of social order, especially in light of the fact that most of the change in the five sectors seems to have been endogenous and dialectical (with institutions producing "self-undermining" side effects), driven by inherent contradictions or accumulating dysfunctions rather than by contingent external shocks or intelligent hegemonic design. Proceeding from here, I will make a case for time and age as important factors in social systems and institutional change, suggesting that a heuristic might be productive that considers social orders as potentially perishable, that is, subject to exhaustion and (self-)consumption over time. Finally, following from my emphasis on the dynamic character of social order and the sometimes endemic, dialectical nature of institutional change, the notion of tipping points will be introduced, referring to moments in processes of gradual change where previously functional causal relations turn dysfunctional— a notion that implies periodicity, in the sense of relations between the elements of a social system or process working out differently depending on the time when they are considered.

Although the language I will be using in the present part of the book does not include formal modeling as in game theory, it is sufficiently abstract to be applicable in principle to institutions in general, regardless of historical and geographical location. This puts my argument at risk of being misunderstood in a number of ways. Since much of the current discourse on institutions in political economy is beholden to some sort of economic functionalism, the same might be suspected here. Or, alternatively, my argument may be misread as implying deterministic causal generalizations, for example, to the effect that all institutions tend toward disorganization; that institutional change is always endogenous and dialectical; that institutions inevitably age and die, and the like. Moreover, as the concepts I use refer mostly to institutional structures and processes, they may appear to deny the role of agency and strategy: exhaustion proceeds whatever actors do, and functions always turn into dysfunctions—strategies do not matter, structure rules supreme, if now in a dynamic rather than a static version. In fact, however, what I have to say is subversive of all of the three: economistic functionalism, scientistic determinism, and agency-free structuralism:

(1) Institutionalist accounts of "models of capitalism" tend to be organized around a concept like complementarity, implying that societies are "systems," that is, that their different sectors, or institutions, are

organically related to one another so as to optimize the joint performance of a collective, "systemic" function. While I do adopt for the time being the language of systems. I do so with the intention to show, drawing on my empirical evidence, that central assumptions made in much of the systems-theoretical "varieties of capitalism" literature do not hold. For example, where the notion of complementarity presupposes a specific configuration of the sectors of a "system," I argue that this configuration cannot be expected to come about on its own through pressures for efficiency, nor can it normally be produced by, as it were, intelligent design. My conclusion is that much speaks for the view that mutual functional enhancement of institutions, as implied by the concept of complementarity, is an exception rather than the rule, and that it, as well as institutional change, can be understood only if central assumptions of functionalist analysis are relaxed or dropped altogether.

(2) At least the way I use it, the language of historical-institutionalist analysis, abstract as it may be, does not make, or aspire to make, statements or predictions regarding institutions as such. Rather than general laws, it offers only suggestions, more or less tested and proven, as to where *also* to look and *what* to look for when dealing with specific instances of institutional ordering and institutional change. In other words, I propose using institutional analysis much more as a heuristic than as a theory. This is based on the assumption that there are properties and regularities in institutions as such that may be operative in very different contexts, so that it may be useful to check if they should be taken into account. For example, in a case of institutional change, one may want to be aware of the possibility that institutions can change under the impact of time, and in this sense age. Empirically, a process of institutional aging may or may not be found: if it is, additional factors have to be brought in to spell out the social mechanisms by which institutional aging was caused, and to explain why it was not, or could not be, prevented by countervailing forces or activities.

(3) Finally, while historical institutionalism rightly takes the logic of institutions and their inherent dynamics seriously, it does not maintain that they are everything, or that they can be fully explained out of themselves. In fact, it is one of my central claims that institutionalist analysis makes sense only if its abstract categories are filled with material content and grounded in concrete historical contexts where the general logic of institutional functioning and development that it may be able to identify meets with motivated actors and

contingent circumstances through and within which it is enacted and actualized.

That this is so should be particularly obvious in the present case, where the importance of time and periodicity suggests a direct link for institutional analysis to temporality and history. Actually Part III of the book will move explicitly beyond the limits and limitations of a purely institutionalist approach, toward a substantive-historical grounding of the analysis of institutional change presented in Part II. The underlying assumption, as well as the proposition to defend, is that in order to account fully for the observed process of systemic change, one has to be aware of it having occurred in a particular historical context, that of the decline of the politically and institutionally domesticated "organized" capitalism of the postwar era. It is here that I will, among other things, return to the concept of "disorganization" to give a material meaning—that of "liberalization"— to its provisional, formal–structural definition. The analysis will show that parallel dialectical change, exhaustion of institutions over time, the gradual shift from mutual support among institutional sectors to mutual subversion, etc. occurred, *not because the institutions in question were institutions,* but because they were located in a specific kind of political economy at a specific time and in a specific place, struggling with specific problems of social integration and system integration. It will point out the driving forces behind the dynamics of disorganization, locating them in a historically concrete constellation of institutions, in characteristic dispositions of actors, and in a particular relationship between rule-making and rule-taking emblematic of the social order and economic regime in question, that is, of contemporary capitalism. Part III, that is to say, will make a case for historical institutionalism to take capitalism seriously while contributing to its analysis by conceptualizing it as an instituted social order, that is, as a system of action within and in relation to social rules.

Notes

1. The milestones are the *Gesetz zur Kontrolle und Transparenz im Unternehmensbereich* (KonTraG, Corporate Supervision and Transparency Act, 1998), the abolition of the capital gains tax for firms divesting themselves of shares in other firms (2000) and the *Wertpapiererwerbs- und Übernahmegesetz* (WpÜG, Securities Acquisition and Takeover Act, 2001). See Cioffi and Höpner (2006).

2. The reorientation of Deutsche Bank toward international investment banking
   began and evolved gradually in the 1980s. In 1984, the bank moved its capital
   market operations to London, and in 1989, it acquired the London broker-
   age firm Morgan Greenfell (Lütz 2002, 234). The process was completed only
   in 1997 when Rolf-Ernst Breuer acceded to the chairmanship (Jackson and
   Höpner 2001).

8

From system to process

The notion of complementarity stipulates a relationship between two institutions within which the performance of one is enhanced by the presence of the other and, perhaps, vice versa (Amable 2003; Crouch et al. 2005; Hall and Soskice 2001a; Höpner 2005b). It belongs in a functionalist perspective on the social world in which social structures are explained by the tasks they perform, and where social systems evolve or are designed to optimize the attainment of a given objective, such as social integration or efficiency in the use of scarce resources. This implies that change in institutions, and certainly endogenous change, is normally tantamount to continuous improvement of institutions in the service of their objective, or to reestablishing the conditions of optimal performance after an external shock that has temporarily upset the functional equilibrium of the social order.

Among the many problems with functionalism is that in social life collective objectives are rarely if ever given, and indeed are typically contestable and in continuous need of definition and revision. Thus, institutional design is made inherently difficult by the fact that the demands that are made on it are complex, contradictory, and often unsuited for technical adjudication.[1] Moreover, as a rule, survival as such, in economic competition as elsewhere, is not enough to guide the evolution of a social order, as there are always alternative modes of survival between which a choice has to be made. The implications of this are many, including that analyzing the relations between institutions in terms of a mutual optimization of their functions underestimates the complexity of social structures while overestimating the computing capacities of institutional designers (Streeck 2004b). It is therefore no surprise that no master designer could be identified in our account of gradual, parallel, systemic institutional change in the German political economy, nor that there was no first and leading sector causing change in the others and acting as a systemic force assuring complementarity between the institutions of the German national "model."

In terms of empirical observations and freed of assumptions of a self-stabilizing tendency toward functional equilibrium, complementarity and systemic stability may be considered to refer to a condition in which the elements, or sectors, of a social order produce *positive externalities* for each other, compensating each other's deficiencies or, more modestly, suspending each other's inherent tensions and contradictions, thereby stabilizing the system as a whole. Negative externalities of one institution for the other, by contrast, would undermine the latter, for example by reinforcing inherent tendencies toward endogenous change. Rather than assuming a priori that social systems are generally governed by a capacity to organize their elements so that they support each other, resulting in a stable overall order that can be expected to restabilize itself after an external shock, I suggest on the basis of my evidence to treat the relations between the sectors as contingent, allowing for mutual functions as well as mutual dysfunctions without prejudgment in favor of either of them. Complementarity would then denote a specific "historical" conjuncture of system elements in which sectors happen to "fit" together and support one another, without however assuming this to be in any way a "normal" condition. Positive externalities are, in other words, allowed to turn negative, and may well do so. Functions may become dysfunctions, implying that complementarity, where it happened to have come about, may also disappear.

Looking for positive and negative externalities instead of complementarity, and allowing not just for functions but also for dysfunctions in the relations between social institutions (Merton 1957), has the advantage that it provides for more varieties of institutional change than just efficiency-improving adaptation. Not only does this do justice to the empirical facts observed in the case at hand. By making it possible systematically to introduce time and history in the analysis, it also opens a new and, I believe, highly productive, dynamic perspective on how institutional configurations, or "systems," including national "models" of political economy, may congeal and dissolve. If a national "variety of capitalism," such as *"Modell Deutschland"* in the 1970s and 1980s, is essentially a fortuitous conjuncture between its component institutions, it is likely to be precarious and temporary: better conceived as a *limited period* in a historical process than as a timeless *self-stabilizing structure*. National models exist, or may be socially constructed to exist, as long as their elements happen to be so configured that their internal tensions and mutual dysfunctions are kept sufficiently in check for the system to "work" and project an appearance of organic coherence. No guarantee can be offered, however, that this will always remain so. Absent a hegemonic designer, a dominant cause or a preestablished principal purpose, it appears that systemic configurations can be no more than fleeting moments in the history of social structures that are mostly messy and always in motion, requiring a great deal of imaginative construction, constructive imagination and, perhaps, wishful thinking, to make them appear coherent or systematic. Any social system, that is to say, even if it lends itself exceptionally and temporarily to being celebrated for what may look like purposeful design for superior functional complementarity, is likely to be short-lived. How long it will in fact live depends on the empirical forces at work in the specific historical setting in which the system is located and out of which it has grown. A national model of capitalism stabilizes itself, not because it is a system, but only contingently: if and to the extent that the social forces at work inside and around it support its stability.

8.1. The "German Model": From Virtuous Circle to Historical Moment

This certainly applies to what was in its heyday referred to as "the German model." It came to be recognized as such in the second half of the 1970s, after a prehistory during which it had gradually evolved out of varying configurations of conflicts, contradictions and external challenges. It lasted only for a short period—roughly a decade—until it found itself, or was found to be, in "crisis." When exactly it came into being, and when it was finally overtaken by history, was and remains hard to say. This, I maintain, is not because of deficient theory or lack of empirical study. Rather, it reflects the very nature of social systems whose origin and demise are and must be to a large extent a matter of convention: of an emerging common sense, typically promoted by political or intellectual entrepreneurs, of the significance of a more or less coherent configuration of social arrangements that may be recognized as a "system" because and as long as it seems particularly good at dealing with a problem widely perceived as particularly important.

Discovery of the "German model" in scholarly writing dates back to the 1980s when British and American diagnoses of "Eurosclerosis," which came combined with demands for a fundamental departure from the postwar European welfare state, were found in sharp contrast to the then superior performance especially of the German economy, as compared to the more liberal capitalism of Anglo-American countries. Social scientists working in the tradition of the neo-corporatist literature of the 1970s perceived an opportunity to establish a theoretical and political alternative to mainstream economics and neo-liberalism, by emphasizing the non-market, social-institutional foundations of national economic success, extending their field of study from wage setting and labor relations to a range of other institutions and their interaction. For example, based on research on industrial relations and industrial restructuring in the world automobile industry, this author in 1985 identified a "virtuous circle of upmarket industrial restructuring" at work in the German case, consisting of five elements: a strategic focus on individualized high-quality production; strong trade unions with an institutionalized presence in the polity at large and in the enterprise; stable employment in an efficient, jointly administered internal labor market; a flexible socio-technical system of work; and a market-independent system of industrial skill generation (Streeck 1987, 455–7). Later versions of what came to be described as "an interactive configuration of policies and institutional structures... ideally matched to, and indeed almost making inevitable, an industrial strategy of upmarket restructuring" (Streeck 1989a, 129) featured a slightly different cast of sectors, such as "a system of 'rigid' *wage determination*"; "a policy of employment protection"; "a set of binding rules that obliges employers to *consult* with their workforces"; "a *training regime*... capable of obliging employers to train more workers... than required by immediate product or labor market pressures"; and "a system of rules regarding the organization of work... obliging employers to design jobs more broadly than many of them would feel necessary" (Streeck 1991, 52–4).

Later yet more institutions were added, for example, an independent central bank foreclosing recourse to inflation and currency devaluation as ways of defending industrial employment and competitiveness (Streeck 1994). Whatever the exact specifications of the model, however, the logic remained the same, with a set of social institutions preventing employers taking the "easy road" at the expense of workers, forcing them to behave in ways that markets would not have demanded while *also* enabling them to adopt difficult and unlikely but all the more successful strategies of adjustment (the "high road") that they could and would not have chosen without the effective support of other institutions in the system.

An example of how the argument ran is the following discussion of the economic consequences of a German-style wage setting regime "that keeps wages higher, and variations between wages lower, than in a free labor market":

Unless employers are willing to move production elsewhere, this forces them to adapt their product range to non-price competitive markets capable of sustaining a high wage level. A high and even wage level also makes employers more willing to invest in training and retraining as a way of matching workers' productivity to the externally fixed, high costs of labor. Moreover, as wage differentials are relatively small, employers have an incentive not to concentrate their training investment on just a few elite workers. In addition, fixed high and even wages make it attractive for employers to organize work in a "non-Bravermanian" way, so that the labor extracted and performed justifies its high price.

(Streeck 1991, 52)

However the argument was phrased in particular, the central point was always that in crucial respects, the behavior of firms in the densely organized German version of capitalism was driven, not by signals of the market, but by institutionalized social rules. Later, in a search for more abstract, "theoretical" language, this came to be described as "coordination" of economic behavior. Moreover, the cost of compliance with institutionalized obligations to act against short-term market pressures was argued to be more than balanced by the beneficial effects of other institutions in the system—an effect that came to be referred to as institutional "complementarity." Thirdly, the typical mode of production of the German economy, "diversified quality production," was presented as the ideal and perhaps the only way out for firms burdened with German-style institutional obligations, provided their management was inventive enough to recognize the economic opportunities inherent in what at first appeared to be no more than costly strategic constraints.

In early writing, it was still emphasized that the configuration of institutions that supported German competitiveness had not been specifically designed for the purpose, and that the functional "fit" in support of diversified quality production between, for example, codetermination and the German engineering tradition had not been a result of deliberate planning:

This configuration had not been intentionally created to meet the new challenges of world-market competition in the 1980s; that it happened to be there was hardly more than a felicitous coincidence. It could have been otherwise, and in any case was either absent or failed to be activated in other industries in the same country, such as ship building. There are also considerable elements of strain and contradiction within the configuration itself which would require separate analysis. (Streeck 1987, 458)

Nevertheless, diversified quality production soon came to be presented as a timeless recipe for prosperity under a less market-driven variant of capitalism, rather than a lucky improvisation making the best of a particular institutional heritage. Increasingly attempts were made to explain the institutional structure of German and, by extension, nonliberal capitalism as a product of a strategic decision, on the part of employers, the government or society as a whole, to seek comparative advantage in profitable markets for diversified quality production, *instead of the other way around.* That the "German model" was successful had to mean that it could not have been a coincidence but had to have been *designed for success;* that it was *economically* successful must mean that it had been instituted *for economic reasons;* and that the elements of the system seemed to enhance each other's contribution to successful diversified quality production appeared to justify the functionalist prediction that, where one of them was present, the others would also be present or would emerge shortly. Moreover, given its apparent functional equilibrium it was hard to see why the virtuous institutional circle of German-style capitalism should have needed class conflict and political mobilization to come about, in the light of how much it benefited the entire nation. Thus functionalist reasoning turned seamlessly into rational choice constructivism, by exchanging the language of systemic equilibrium for one of intentional action, turning what was first conceived as the unintended outcome of the interaction between complementary institutions into the intended objective of rational actors endowed with far-reaching political and cognitive powers of institutional design. By the same token, what had figured in early analyses as a more or less coincidental constellation of institutions making, at a particular moment in history, for a labor-driven sort of industrial adjustment, was redefined as a result of technocratic design and redesign of social institutions in the service of high economic performance.

Empirically, the functionalist interpretation of the "German model" was always disputable, and not only with respect to its applicability to all rather than just a few sectors of the German economy. Critical questions began to be asked with the decline of German economic performance in the 1990s, which was bound to appear confusing to those who had considered "diversified quality production" as a perennially superior strategic choice rather than a constrained expediency. Explanations for the decline of German economic fortunes, if it was not altogether denied, included changing external conditions ("globalization") and the shock of unification; mostly a return to the golden days of the 1980s was considered impending. Of course, what was even harder to reconcile with the reified version of "diversified quality production" was that it was the employers and not the unions that in the 1990s began openly to attack the pillars of a "model" that had supposedly served them so well and that in a rational-functionalist worldview they should have done their best to defend. In fact what had been overlooked or denied from the beginning in functionalist analysis was that, as we have seen, pressures for change emanating especially from employers had started long before the 1990s; that the "model" had if at all been imposed on rather than created by capital; and that employers had throughout its lifetime to be bought in at rising costs for the "model" to function at all.

I argue that it is only in a strictly historical and dynamic, nonfunctionalist perspective that the rise and fall of the "German model," as a definite period in a continuing process of institutional construction and deconstruction, can be fully accounted for. A stylized narrative of its evolution, cutting across the institutional settings whose histories were presented separately in Part I, would reconstruct its object as a historical era, with uncertain beginning and end, in a stream of events during which certain features of the social world temporarily gelled into an identifiable gestalt until they evolved further and their conjuncture gave way to something new. A narrative of this sort would start with the observation that in Germany, the foundational conflict in postwar democratic capitalism between free collective bargaining and public responsibility for full employment was for a while suspended by the enormous economic growth that came with reconstruction. When in the 1960s an encompassing wage setting regime had established itself after a long period of conflictual institution-building (Manow 2001), the first postwar recession in 1966 and 1967 caused a change of government, ushering in a social-democratic attempt at Keynesian reflation combined with a voluntary national incomes policy. The latter was thwarted by the unexpected level of labor militancy after 1969. Subsequently, the independent central bank of the Federal Republic of the time imposed a rigid policy of monetary stability on a political economy in which industrial trade unions had attained the historical peak of their political and economic power. Together this forced firms to restructure in the direction of advanced niche production for international premium markets (Streeck 1991), by drawing on a range of specifically German cultural and institutional resources that had been temporarily submerged during the "Fordist" epoch. To secure the social peace necessary for internationally competitive "diversified quality production" in the wake of the labor unrest of the late 1960s, the government for its part, extending a practice that had first been introduced in the early 1960s, offered the "social partners" a social policy of defensive labor supply management to serve as a functional equivalent to monetary and fiscal expansion.

By the late 1970s, everything seemed to have come together to constitute a model political-economic system capable of being successful in world markets while paying workers high and not too unequal wages, training them well, and affording them a strong voice at the workplace. Inflation was low, and so was unemployment. Wage settlements were in line with and indeed helped drive increasing productivity; trade unions and employer associations were well-organized and behaved as responsible private governments in a wide variety of areas, including training, where they relieved the state of otherwise difficult or unsolvable problems of policymaking and rule enforcement (Streeck and Schmitter 1984). State, business, and labor worked together in "social partnership," with an encompassing trade union movement organizing nation-wide solidarity, and with a network of large firms which, in addition to supporting comprehensive organization in strong business associations, accepted responsibility for a range of public goods, most important among them enhancing the international competitiveness of the German economy. In 1976, then, Chancellor Helmut Schmidt found it expedient to introduce "*Modell Deutschland*" into the German and international political language—projecting an image of effective cooperation between technically competent government and well-organized and safely established, and therefore almost inevitably cooperative, social classes, jointly managing the new risks and exploring the new opportunities associated with a changed world after the end of Bretton Woods and the rise of OPEC, without causing social inequities and avoiding political disruptions of the sort that had shaken democratic capitalism a decade earlier.

With hindsight one realizes that "*Modell Deutschland*" was no more than a short span of time in a continuous historical process when a number of elements of the German institutional legacy happened to fit together particularly well. Empirical observation reveals that what was presented to the world as a coherent, historically fixed, functionally self-reproducing model of a socially domesticated modern capitalism carried within itself an abundant supply of seeds of destruction. What made for the perception

113

of stability was simply that the system's many internal contradictions, within and between its different institutional settings, needed time to mature, after their lucky suspension in the years following the shocks of 1969 and 1972. Already Schmidt's public narrative in the mid-1970s of responsible and cooperative social partnership was as much a collective imaginary, a purposefully created political myth, and even an attempt at faith healing as it was a description of social reality (Streeck 2006a). A particularly glaring illustration of this was Helmut Schmidt's *New York Times* op-ed article, "The Social and Political Stability of West Germany," published on May 2, 1976, during the run-up to the federal election, which was fought and won by the Social Democratic Party under the slogan *"Modell Deutschland."*[2] Its final paragraph reads:

All these rights enjoyed by workers and their representatives give them a greater understanding of the workings of the firm and industry and of the effects of business decisions. This, I believe, creates a climate in which labor refrains from excessive demands and generally asks only for what is reasonable. This belief has been repeatedly confirmed by experience, especially in the difficult year of 1975. And when looking ahead at labor negotiations in 1976, too, union leaders unequivocally stated that their demands would once again be guided by the productive capacity of our economy.

Note that 1976 was the year when the government had passed a law on enterprise-level codetermination that remained far behind what the unions had demanded. Note also that one reason for the resignation of Schmidt's predecessor, Willy Brandt, in 1974 had been an inflationary public sector wage settlement, following a crippling strike, which had in turn caused the Central Bank to adopt the highly restrictive monetary policy for which it later became famous or, as the case may be, infamous. While publicly the government complained about the threat of rising unemployment caused by the Bank's rabid monetarism, in private its ministers, even those with a union background, were grateful for the Bundesbank doing a job they themselves could not do for political reasons (Scharpf 1991). In fact, in 1977, one year after Schmidt had been returned to office, the unions used the opportunity of the employers taking the codetermination law of 1976 to the Constitutional Court to withdraw from participation in *Konzertierte Aktion,* the tripartite body that was to organize a voluntary incomes policy that had, however, become increasingly perfunctory over the years.

Conflicts were everywhere in "Model Germany," although for a time they could be overlooked or kept latent, having not yet developed to a point where they could discredit the model's proud image of itself. In reality *"Modell Deutschland,"* where it was more than a political slogan, was a provisional, improvised, inherently perishable although temporarily quite effective, nationally distinctive answer to new internal tensions and external challenges to the postwar social order—a response that for a while happened to fit a changed but also continually changing environment well. Yearly fiscal deficits and growing public debt were only one symptom of the underlying problems. In the early 1980s, unemployment went up sharply and refused to go down even when the economy temporarily recovered. The unhelpful and indeed aggressive response in 1982 and 1983 of the Kohl government to the bankruptcy of *Neue Heimat*, the unions' huge housing concern, was, probably rightly, perceived by the leadership of the DGB as a not-so-covert attempt to destroy their economic base and their public reputation.[3] The 1984 strike in the metal sector, called in reaction to both a deteriorating labor market and rising government hostility, exacerbated the developing crisis of the social security system and, as we have seen, profoundly changed the terms of cooperation between capital and labor at the workplace. It also set in motion the subsequent decentralization of the collective bargaining system. Union membership had already started to decline, and gradually the same began to be true for works council coverage. Internal union divisions became insuperable in the wake of the 1984 conflict, leading to negotiations on union mergers, initially secret, which would effectively preclude a return of the union federation, the DGB, to political significance. Moreover, tensions within *Gesamtmetall* began to build after 1984, setting in motion a slow but steady decline of its membership and industrial power.

By the late 1980s, the Kohl government contemplated deep reforms in social security, ready to go to battle with a union movement which, while losing members, continued to insist on fighting unemployment by reducing the supply of labor at the expense of both private firms and public coffers. Even the emerging leader of the SPD, Oskar Lafontaine, publicly attacked the unions in 1988 for their insistence on reduction of working hours without reduction of pay. Simultaneously, large German firms were getting ready for the "completion of the Single European Market," as envisaged by the Delors European Commission for 1992; Deutsche Bank was slowly beginning to move into investment banking; and first steps toward the privatization of public enterprises were being considered. Then came German unification, for which the government dearly needed peace on its West German domestic front. For another half decade, this kept in place and even reinvigorated an institutional configuration between collective bargaining, corporatist interest organization, and the welfare state that had long begun to generate not just ever higher deficits, but also rising unemployment and growing social divisions. With the end of the short economic boom after unification, it became increasingly visible that under the surface of a series of tripartite meetings at the Chancellor's Office in the first half of the 1990s,[4] the decay of the "German model" that had begun in the old Federal Republic about a decade earlier had continued. By the mid-1990s, the various lines of institutional change that had started long before unification had resumed at an accelerating pace, as though to catch up for time lost. With the failure of Kohl's "Alliance for Jobs" in April 1996 at the latest—one-and-a-half years after the election and in the wake of no less than nine fruitless meetings since January 1995 with the "social partners" on reforms to improve the German *Standort*—the transformations under way in different settings of the German political economy began to reinforce one another, setting in motion an encompassing process of "self-disorganization" that was to thicken into a broad stream of rapid institutional change during Gerhard Schröder's second term as Chancellor.

Looking closely at the "German model" over a longer period, one sees much more change than stability, and indeed if there was anything permanent, it was that all elements of the system were continually in motion, individually and with respect to their mutual functions and dysfunctions. Since change proceeded slowly and developments took their time to make their significance felt, many contemporary observers were misled to read more continuity and complementarity into what they saw than there actually was, clinging to a static image of a "system" that had long served them well, regardless of a growing number of observations that would have been more compatible with a different, more conflictual, and less well-ordered view of the social world. Thus, as time passed, the "German model" imperceptibly turned into an idealized memory of a period in history when by lucky coincidence and, perhaps, the skilful opportunism of political leaders of the likes of Helmut Schmidt and Helmut Kohl, a set of evolving institutions happened to function together in a way that temporarily suspended their inherent fragility and supported their positive externalities for one another, or in any case made it possible to overlook pragmatically the accumulating evidence of instability and ongoing transformation.

Representing as a stable state, and thereby reifying, what is in reality no more than a short stretch of time cut out of a continuous flow of history is tempting, since a static model of society is easier to communicate than a dynamic one. Moreover, sense-making in political analysis is usually, and perhaps inevitably, loaded with practical intentions, which are often directed toward making desirable conditions more permanent than they otherwise would be. One reason why many observers of the "German model" were driven to describe what they saw, or what they had constructed from what they had seen, as stable and lasting was that they wished to demonstrate that social egalitarianism and political solidarity were compatible with a capitalist economy even after the end of the Golden Age, and that in particular strong unions and self-confident social democracy, as they had emerged from the formative 1960s in Europe, were no obstacle to economic prosperity and competitive success under capitalism. Here as always, realism and constructivism are not easy to distinguish since even the most motivated reconstruction of the world must bear some resemblance to what reasonable observers perceive to be real. In fact the problem of social "models" as stylized images of a real world working well is not so much that they are or could be invented freely. Rather, it is that the rhetoric of models tends to freeze conceptually and rigidify into a static design what can be no more than a selective collection of observed functional relationships, carved out of a steady and inherently messy flow of events by motivated participants hoping to impose on it a durable institutional master plan and a unified functional purpose.

Much of the literature on the "German model" of the 1970s, that is to say, can be read as inspired by a sentiment similar to that for which Faust, would he ever feel it, had agreed to surrender his immortal soul to the devil: "Then to the moment I'd dare say: Stay a while! You are so lovely!" (Goethe, Faust II, V.).[5] Like Kuhn's "normal scientists" (Kuhn 1970) stretching their paradigms, if necessary beyond recognition, in order to accommodate empirical measurements with which they would otherwise be incompatible, numerous students of the "German model" well into the 1990s tried to salvage their received frame of interpretation in which Germany figured as a demonstration case of a capitalism both competitive and benevolent, by adding to it an ever longer list of ad hoc exceptions and extensions, immunizing their model against disappointment by declaring ongoing change to be immaterial or, ultimately, denying that it had occurred or was occurring at all.[6]

More often than not, proving a possibility is motivated by a wish to help make it come true. The same wish may also account for a tendency in much political-institutional scholarship to overstate the capacity of human actors to arrest the flow of history and purposely create institutional structures that, being superior to others, are likely to remain stable for a longer time. However, few if any political-economic configurations, model or not, owe their existence to provident institution-building. Certainly the "German model" of the 1970s emerged, not by "intelligent design," but as a fortuitous momentary combination, or recombination, of a number of institutions, each of which had its own history and historical dynamic.[7] More or less accidentally, in the decade from the mid-1970s to the mid-1980s, these happened to complement each other in a way that responded well to a series of external challenges, of a sort altogether unforeseen in the immediate postwar decades. Statesmanship did play a role in that there were in leading positions at the time individuals who recognized that the institutional material at hand lent itself to strategies and purposes that happened to fit some of the contingencies of the day, at least for the day. Good luck, however—or, in the language of Machiavelli, *fortuna*—was no less important than was the statecraft— the *virtù*—of someone like Helmut Schmidt. A few years later, the same institutional tendencies and dispositions whose contradictions and negative externalities had for a while been neutralized had further unfolded, and conflicts and dysfunctions that had been invisible or pragmatically considered insignificant inexorably came to the fore.[8] While one might want to know, in the words of Alexis de Tocqueville, how a sick man might have been saved, having understood the malady of which he had died,[9] such treatment, too, would clearly have worked only with a good deal of luck in a world in which the real consequences of social institutions and political-institutional design can normally not be fully known in advance.

Inspection of the fate of the "German model" over a longer time span reveals that stability, even if construed to be based in functional complementarity, is no more than an unrealistic expectation when dealing with the social world. The normal state of a social structure is that it is changing. Stability is essentially a convenient invention of overwhelmed observers needing to simplify the world to be able to speak about it. It is true that some constructions of a social situation as stable may be more than others based in fact, for example if, temporarily, the positive externalities of institutions inside an institutional complex outweigh the negative ones. Even in the best of circumstances, however, stability can never be more than transitory. Rather than reading into the real world an exaggerated degree of order somehow rooted in the presumed functional advantages of complementarity, institutional analysis should more modestly undertake to trace the evolution over time of the positive and negative externalities created by social institutions for each other. This is because no social arrangement can be designed, if it can be designed at all, to fit all exigencies that may arise in its environment, or to anticipate the totality of the consequences of its own operation for itself, for its environment, and for its relationship to it. *The uncertainty of the world always exceeds the flexibility of any structure in the world.* Societies are processes, and social systems are cross-sections, constructed by motivated observation, of a process by which society is permanently constituted and reconstituted in history: they represent a condition that, strictly speaking, has already passed. Dynamics precede statics, and time is, as I will argue next in more detail, a fundamental constituent of society and its institutional order. As Heraclitus of Ephesus, the first to recognize the primacy of process over condition, put it: "All things are in motion and nothing remains still."[10]

Notes

1. More on this in the final chapter.
2. The article is documented by Peter Katzenstein in his "Policy and Politics in West Germany" (1987, 156–8).
3. I draw here on interviews Christine Trampusch and I conducted with union leaders of the time.
4. According to data gathered in joint research with Christine Trampusch, there were no fewer than 23 *Kanzlerrunden*—tripartite meetings of government, business associations, and trade unions convened and presided over by the Chancellor—between February 1990, almost a year before the accession of the *Neue Länder* to the Federal republic, and September 1994, immediately before the federal election. The subjects of the meetings included the numerous political and economic challenges connected to German unification.
5. "Werd' ich zum Augenblicke sagen: Verweile doch! du bist so schön!"
6. A few examples among many are Abelshauser (2006), Busch (2005), Dyson (2001), Harding (1999), Jürgens and Krzywdzinski (2007), Lane (2000), and Vitols (2006).
7. "Nothing in the above is to suggest that the institutional configuration that made up the 'German system' in the 1970s and 1980s was created in one piece, or created for the economic purposes that it came to serve. Some of its elements were pre-Wilhelminian, others were introduced by the Allies after 1945, and still others originated in the politics of the Federal Republic, sometimes drawing on and modifying older arrangements, and sometimes not. Moreover, each element, for example the banking system, was subject to its own historical dynamic. All were and continue to be changing, for

119

their own reasons as well as in reaction to each other, and certainly there can be no presumption of a preestablished fit between them, even though one might want to allow for some reinforcement effects of the 'model's' historically contingent, social and economic success. That its parts happened to perform together so well during the period in question must be attributed at least as much to *fortuna* as to *virtu*" (Streeck 1997*b*).

8. This will be elaborated below, from a variety of perspectives.
9. I owe the reference to Tocqueville to an as yet unpublished manuscript by Richard Swedberg. Tocqueville's *bon mot* is found in the Foreword to his book of 1856 on "The Old Regime" (1983, xii), where he uses it to describe the task of social science as he saw it.
10. Heraclitus (540–475 BC), for good reasons, was called "the Obscure" already by the ancient Greeks. Even Platon, in the Cratylus dialogue, had to guess what Heraclitus had really meant: "Heraclitus, I believe, says that all things go and nothing stays, and comparing existents to the flow of a river, he says you could not step twice into the same river."

9

Endogenous change: time, age, and the self-undermining of institutions

Change in institutions is the intended or unintended result of individual and collective action in the context of institutions, that is, in compliance with or defiance of social rules. Understanding institutional change therefore requires exploration of the relationship between social rules and social action, in terms that can account for human action as rule-making, rule-taking, and rule-breaking, spelling out what it means to follow a rule or not, and how this reflects on the rule itself. No action-theoretical framework of this sort can and needs to be developed here. For present purposes, it is enough to note that norm-following behavior is never completely determined by the norms it follows, and therefore always retains agentic properties. Because of their compulsory and, indeed, compulsive creativity, actors' responses to social rules remain ultimately unpredictable, not just for the observer but also for those who have designed the rules to which actors are responding. Moreover, agents acting in the context of a social order face long chains of causation that they cannot normally fully understand or, if they understand them, take into account when acting. This makes for all sorts of unanticipated consequences and emergent aggregation effects.

Rather than trying to analyze these in general terms, I will more modestly explore and perhaps specify some of the mechanisms responsible for endogenous institutional transformation as observed in my five sectors. Above all, I want to show how engagement of gradual change in particular may alert us to the central importance of time for social structures, and in fact suggest a shift from a system to a process perspective on social order. A process perspective, in turn, as applied in the preceding chapter to "*Modell Deutschland*," invites speculation on institutional life cycles,

121

drawing attention to the possibility of birth, growth, decay, and death of institutions, and generally on periodicity in social order. Gradual change, by definition proceeding slowly, takes time, making the time that passes as a changing institution moves from one condition to another an element of the social situation, in a somewhat paradoxical fashion. While slow change allows actors to perceive a changing situation as stable, or regard the changes they observe as merely temporary and ephemeral, it forces social science to widen its time horizon. In particular, it makes it impossible to pretend, as does correlational analysis, that cause produces effect essentially immediately without delay and friction; that the time that passes between cause and effect is short enough to be negligible; and that "independent" and "dependent" variable are tightly coupled when in fact their relationship may realize itself only with time. In other words, understanding gradual change requires a departure from the correlational machine model of society implied by standard variable sociology which, just like neo-classical economics (North 1997), tends to treat time, and transitions in time, as too short to be worth attention or make a difference. Once that departure has been made, and chronological time is recognized as a defining element of social relations, the door is open for historical time to be taken seriously in social theory, conceived as the unique, irreversible, and irretrievable period that a specific process needs in order to unfold.

Time and process are familiar concepts in the literature on social mechanisms. According to Mayntz (2004), social mechanisms are "recurrent processes," represented in terms of "generalizable properties abstracted from concrete (historical) processes," "linking specified initial conditions and a specific outcome," in particular with respect to the macro- or meso-level of a social system. Put otherwise, mechanisms "state how, by what intermediate steps, a certain outcome follows from a set of initial conditions" (Mayntz 2004, 241). I leave aside the question, central to the unending feuds in sociology over the ontological status of the social world, whether the establishment of a causal link between the condition of a causally "independent" institution A and that of a causally "dependent" institution B necessarily requires recourse to the micro level of individual action.[1] More important is the fact that mechanisms are typological generalizations of processes stretched out and developing *in time*, rather than statements on apparently timeless correlations between variable properties of social structures. Put otherwise, the better a causal mechanism is understood as a sequence of intermediate causes and effects, the more obvious it becomes that its operation requires time, suggesting a switch from a cross-sectional to a diachronic perspective on causal relations in social systems. Mechanisms, in other words, *conceptualize causation as change*. Moreover, they would seem to be especially well suited to deal with gradual change, where the objective is to specify as a sequence in time the process connecting different conditions of the same institution at different times, t_1 and t_2. "Temporality," according to Mayntz, "is clearly a characteristic of social mechanisms" (Mayntz 2004, 242).

A diachronic perspective suggests itself in particular for the analysis of *endogenous* gradual change, especially where endogenous change proceeds in a "dialectical" fashion. Having emphasized the multiple instabilities and the processual nature of social systems, based on my empirical accounts of parallel and equidirectional yet non-teleological and ungoverned change in neighboring institutional settings, I will now look more deeply at how social action within an institution may cause effects that undermine that same institution, through gradual accumulation of intended or unintended consequences incompatible beyond a certain point with the institution's continued operation or existence.[2] As such accumulation takes place over time, one may feel tempted to go as far as to treat the passage of time itself in certain institutional settings as a mechanism producing change: the longer a self-undermining institution has existed—the older it is—the more likely its self-destructive effects will have sufficiently accumulated to disable it. One implication would be that to the extent that institutions are subject to dialectical self-undermining, they have a limited lifetime as they become exhausted and "spent" while being used, or better consumed. At the end of this chapter, I will explore some further ramifications of this intuition.

9.1. Dialectical Change

Most current theories of institutional change tend to treat institutions as social artifacts purposely designed by rule-makers to govern the future behavior of the rule-makers themselves or of others on whose behalf they have a capacity to act (for many others, see Campbell 2004). This is particularly the case for those discussions of institutional change that have originated in political science, where the central subject is, of course, governance. Even where the perspective of policymakers prevails, however, design and redesign of institutionalized social rules appear far from straightforward. In fact, most of the literature on the subject, taking off in one way or another from the notion of path dependence, emphasizes the impact on the form of institutions and the direction of institutional change of already existing institutions that constrain what institutional designers can do. Both "layering" and "conversion," the two types of gradual change identified in Thelen's seminal essay (2002), are stylized representations of institution-building practices of policymakers who are prevented by the existing social order and the interests embodied in it from creating entirely new institutions from scratch. Rather than trying to do so, and very likely being defeated over it, skilled actors who want to achieve real change are likely to leave existing institutions intact while attaching new elements to them that gradually alter the status and structure of the institutional setting as a whole ("layering"). Or they may undertake stepwise to devote old institutions to new purposes, instead of trying to undo them and create new institutions in their place ("conversion").

A limiting case of a design perspective on institutional change is "drift," as described by Hacker (2004) and included in a later, extended typology (Streeck and Thelen 2005). Institutional change occurs in the form of drift when a changing environment distorts the intended effects of an institution in a way that fits the interests or intentions of agents with power over its design. This enables them to promote change in the way the institution works out in its social enactment by leaving its structure unchanged, that is, by doing nothing to readjust it to its original purposes. In the typology, drift is described as the result of deliberate, strategic neglect of institutional maintenance when external change produces slippage in institutional practice "on the ground." What changes, then, is not the rules but their outcome, due to change in the external conditions under which the rules are applied.

Analysis of drift directs attention to the independent contribution of the situational enactment of institutions to institutional change, and in particular to the role of the actors subject to an institution as producers of unanticipated side effects of rules and rule-making (Streeck and Thelen 2005). In this perspective compliance or, for that matter, noncompliance with social rules, rather than being taken for granted, appears as active participation in their creation, maintenance, and transformation, and must therefore be included in theories of institutional change. In fact, taking a wide variety of often unpredictable forms, the responses of rule-takers to institutionalized expectations may set in motion processes of change entirely unexpected and often highly undesirable from the point of view of elite rule-makers.[3] While rule-making has been extensively explored in political science institutionalism, which tends to focus on how political elites create, recreate, abolish, or reform social institutions, rule-following, and its effects on the rules being followed is much less well understood.[4] Taking enactment seriously as a contribution to institution-building requires taking into account, for example, inconsistencies in rules, or unforeseen changes in the external conditions of implementation, that demand creative rule application in good faith but also allow for inventive reinterpretation in bad faith; limited possibilities for compliance, as well as emergent opportunities for non-compliance; political contestation of the legitimacy of a given institution; and the wide variety of empirical motives for compliance, reaching from fear of sanctions to material interests to internalized cultural values.[5]

More generally, distinguishing between rule-makers and rule-takers opens a perspective on a sort of institutional change that proceeds independently from and against the intentions of those supposedly in control, through deviant local enactment or the slow accumulation of anticipated or unanticipated consequences of an institution's routine operation. In the previously quoted catalog of fives types of slow institutional change (Streeck and Thelen 2005), this latter possibility is most closely represented by a mechanism of change called "exhaustion." Exhaustion refers to a process by which an institution "withers away" through "self-consumption"; through decreasing returns due to its costs increasing with its expansion; or through overextension diminishing its capacity to do what it was originally invented to do. Change of this sort appears truly dialectical to the extent that it is driven by the regular performance of an institution's intended functions, or by behavior in line with institutionalized rules. It is also truly endogenous, with rule-following or rule-using inside an institution being the source of increasingly destructive tensions and contradictions. Moreover, dialectical change, where there is a potential for it at all, seems all the more inevitable as it comes about as a side-product of the very benefits for the sake of which an institution was created or is supported by those in control of its design. Looking for dialectical effects of this kind thus appears to be a highly promising strategy when having to account for endogenous institutional change, that is, for change obviously not caused by contingent events outside of an institution or a system of institutions.

9.2. Self-Undermining Institutions

As it happens, dialectical processes of self-undermining, self-consumption, self-exhaustion, overextension, and the like abound in our five narratives of endogenous sectoral change in the German political economy. Among the examples are:

(1) Nationally coordinated collective bargaining by industrial sectors created and reproduced a high average wage level combined with a flat wage structure. Inclusion of the service sector in the encompassing wage setting regime stifled job growth while employment in manufacturing was shrinking, although at a lower rate than in most other countries. The unintended, ultimately self-destructive result was a declining employment rate at a time when more and more people were seeking participation in the labor market. The growing number of labor market outsiders might have sought and found ways to undermine centralized wage setting and the rule-making power of the social partners, had they not been absorbed by a restrictive management of the labor supply through an expanding social policy. This, too, however, was no more than a temporary stopgap that increasingly failed to protect the stability of the collective bargaining regime.

(2) Industry-level wage setting continuously increased the pressure on small firms as it narrowed the wage spread and forced small firms to invest heavily in the productivity of their workforce. The longer the regime was in operation, the less slack was left in small firms, and the more they approached the limits of their capacity to adapt to an ever-tightening labor constraint. Temptations to defect from employer associations to escape encompassing wage setting became stronger with time, especially when it turned out that collective agreements on working time flexibility and social policies promoting early retirement were less suitable for small firms than for large firms. Rising discontent was for a while contained by "patriotic" behavior on the part of large firms habitually purchasing their supplies from long-established domestic supplier networks. When this changed due to changing market conditions, defection of small- and medium-sized firms from industry-wide collective bargaining and encompassing employer associations became widespread. A supporting

factor may have been that in the course of adjusting to the pressures of increasingly demanding employment conditions, firms may have become more sophisticated over time with respect to managing their human resources, increasingly enabling them to deal with their industrial relations individually and on their own.

(3) As industry-wide collective bargaining gradually expanded into complex subject areas such as the regulation of working time, employer associations, and trade unions had to concede increasing local discretion to individual employers and the elected representatives of their workforces, that is, the works councils. Originally, decentralization of this kind made it possible for unions and employer associations to continue to negotiate all major elements of the employment relationship between them at the industrial level. While delegation of specific bargaining rights to local agents initially stabilized the collective bargaining regime as a whole by increasing its flexibility, however, it simultaneously led to individual employers and works councils learning to negotiate for themselves, and perhaps to appreciate the advantages of firm-specific rather than general regulation of employment conditions. In the process, works councils became less prepared to limit themselves to supervising the implementation of the industrial agreement, demanding an ever greater role in setting the employment conditions for their clients. Many employers, in turn, acquired the confidence and the skill to deal with worker representatives on their own, especially in periods of economic crises when they saw the opportunity to extract concessions that they would not have received from the industrial union.

(4) German trade unions used to negotiate wages and working conditions not just for their members but de facto for all workers employed in their domain. Coverage by industrial agreements vastly exceeded, and continues to exceed, trade union membership, effectively turning the collective agreement into a collective good. As a consequence, German unions early on had to take countermeasures against membership loss, including securing organizational support from employers and the legal system helping them recruit and retain members. Rising tensions with employers, caused by the accumulating results of industry-wide collective bargaining, began to undermine this mechanism as early as the 1980s. In this way, an essential condition for the functioning of the encompassing collective bargaining system—the organizational strength of industrial unions—was weakened in the course of the system's normal and intended operation. Moreover, as industry-wide collective bargaining covering de

facto all firms and workers regardless of membership in employer associations and trade unions became firmly established, workers and employers increasingly learned with time that what they expected from the bargaining regime—good and secure working conditions and industrial peace, respectively—was to be had also if they remained "free riders." It is likely that this contributed to the membership crisis of organized business and labor which, in turn, undermined the collective bargaining system.

(5) Industrial trade unions must serve a highly heterogeneous membership, the majority of which stand to benefit from a policy of wage leveling. Industry-wide collective bargaining, therefore, has traditionally tended to compress the wage structure. The longer wage leveling proceeds, however, the more grievances accumulate among earners of higher wages who see their differentials being eroded. With time, incentives grow for elite groups of workers or the works councils of large and profitable firms to break away from industry-wide bargaining and seek separate settlements. This may still be manageable for the national trade union leadership as long as industry-wide collective bargaining is otherwise unchallenged and institutional opportunities for separate bargaining do not exist, or are not provided by employers or the courts. The less this is the case, however—for example, if the works councils of large firms can credibly threaten to withhold support, or if a wide variety of alternative forms and arenas of negotiating employment conditions opens up—trade unions must become more attentive to the demands of their members at the upper end of the wage structure. Even then, sectional organization and bargaining, in reaction to wage leveling having gone on for too long, may become impossible to prevent entirely.

(6) Using a Bismarckian social security system to reduce the supply of labor causes increases in labor costs, which in turn increases the number of workers that need to be taken out of the market. Over time, as the practice of publicly funded retirement from the labor market expanded, a self-reinforcing spiral of unemployment, its management by restricting the labor supply, rising labor costs, and further unemployment was bound to evolve. Exacerbating the problem it was supposed to solve, social policy deployed to fighting unemployment by reducing the labor supply became self-defeating as it continued to be pursued.

(7) To promote social peace, the German state for a long time parceled out social policy to organized business and labor. To a very large extent,

the social security system was governed by the "social partners," who also effectively controlled legislation in the Bundestag. Driven by an ever-growing need for public money to underwrite the labor market regime and keep the social security funds solvent—which in turn reflected the political imperative to preserve the peace between unions and employers under comprehensive collective bargaining—social security expenditures continued to rise, forcing the government to make growing parts of the federal budget available to cover the rising deficits of the social security system. Borrowing soon became the method of choice for procuring the necessary funds. Funding present political priorities by incurring public debt involves transferring resources from the future to the present, which if continued must with time exhaust future capacities to address newly arising needs; for this reason, if not for others as well, it can be viable only temporarily. High economic growth or low interest rates may delay the day of reckoning, but when resources for discretionary spending shrink and new debt is entirely consumed by servicing old debt, public finance is no longer available to suspend the conflict between capital and labor on the conditions of employment in a changing market economy.

Of course, other mechanisms, less self-propelling in character, were also at work. Change in the economic environment, in particular increasing competitive pressures in world markets, eroded the patriotic procurement policies of the large firms that dominated the employer associations, and thereby intensified small firm dissatisfaction with the collective bargaining regime. New opportunity structures in expanding markets contributed to the dissolution of the German company network, by changing the cost–benefit calculations of large firms with respect to the individual pursuit of profit as opposed to the collective pooling of business risks under national auspices. Also in evidence were several of the already well-catalogued elite responses to institutional configurations that had become dysfunctional (Streeck and Thelen 2005). Dormant institutional resources were mobilized to take over tasks that other institutions had become unable to discharge, for example when unions and employer associations were urged by the government to conclude collective agreements on supplementary pensions, to make up for declining public pension benefits ("displacement"). New elements were attached to existing institutions with the intention to alter their status and structure, as when a "third pillar" of individual, defined-contribution retirement pensions was added to the public pension system ("layering"). Also, as the old wage setting regime disintegrated, attempts were made to turn the works councils of large firms into agents of company-based productivity bargaining and, sometimes, co-management ("conversion"). In most cases, however, endogenous, self-generated pressures for change had to build up and mature before elites were willing or able to redesign traditional institutions, mostly by recycling existing ones.

9.3. Time, Age, and Change

As pointed out, one implication of the concept of dialectical change is that it directly links stability and change in institutions to time. The passage of time figures as an important causal factor in the self-undermining of institutions as analyzed by Avner Greif (2006, Chapter 6, Greif and Laitin 2004). Greif shows how institutions may be destabilized by the incrementally accumulating effects of their enactment on the "parametric" conditions of that enactment. While Greif undertakes to provide a game-theoretical "micro-foundation" for change of this kind, he acknowledges that "the conditions under which (self-undermining) may occur are not yet clear," and he notes that "no general theory identifies attributes of institutions that lead to undermining" (Greif 2006, 181). Of course, as stated in Part I, the figure of thought that Greif suggests is as such far from new—see, for example, Max Weber's explanation of the decline of the "Protestant ethic" as a result of the accumulation of wealth to which it had given rise; his parable of the "routinization of charisma" causing, the transformation of a social movement into a bureaucracy after the death or retirement of its founding generation; Marx's theorem of the gradual decline of the rate of profit, and the resulting final crisis of capitalist accumulation caused by its own progress; or Schumpeter's notion of modern capitalism as a system of innovation defeating itself by the continuous rationalization to which it is devoted. Among modern authors, Mancur Olson stands out with his account of capitalist stagnation as a result of the accumulation over time, under democratic auspices of freedom of association, of "distributional coalitions" (Olson 1982). Another way the passage of time may drive endogenous dialectical change, already invoked above in relation to the growing collective action problems of trade unions and employer associations, might be the build-up of experience with the way an institution works in practice, teaching those subject to it how it may be evaded, or that evasion has less serious consequences than originally imagined.[6] Time may also be considered a source of change in legal systems, which tend to become more complex the longer they exist, due to accumulating specifications of general norms by judicial precedent and legislative amendment.[7]

Self-undermining endogenous change in a social institution may be regarded as setting a limit to its *lifetime,* at least in its original form, just as an institution's accumulated self-undermining effects may indicate its *age* and the extent to which it has already consumed itself in the performance of its functions. The idea of a life cycle (Greif 2006, 180), or a limited shelf life, of institutions fits well with the notion of *periodicity* in social orders and political-economic regimes. Under periodicity, the institutions that govern a social order at a given time are assumed to be different, or to work differently, from those that did the same in the past, and they are expected to die off at some time in the future to give way to other institutions that function differently again. The implication is that all institutions and social orders are in principle *perishable:* they can last only until they are used up. Institutional change in this sense amounts to historical change: the rise and fall over time, or the succession in time, of institutions that are *substantially different* from one another. A life cycle perspective on institutions, then, considers all social arrangements *in the light of their mortality,* or their *future death*—which at the very least should be a healthy antidote to the appearance of eternal youth of social institutions projected by standard variable sociology, with its static property space and time-indifferent relations of timeless, instant causality.

Obviously, there are many different ways in which time may bring about institutional change. As Greif writes, "the mechanism that brings about institutional change once the behavior associated with an institution is no longer self-enforcing depends on the nature of the quasi-parameters that delimit self-reinforcement" (Greif 2006, 168). As our five sectors show, institutional self-exhaustion may be driven by a variety of mechanisms, and a convincing typology of processes of self-propelled institutional aging is still lacking. Resisting the temptation to try to develop one, I limit myself here to pointing out the essential contribution of the passage of chronological time to some of the processes of institutional change we have empirically observed, and the usefulness, resulting from this, of the assumption that the time for which an institution can function the way it was conceived may generally or in specific cases be finite.

To be clear, rather than suggesting that all institutions inevitably age and die of aging, I much more moderately propose considering aging, or the passage of time as such, as *one mechanism of institutional change among others*. As pointed out above, a mechanism is not a theory but a generic type of causal connection between social and structural conditions that can be expected to be found in a variety of social settings (Mayntz 2004). While much might be said in favor of the view that time is limited for all institutions, and for a generalization to the effect that all social orders are mortal, all I am proposing here is that aging with the passage of time may be one mechanism of institutional change among others that one might want to include in a heuristic checklist of what to look for and perhaps find in analyzing empirical observations. Whether or not time passed is in fact found to be a causal factor in institutional transformation depends, again, on the historical setting in which the institutions are located whose fate is being traced. If that setting happens to be a capitalist political economy in which cooperation between capital and labor requires a restrictive management of the labor supply, which in turn requires steady infusion of public money in the social security system; and if the necessary funds are easier to mobilize from future than from present citizens, chances are that public debt will gradually accumulate until a level is reached when new debt can no longer be incurred without causing unacceptable problems elsewhere in the system. At this point, the political resource of funding social integration and political stability by borrowing will be exhausted. Similarly, if, and to the extent that, public subsidization of social peace gradually eliminates the government's fiscal discretion, by forcing allocation of an ever-rising share of public expenditure to a small number of fixed purposes, this amounts to the consumption of a finite and nonrenewable resource, after which the old political game can no longer be played and a new regime must be invented to provide for social order.

Including time among the sources of institutional change is far from monocausal determinism, even though it is true that time is the same for everyone and its progress is by definition unstoppable. Even in Olson's theory, where "institutional sclerosis" in the form of a gradual proliferation of organized interests (Olson 1982) is regarded as inevitable, the disease can from time to time be reversed if citizens can be persuaded periodically, quoting Thomas Jefferson, to "water the tree of freedom with the blood of tyrants," for example of trade union leaders. Also, economic growth or inflation may reduce public debt, without present citizens having to be asked to pay it back, making it possible *for the time being* to continue subsidizing social peace with borrowed funds. Even if a gradual build-up of pressures for change over time does not actually result in change, however, this need not mean that it was without effect, or that it does not exist at all. Marx's "law" of a secular decline of the rate of profit due to a secular increase in the "organic composition of capital"—a growing capital–labor ratio—may not in fact have resulted in a declining profit rate (although this remains a matter of debate), because of a number of "countervailing forces" such as technological progress or an increase in what is today called "human capital," factors which Marx himself had gone to great lengths to spell out (Marx 1966 [1894], Chapters 14 and 15). What matters then is that the presence of these forces, and the investment in it of considerable effort and resources, may be explained *as a reaction* to the presence of and the continuing effective pressure from the tendency for a decline in profitability. As an invisible underlying force, that tendency may consume a large share of the attention and explain much of the political and economic effort in the society on which it works, even though it never produces its supposed effect. Or, to take a more familiar example, industry-wide collective bargaining, as we have argued, leads to wage compression, which may gradually exhaust support for it and thereby undermine it as an institution. But wage bargainers can take this into account and, as in Germany in the 1980s, switch back and forth from flat-rate to percentage wage increases, allowing wage compression in some years to be mitigated so it could continue to be pursued in others. Progress toward institutional self-undermining may thus be slowed down and, with luck, entirely suspended, at least for the time being. Again, however, this does not deny the effectiveness of pressures for endogenous institutional demise, if only in that they cause political and economic capital being expended on measures, often quite elaborate ones, to delay or prevent it.

In conclusion, part of the secret behind the parallel development of the five institutional spheres we have traced in Part I, in the absence of a dominant functional purpose as well as of hegemonic political control, may be the passage of time and the aging of institutions over time. As an institution ages, its accumulating effects and side effects may change the conditions of its reproduction, so that they begin to undermine it.[8] Deterioration may for a while be prevented by positive externalities of other institutions providing support, but these may become increasingly dysfunctional as well. Depending on "the nature of the quasi-parameters that delimit self-reinforcement" (Greif 2006, 168), different sectors of a national political economy may become dysfunctional at roughly the same time, leading to mutual support giving way to mutual destabilization. At this point, one could speak of the end of a historical period, when all attempts to prolong and repair the old order are bound to fail, even though the gradual nature of progress toward this end may hide this condition for some time.

Notes

1. Mayntz' position is that while it may sometimes be useful in tracing causal chains to go down to the bottom of the Colemanian bathtub, it may not always be possible, and in fact may not add much explanatory power: "Structures exert their effect through the actions of individuals, but assuming a general action orientation of individuals (for instance rational choice), it is the nature of the structural arrangements within which they act that determines the effect" (Mayntz 2004, 252). My only reservation is that I would prefer to speak of conditioning rather than determination, as I consider it in the nature of institutionalized norms that they cannot be fully determinative of human action since they require creative enactment. I also doubt whether the assumption of a rational choice disposition on the part of actors is instructive enough as long as it treats learning, discovery, hedging in the face of uncertainty, and the like as ephemeral. Generally, the more agency one assumes, or must admit, the less reliable will be a prediction of future structures from past or present structures. One could also say that recourse to the micro level is dispensable (only) when action is routine and its course can be taken for granted, which empirically it often can.
2. As mentioned above, this is what Greif and Laitin (2004) call "parametric change."
3. This effect has long been familiar to sociologists studying law as a form of social action. For an outstanding example, see Stryker (1994, 2003). See also Edelman (2004).
4. Similarly Carruthers and Halliday (1998).
5. The best treatment of compliance and its fundamental importance for social order is still Etzioni's "Comparative Analysis of Complex Organizations" (1961). I will return to this briefly in Part III.
6. This might well be put in terms of a theory of learning. Time is, of course, an essential factor in learning theory, although this is not always recognized in its full significance.
7. Time has recently attracted growing attention by social scientists. See Büthe (2002), Kay (2006), and of course, Pierson (2004).

8. In addition to self-undermining in a strict sense, objectives or constituencies not originally represented may gather strength as time passes and acquire the capacity to upset extant institutions or the balance between them. Also, in substantive terms, endogenous institutional change may be driven by dilemmatic contradictions between social objectives that, although equally required for the reproduction of a social order, cannot be pursued or attained simultaneously. I do not pursue these issues here and postpone them to the substantive-historical analysis in Part III.

10

Time's up: positive externalities turning negative

We have seen that interactions between the five sectors whose development we have traced changed over time from mutual support to mutual destabilization. For a while, positive external effects seem to have prevailed between institutional settings, arresting endogenous tendencies toward disorganization and keeping in check whatever negative externalities there may also have been. This, we have seen, is what a "system," or in the present case, a socioeconomic "model," is all about. By the mid-1990s at the latest, however, tipping points were reached where positive externalities turned negative; mutual reinforcement gave way to mutual obstruction; and support for existing forms of social order was succeeded by active disorganization. Where sectors had produced positive externalities for other sectors, they now generated side effects for them that were destructive. In some cases, the resources needed to support organization elsewhere in the system were exhausted, or the accumulated costs of mutual support rendered its continuation increasingly impossible. One may add that new opportunities emerged on the outside as well, weakening the motivation of crucial actors to continue using their resources to discharge their obligations within the system. Disorganizing tendencies were thus reinforced across sectors when the equilibrating mechanisms that had for some time suspended them ceased to work due to internal exhaustion or changed external circumstances.

Reconstructing the transformation of the "German model," I have suggested that time, referring to both chronological and, as we will see later, historical time, may be an essential element in social systems, which are better conceived as processes. To recall, where costs are incurred in the service of institutional stability, they may accumulate until a moment is reached when support is disabled. Also, to the extent that sustaining a social order requires resources that may become exhausted with time, the stabilizing functions performed with such resources can be performed only so long. This suggests that the age of a social system may be one of its defining properties, as it may affect how long the system is likely to remain capable of resisting endogenous and exogenous pressures for fundamental change. Thus, age may affect the capacity of individual institutions to contribute to systemic stability and performance, that is, fulfill their "complementary" functions in relation to other institutions. For a limited time, the effect of one institution on another may be positive and supportive, but when that time is over, the positive effect may disappear or turn negative and destructive. In such a case, the evolution of a social system ceases to be linear, and a variety of tipping and turning points may be expected to appear in the causal connections between system elements.

This is not to say, of course, that age always has this effect, or that institutions could not be rejuvenated. Time and age do affect social structures, for example, when legal systems become ever more complex as precedents accumulate and all manner of exceptions and qualifications are added while a norm is applied to ever-new and different cases. In the present study we have found what seemed to be a tendency for specific institutions to become more difficult to maintain the older they become. Examples are a flat wage structure imposed on firms by industry-level collective bargaining, the subsidization of social peace by means of public debt, or the enforcement of collective obligations on actors increasingly more adroit with time as to how to evade them. Still, why time works the way it does in a given case is ultimately explained only with reference to the substance of the social relations in question. The decay of the "German model" that we have observed may from this perspective appear as a gradual maturation of tensions and contradictions in a capitalist political economy between, ultimately, the private appropriation of the surplus and the social, or public, organization of its production—tensions and contractions that can be suspended only for a limited period of time. Managing them may, for instance, demand ever-new answers to questions like whether and how to take care of the casualties of an ever more volatile and expanding labor market; how to ensure cooperation between the classes by absorbing some of the costs of uncertainty without interfering with the private appropriation of its benefits; how to adjust and readjust continuously the distribution of risk and uncertainty between individuals, classes, and the collectivity; and how to regulate and enforce the contributions of the citizenry, corporate, and individual, to the maintenance

137

of the commons of a workable social order. Here it seems reasonable to assume that the concrete nature of the problems to be resolved, as well as the efficacy of the solutions devised for them at a given moment, are likely to change over time, for reasons grounded ultimately in the social order itself, requiring ever-new efforts on the part of public policy without any guarantee of success.

So far this study has tried to describe in formal and general terms—as it were, phenomenologically—a complex process of systemic institutional change: how a social order originally characterized by internal complementarity slowly decayed with time. In a very remote sense, this may be compared to a descriptive account of the transformation of a chemical compound with a limited lifetime, or a definite half-life period. No claim is implied that all social structures develop in the same way, from complementarity to mutual subversion; undoubtedly many may evolve quite differently. Nor can a description of this sort say anything about the forces driving the observed process. As suggested several times, one may suspect that the institutional change found by our empirical research reflects inherent underlying social tensions specific to the capitalist mode of production, in a sense that would need to be elaborated in detail. An attempt to make progress to this end will be made in Part III of this book.

10.1. Systemic Decay

In various ways during the period of observation, interinstitutional relations between extant German institutions of collective bargaining, intermediary organization, social policy, public finance, and corporate governance gradually turned or suddenly pivoted from mutual support to mutual obstruction. In the following, I will draw out some of the lines of institutional change where this applies.

(1) Until the 1980s, sector-wide collective bargaining with strong trade unions supported encompassing employer associations, and in particular enhanced the capacity of the latter to recruit members. Firms of all sizes benefited from central regulation of wages and employment conditions, as it kept distributive conflicts out of the workplace and saved firms transaction costs when making employment contracts with workers. If a firm nevertheless decided to stay out of or defect from the association, perhaps because of discontent with the substance of industrial agreements, it was regularly singled out by the sectoral union for particularly aggressive treatment, until it saw the light and returned under the protective roof

of the association. Usually when this happened, the sectoral employer association looked on in benevolent silence. Just as encompassing organization of employers made sector-wide collective bargaining possible, so regulation of employment conditions at the industrial level sustained strong intermediary organizations of employers and, by extension, an effective capacity of unions to represent workers in a wide variety, and indeed de facto the totality, of sectoral firms.

As we have seen, this ended when dissatisfaction among small firms with the accumulating results of industry-wide collective bargaining increased in the 1980s while simultaneously rising unemployment detracted from the unions' power to punish firms for leaving the employer association. Additionally exacerbating the divisions within employer associations were growing opportunities for large firms to purchase their supplies abroad. Combined with rising international price competition even in German firms' traditional markets for diversified quality production, this caused a lasting deterioration of the relations of large export-oriented manufacturers with their German suppliers, many of which were organized in the same employer associations. Increasingly, their leaders failed to bridge the growing divisions of interest in their ranks caused by their continuing support for the old collective bargaining regime. Declining employer association membership contributed to shrinking the core of the traditional industrial relations system, and the same held for employer associations, faced with rising numbers of defections, setting up special divisions for firms unwilling to be covered by the industrial agreement. Where in the past, encompassing collective bargaining had provided for almost complete organization of firms in employer associations, which had in turn kept the collective bargaining system unified and organized, now employer associations went through an organizational crisis which caused increasing fragmentation of the collective bargaining system. The latter, in turn, forced employer associations to make changes in their organization responding to rising dissatisfaction with the sectoral wage setting regime, thereby advancing its disintegration. By the mid-1990s at the latest, the evolution of the collective bargaining system had begun to weaken rather than strengthen employer associations, just as these had begun to develop in a direction which accelerated the disorganization of the German industrial relations system.

(2) Just as unions had for a while assisted the organization of employers in employer associations, so had employers indirectly contributed to unionization, making for a relationship of mutual support that contained the centrifugal tendencies inevitably affecting "mature" trade

unions whose political achievements represent collective goods for workers (Olson 1971). Among other things, employers had usually tolerated the works council system being used by unionized council members to enhance unions' organizational security, in particular by using it for recruiting members (Streeck 1982). Over time, however, relations between the organizations of business and labor turned from mutual support to mutual obstruction, in a number of ways. While unions lost the capacity to drive defecting firms back into sectoral employer associations, the latter, through the creation of their new *OT* sections, developed a capacity to assist firms in efforts to become or remain union-free. In the late 1990s, under pressure from their small-firm members, employer associations also resisted legal reforms of the works council system intended to improve its fit with a changed business environment. This was motivated by speculation on continued drift further undermining, among other things, the capacity of trade unions through works councils to monitor the implementation of collective agreements. At the same time, both at the firm and the political level, employers also tried to strengthen the role of works councils as agents of workplace-level wage setting, hoping gradually to replace unions, who have a right to strike, with an interlocutor obliged by law to maintain industrial peace. Where employers succeeded in forging workplace-level "alliances for employment and competitiveness" outside established channels of industry-wide collective bargaining, unions' organizational position, and with it their capacity to convince workers to join them, was further weakened. The same would have applied had a different outcome of the 2005 federal election made it possible for proposed legislation to come into force which would have made it legal for works councils to sign wage agreements in deviation from the sectoral agreement, provided a certain percentage of the workforce had agreed to it in a formal vote.

(3) As noted several times, German social policy after the mid-1970s had become increasingly subservient to holding the collective bargaining regime together and preserving the peace between organized business and labor. It was used in particular by the "social partners" in alliance with the government for taking a growing number of workers out of the market who were unable to find access to high-paid employment in a flat wage structure. We have seen that while for a time this contributed to the stability of centralized wage setting, it also added to the costs of labor, and thereby fueled conflicts of interest between large and small firms. Although it is probably impossible to say with certainty at what point the economic disadvantages of a further increase in social security

contributions and, as a result, in nonwage labor costs, exceeded the political and economic benefits of additional labor being taken out of the market, indications are that the tipping point, at least for the internal politics of employer associations, was reached in the mid-1990s when social security contributions exceeded 40 percent of the gross wage. This is indicated by the fact that it was then that the willingness of employer associations to let their members be taxed by the state to pay for defensive labor supply management finally came to an end, giving way to calls for a fundamental restructuring of wage setting to allow for greater wage dispersion, the decentralization of wage determination to the firm level, and de-unionization.

(4) Over time, the evolution of social policy also had destructive effects on the intermediary organizations of capital and labor and their relations with each other and the state. Rising pressures on the government to return public spending to public control broke up the corporatist alliance between the state and the social partners, causing a rift that turned out to be unbridgeable, first under Kohl and then under Schröder. Divisions over how to allow the state to rein in continually rising expenditure on social security reflected and reinforced the emerging conflicts at the time over the conduct of industrial relations at the sectoral and firm levels. Trade union resistance to social policy reform cost two chancellors their office, first Kohl in 1998 and then Schröder in 2003. In the latter instance, however, the government had had enough time to make far-reaching changes both in social spending and in the institutional infrastructure of the social welfare state, attacking in particular the role of the social partners in its governance and thereby adding to the disorganizing effects of the decomposition of the collective bargaining regime on unions and employer associations. Especially after 2002, social policy not only ceased to offer organizational and political support to organized business and labor, once and for all dissociating itself from its corporatist legacy, but was actively deployed to advance their disorganization.[1]

With hindsight, the eventual exhaustion of the capacity of social policy to serve as a receptacle for surplus labor would appear to have been entirely predictable. Like social security contributions, the subsidies of the state to the social security system could rise only up to a certain point. Having the social welfare state absorb a growing amount of labor that could not be accommodated in the employment system could never have been more than an improvised interim solution, and was always limited by the finite capacity of the state to pay. Still, business, labor, and the government became addicted to it, step by step testing out jointly or in friendly competition with each other how far defensive management of the labor supply at public expense could be driven before it hit the wall. Such brinkmanship was undoubtedly helped by the fact that the end point was uncertain and that new steps along the old path could be taken one by one, appearing less difficult and dramatic than a change of direction. As all three parties moved inexorably toward the inevitable breaking point, it was, and had to be, the government that first got ready to turn around and attack its former allies. Then, however, the decay having gone on for so long, the only alternative to the old model was its radical rejection, which included not just cuts in benefits but also a wholesale departure from the corporatist institutional structure of postwar German social policy.

(5) As social policy claimed a growing share of the federal budget, deficits became endemic and public debt accumulated, causing irreversible changes in the management of public budgets as they shifted from a regime of easy money to one of fiscal austerity. Accompanying this shift was extensive privatization, that is, the mobilization of private resources for purposes that had once been tasks of the state and the government. By having recourse to privatization in diverse policy areas and in a wide variety of legal forms, the German state, actively contributed beginning in the mid-1990s, to the disorganization of wage setting, of corporatist intermediary organization, of the institutional and organizational field of social policy, and also of the German company network, far beyond the impact of the retrenchment of social policy.

As to collective bargaining, privatization of state assets upset the wage setting regime of the public sector, uniquely encompassing even by German standards, thereby disempowering trade unions and making them reorganize in ways that further detracted from their national unity. Privatization in social policy weakened the role of unions and employer associations in the governance of the policy area by permitting competition by private firms, especially in pension insurance. As the impact of associational self-government of the sector was reduced by privatization and private competition, intermediary organizations of capital and labor found their privileged corporatist status diminished. Also, privatization of state assets required modernization of German financial markets, which advanced the disorganization of the German company network by facilitating mutual divestment, enabling firms looking for capital to turn from their *Hausbanken* to the markets, and forcing them to pay more attention to their return on capital and the price of their shares.

Privatization was closely related to internationalization, which refers to a property of markets and production systems as well as a strategy of governments in dealing with their domestic political economies and the latter's declining governability. Obligations entered into in the context of international organizations such as the European Union to open up domestic markets for foreign competition provided legitimation for selling off the public infrastructure to raise money to reduce state deficits for the time being, against the resistance of sectoral producer interests. Admitting foreign competition in domestic markets for services not only put pressures on domestic trade unions to make concessions in wage bargaining, resulting in an increase in the wage spread, but also added to the German economy de facto a union-free sector located abroad. Reforms in capital markets and corporate governance designed to make it attractive for German investors to buy shares in the formerly public enterprises, in order to maximize the yield to the state from their privatization, invited foreign investors into the German capital market, and were in fact passed with exactly this outcome in mind. More examples could be added to show that under contemporary economic conditions and in the context of membership in the European Union, privatization and internationalization are inseparable, the former always and inevitably also involving the latter, and with it its disorganizing consequences for a nationally organized political economy.

(6) The changing practice and, later, the reformed legal framework of corporate governance in Germany contributed to the disorganization of collective bargaining, of intermediary organization and, in part, of the state as banker of last resort for the corporatist postwar order. In the past the company network had in a variety of ways shielded its members from competition, helped firms survive periodic losses, secured access to credit at low rates of interest, and protected firms from takeover, in effect enabling them to operate at a low level of profitability and employ large workforces with high job security and high wages. Indirectly, this helped sustain industry-level collective bargaining, which in turn left large firms enough of their profits to invest in training and in internationally competitive technologies and products. It also supported strong business and employer associations dominated and funded mainly by large firms interested in effective collective representation, in relation to both trade unions and the state.

Exit from the network, first by the big banks and then by large industrial firms, very much reversed these relationships. In the 1990s, deprived of their protection from the pressures of product and capital markets, large firms began to squeeze their suppliers or turned to foreign sources altogether, undermining the internal cohesion of German employer and business associations. Large firms also sought alliances with their core workforces, represented by their works councils, to increase productivity and profitability in response to new risks and opportunities in international markets, which eroded not just the reach of industrial collective agreements but also the internal cohesion of trade unions. As firms found themselves forced to fend for themselves, with the state less and less willing and able to protect them against foreign competition, they also became less willing to pay taxes in Germany, extracting from successive governments of different political colors deep cuts in corporate taxes that contributed to making the state end support out of public funds for the postwar compact between business and labor.

The disintegration of the German company network was not caused by pressures from the domestic political economy. The flat German wage structure and the rising nonwage labor costs were immaterial to the decision of Deutsche Bank to turn to investment banking, or of Allianz to raise its rate of profit. But once disintegration was under way, firms discovered and perhaps needed new opportunities to defend themselves against the ever-growing costs of the German welfare state. Departure from *Deutschland AG* being by and large identical with expansion into the international economy, it created, in addition to new risks, hitherto unknown opportunities to leverage international competition against domestic constraints on the use of firms' resources. That the state by the late 1990s reached the limit of its capacity to extract resources from the economy with which to subsidize the continuation of the postwar social contract and its institutions is no accident: it coincided with the accelerating internationalization of the German economy, in particular of its large firms, for which national solidarity had lost its value, while invoking international pressures against union or state demands constituted an irresistible temptation or even a plain business necessity.

10.2. A Slowly Grinding Force

Summing up, mutual stabilization of the various institutional spheres of the postwar "German model" worked only for a limited period of time. After this, complementarity in a variety of respects turned into subversion, generated by an endogenous, system-wide dynamic of core institutions of the postwar political economy that apparently made it impossible for them to remain the way they had once been designed, or to continue to perform the functions once assigned to them. In part and importantly, this was because the positive contribution of some institutions to the stability of others that underlay *Modell Deutschland* depended on resources that turned out to be finite and nonrenewable, such as sufficient free space in public budgets to accommodate growing demands for material support. When such resources had been consumed, as they had to be at some point unless effective countermeasures were taken, existing patterns of social order, political-economic "model" that they may have been for a limited time, were no longer viable, and consequently disintegrated. Unlike what functionalist theories would have predicted, there was no negative feedback among institutional settings that would have returned "the system" to its "model" equilibrium. In fact, over time, sectoral change trajectories reached and crossed tipping points at which positive externalities between sectors turned negative, and institutional settings, instead of enhancing each other's stability, began to undermine it.

Inspection of the parallel lines of sectoral institutional change that we have reconstructed in our empirical accounts shows that in the second half of the 1990s, a number of initially separate processes of slow disorganization that had long been under way rapidly accelerated and became systemic, reaching a point where they overlaid one another like the amplitudes of waves in constructive interference. Just as in the 1970s and early 1980s a temporary conjuncture of sectoral institutional conditions had lent itself to theoretical and practical "modeling" in terms of structural stability, functional complementarity, and high economic performance, in the 1990s and early 2000s a different conjuncture emerged out of continuing gradual change that bundled sectoral change in the different institutional settings of the German political economy together into a systemic process of self-reinforcing and self-accelerating disorganization. The decline of trade unions and, later, employer associations; the attrition of sector-wide collective bargaining; the over-commitment of the social security system to the preservation of social peace; the exhaustion of public finance and the transformation of corporate governance had all started in the 1980s or earlier. For a limited time, the slow speed of their progress had left open the possibility for observers as well as participants to consider them—one by one and in isolation from each other—as temporary fluctuations within a timelessly stable system. However, when in the second half of the 1990s, sectoral changes coagulated into a broad stream of rapid transformation, this interpretation, optimistic from the perspective of those who hoped for the postwar blueprint of a socially embedded capitalism to remain applicable in the twenty-first century, became less and less convincing.

Our analysis has shown that systemic change was not driven by a master sector pulling the rest of the system along, so as to preserve institutional complementarity and make the system as a whole fit for changed functional requirements. As organized business was among the institutions that were disorganized in the process, there was also no master class capable of collectively pursuing disorganization as a hegemonic project. Nevertheless, although sectoral dynamics, while reinforcing each other, proceeded independently, they did not proceed at random, and indeed moved in parallel in the same direction. Systemic disorganization thus appears to have been overdetermined, in an intriguing way, by similar causes originating and operating independently in different settings. Looking at it as a historical trend, one wonders what the slowly grinding force may have been that made for the uniformity of change across sectors by directing an apparently redundant variety of causes of change, evolving apparently separately and independently, to a point where they began to reinforce each other after enough time had passed for them to mature. It is in search of that underlying force that I will now, in Part III, return to the concept of disorganization, in an attempt to fill its formal definition with a substantive-material meaning by locating it in the historical context of the evolution of the postwar political economy of capitalism.

Note

1. Threats by the Schröder government to curtail free, that is, union-led collective bargaining and enhance the rights of works councils to negotiate firm-specific wage settlements had the same effects, even though they were not realized in the end. The respective policy proposals were, however, gladly taken over by the Christian Democrats and remain in their collections of tools of political torture.

Part III

Liberalization: Re-Forming Capitalism

11

Disorganization as liberalization

To characterize the direction of institutional change in five sectors of the German political economy, I have found it useful provisionally to draw on the concept of disorganization. Avoiding its all-too-general, postmodernist meaning of everything solid in modern society melting into thin air (Lash and Urry 1987), I used disorganization to denote an empirically observed trend in Germany's political-economic regime away from centralized authoritative coordination and control toward dispersed competition, individual instead of collective action, and spontaneous, market-like aggregation of preferences and decisions. By invoking the concept of disorganization, I implicitly though not without intention related my inquiry to the notion of "organized capitalism." That notion is deployed by a variety of literatures for a range of historical forms of a capitalist economy governed, in addition to markets, by various market-overriding social and political institutions. In the current chapter, I will make use of the concept of organized capitalism to infuse historical-political substance into my analysis of formal institutional change ("organized" vs. "disorganized"), aiming at a clearer understanding of the nature of the ongoing "disorganization" of postwar capitalism in Germany and, perhaps, elsewhere.[1]

A discussion of the history and the diverse and changing meanings of the concept of organized capitalism is beyond the capacities of this essay.[2] For present purposes it is enough to remember that in all its different versions, organized capitalism relates to a combination of public and private arrangements for governing a capitalist economy, in particular of the behavior of large firms, with state bureaucracies coordinating their activities in one form or another with corporations, cartels, or business associations[3] (Winkler and Feldmann 1974). Such coordination between the state and large industry was concerned with two broad categories of

Table 11.1. Organized capitalism: domains of organization, collective objectives, and organizing practices

	Efficiency	Solidarity
Public (state)	Economic planning	Social and economic protection
Private (economy)	Trust-building	Collective commitments to cooperation and the national interest

objectives, which may be summarily described as *efficiency* and *solidarity* (Table 11.1). Organization of capitalism, whether by the state or by capitalist firms themselves, was to overcome what was in the nineteenth and early twentieth centuries widely perceived, on the Right as well as on the Left, as an inherent "anarchy" of the capitalist mode of production, which was seen as deriving ultimately from economic behavior being regulated by free markets.

Capitalist anarchy was regarded as adverse to *both* efficiency and solidarity. With respect to the former, it was apt to destroy vast sums of capital in cyclical crises. Modes of organization of capitalism that were to prevent this included economic planning, directive or indicative, usually under the auspices of the nation-state as well as of conglomerate firms, cartels or monopolies ("trusts") created in the private sphere—which, however, as a rule required permission or toleration by the public power (Table 11.1). With respect to solidarity, the dynamics of self-regulating markets and the crises they were believed to cause threatened to cut off workers and their families from their means of subsistence, giving rise to widespread misery and divisive class conflict. Free markets also laid the national economy open to foreign interests, thereby weakening the cohesion of the nation as a community and potentially depriving it of the means to secure its economic and military survival. Organizing practices used to safeguard solidarity included authoritative social and economic protection by state intervention and negotiated collective commitments to cooperation and social peace by organized business and labor.

In order to enhance economic efficiency and stability and protect national solidarity and national power, societies organized their capitalist economies using public and private instruments to impose obligations especially on large firms to observe not just their own interests in profitability, but also collective societal interests, as defined by the politics of the nation-state, in both efficiency and solidarity. Instruments for making capitalist firms publicly accountable included controls on investment; protective legislation for workers and industrial sectors; encouragement of trade unions and the institutionalization of workers councils; as well as collective political commitments, agreed between the state and capital and enforced by lead firms or powerful business associations, not to act against vital national interests in internal economic and political stability and external security. Organization in this sense turned liberal into non-liberal capitalism (Streeck 2001b). Whereas the latter undertakes "to infuse social obligations in economic transactions" (ibid., 4), the former "sets economic transactions free from obligations other than to serve the interests of those immediately involved" (ibid., 5). Disorganization—the move from organized to less organized versions of capitalism—would then be tantamount to nonliberal capitalism becoming more liberal through a process of *liberalization*.

What does the concept of organized capitalism, and with it the distinction between nonliberal and liberal capitalist political economies, contribute to the analysis of institutional change as observed in five sectors of the German political economy? And, vice versa, what can institutional analysis, concerned with the properties and dynamics of institutions as such, teach us about the current development of modern capitalism as a social formation? In the following I will point out, as a first step, that empirical study of *disorganization as a process of institutional change* reveals that liberalization is not necessarily identical with de-institutionalization. Instead, it may, as it seems to in the present case, amount to a transition to a more contractual and voluntaristic kind of institutionalized social order. This I take to mean that, while *the coordination of a coordinated market economy* may be accomplished not just by obligatory but also by contracted institutions, the *organization of organized capitalism*, relying as it does on authoritative enforcement of social obligations on market participants, can be achieved only as long as society provides for institutions capable of defining and imposing an obligatory public order. Liberalization, in other words, sets actors free from institutionalized obligations, allowing solidarism to be overruled by segmentalism (Thelen 2004), but does not preclude and is not incompatible with coordination in a "coordinated market economy," provided such coordination comes about voluntarily and from below.

A crucial observation presented in Part I was that the disorganization of the German company network and the reorientation of large German firms in the 1990s toward a new, more shareholder-oriented business strategy labeled "shareholder value" was not accompanied, as one might have expected, by a replacement of collectively organized industrial relations with atomistic labor markets and individualized employment contracts

151

(Höpner 2005*b*). Nor does such replacement seem to be in the offing, certainly not at the large firms and even after these have emigrated from the German company network to become more exposed to international markets than ever (Thelen 2000). Instead, large German firms have sought, often successfully, and continue to seek close cooperative alliances with their core workforces (Rehder 2003). To this end, they have converted elements of the old industrial relations system, especially the works councils, into pillars of a more decentralized, segmental, company-based labor relations regime.[4] In addition, most of them continue to adhere to the established regime of sectoral collective bargaining while promoting its gradual rebuilding, so as to make it more flexible without undermining its function as a protective shell against domestic labor conflicts. In short, more market-driven business strategies, including orientation of firms toward international capital markets, have turned out to be compatible with institutionalized coordination with labor, albeit in the framework of more customized institutions whose center of gravity has moved from the sectoral to the enterprise level.

The persistence of institutionalized nonmarket coordination with labor in firms increasingly exposed to capital market pressures constitutes an anomaly if one expects liberalized capital markets to remake industrial relations and all other sectors of a coordinated market economy in their image (Hall and Soskice 2003). At the same time, while the trajectory of German industrial relations is not appropriately described as a move from institutionalized coordination to free markets, the shrinking and softening of the core of the German industrial relations system and its slowly becoming enveloped in a variety of new, "fringe" industrial relations regimes does appear to represent significant change in what once was a centralized and unified nationwide wage setting system. In the course of that change, comparing the situation in the 1970s to that in the early 2000s, governance by the social institutions that regulate the employment relationship became less obligatory and more a matter of choice, which among other things accounts for the much increased diversity in institutional arrangements. Also, as a result of gradual disorganization, relevant institutions of industrial relations became more responsive to markets and the situation of actors in them, and correspondingly grew less responsive to national ideas about a desirable wage spread, social justice, and the legitimate claims of workers as citizens regardless of the place where they happened to be employed, and irrespective of current conditions in volatile product and labor markets.

In other words, the disorganization of the German system of labor relations liberalized it, in the sense of making its traditional core less obligatory, rendering adherence to it more voluntary, and providing more flexibility for those remaining in it. Today, firms hold on to industry-wide collective bargaining to the extent that it appears more efficient to them than wholesale replacement of institutionalized coordination with market relations, and provided they are given enough space to modify and supplement the system with customized rules fitting their special needs and interests. In addition, firms have the possibility, and can reserve the option, to exit from the system should another mode of employment regulation turn out to be more expedient. As a side effect, this increases their power inside the system, in relation to trade unions and, indirectly, to works councils. In the course of disorganization-cum-liberalization, which mode of regulation firms adopt has increasingly become a question of what they regard as efficient, the more so since the capacity of the state or of organized collectivities to impose collective obligations on their individual interests or those of individual workers has declined.

Disorganization as liberalization, then, turns institutional design over to interested parties acting under the pressures of markets and competition. At its core is the liberation of economic actors from noneconomic obligations, replacing social duty with interested choice, also with respect to the way transactions are governed, and setting actors free for individual pursuit of optimal market performance. Institutional change as involved in liberalization thus appears as a change in the way institutions are constituted, or in the type of institutions that govern social action. Previously obligatory institutions *de jure* or de facto become voluntary arrangements that actors may adopt or reject depending on whether they fit their interests. Change in institutional type as associated with liberalization entails an increase in choice, and ultimately a transition to a social order ideally built and continually rebuilt "from below." Liberalism and liberalization are compatible with, and indeed may require, a broad range of institutions, provided these either protect the freedom of markets or can be voluntarily contracted between consenting trading partners interested in enhancing their exchange, as opposed to being extraneously imposed on them to make them do things that they do not at first regard as being in their interest.

Martin Höpner, reflecting on the fact that at least in the German case, liberalization has proved far from identical with de-institutionalization, has suggested distinguishing between *organization and coordination as two independent dimensions of nonliberal capitalism:* coordination, as in what

Hall and Soskice call "coordinated market economies" (Hall and Soskice 2001*a*), and organization, as in "organized capitalism" (Höpner 2007*b*). This enables him to argue that continued *coordination*, as witnessed in German industrial relations, need not be proof of continuity in *organization*. Comparing 20 OECD countries, Höpner in fact demonstrates that organization, defined as the existence of political institutions above the enterprise level capable of exercising public control over private business,[5] and strategic coordination in the sense of nonmarket governance of economic transactions (as in Hall and Gingerich 2004), vary independently, making it possible in principle for a market economy that used to be both organized and coordinated, *to remain coordinated while becoming less organized*. Höpner suggests that we relate coordination to a *logic of production*, explaining it out of adaptive exigencies of an efficient conduct of business, and organization to a *logic of power*, concerned ultimately with the political decision as to who gets what and how much and from whom.[6]

Highly enlightening as Höpner's distinction between organization and coordination is, I would like to emphasize, not the extent to which the functionalist equilibrium theories of the "varieties of capitalism" literature can be upheld, rejected, or upheld and rejected at the same time, but the generic differences between the types of political-economic institutions that govern nonliberal and liberal capitalism, respectively— or, in the present case: the German political economy at the beginning and the end of its liberalization, reconstructed as a process of institutional change. For this it seems useful to draw on two powerful strands of institutionalist theory: classical sociology, referred to here for the sake of brevity as the Durkheimian perspective, and modern institutional economics, associated in shorthand with the name of Oliver Williamson. I suggest conceiving of the transition from organized to disorganized, or from nonliberal to liberalized, capitalism as one from *Durkheimian* to *Williamsonian* institutions, or as a process in which Durkheimian institutions gradually become more Williamsonian. In much institutionalist writing, the two types are not clearly distinguished, hiding differences that, I suggest, are of fundamental importance for institutional analysis, and generally for the understanding of the political economy of modern capitalism (Table 11.2).[7] Durkheimian institutions authoritatively constitute an obligatory public order that in principle exists apart from and beyond the choosing of those subject to it. To them, they are "social facts" (Durkheim 1968 [1894], Chapter 1): a constraining external reality that they are not in principle free to adopt, reject, or change.[8]

Table 11.2. Two types of political-economic institutions

Durkheimian	Williamsonian
Authoritative organization	Voluntary coordination
Creation of obligations	Reduction of transaction costs
Public order	Private ordering
Government	Governance
Obligational	Voluntaristic
Exogenously imposed	Endogenously contracted
Third party enforcement	Self-enforcement

In the modern world, designing and redesigning such institutions is done not by private contract, but through a public constitutional process. By imposing on actors obligations that they would not voluntarily accept, Durkheimian institutions exercise governmental authority.[9] Whether or not an individual fulfills or violates institutionalized obligations of this kind is of interest, not merely to the directly injured party if there is one, but to the community as a whole; it is, in other words, not just a private but a public affair. Sanctioning, therefore, is in the hands of a *third* party representing, somehow, the whole of society, and that such a third party can be called upon to restore order is a defining element of a Durkheimian institution.[10]

Williamsonian institutions, by contrast, are devices for nonmarket though market-responsive and indeed market-driven coordination of economic behavior. They are purposely and voluntarily constructed by market participants to increase the efficiency of their exchanges. Williamsonian institutions include the private hierarchies of Coasian firms, as distinguished from the public hierarchies of the state devoted to enforcing obligations on and to the collectivity as a whole. They may also include trade associations, subcontracting networks, cartels, or arbitration procedures contractually instituted to settle commercial disputes more efficiently than public courts of law. While Durkheimian institutions may *contain* markets, Williamsonian ones *grow out of* markets, for example, when they promise to lower transaction costs below the costs of market exchanges. Where public institutions provide *government*, Williamsonian institutions offer *governance* through "private ordering" (Williamson 1987). Unlike Durkheimian institutions, they arise "from below" through voluntary agreement, representing shared rational interests in optimally efficient trading relations. Williamsonian institutions are therefore typically self-enforced, in the sense of rational choice institutionalism, as all parties are interested in their good performance and further existence. They also lend themselves to being conceptualized in efficiency-theoretical terms.

A few brief elaborations may be in order. For the sake of simplicity I have left aside contract and regulatory law, that is, obligatory institutions designed to enable the free play of market forces. While they are Durkheimian in the way they are created and enforced, their function is to make possible contractual agreement between consenting market actors (Durkheim 1964 [1893], Chapter 7). Contract law in particular consists of legal instruments, enforceable in court, that are provided by society to private actors for use at their pleasure (*dispositives Recht*). Sometimes such use is made conditional on the assumption of social responsibilities or on moderation of the terms of contracts between unequal parties, but less so as a social order becomes more liberal. Which aspect one emphasizes, contractual freedom or obligatory solidarity, depends to an extent on what one wants to prove. Durkheim was interested in the noncontractual conditions of a regime of private contracts, that is, in what he considered to be the indispensable obligatory underpinnings of liberal voluntarism. Modern "neo-liberalism," by contrast, plays down as much as possible the role of public intervention, especially by government, suggesting the possibility or even reality of a social order that is enforced either entirely by itself or, at most, by civil law courts.

Political scientists sometimes fail to understand the nature of regulatory and contract law, and generally the distinction between market-distorting and market-making legal regulation. This leads to the frequently heard but still fundamentally misleading claim that the role of "the state" remains undiminished in comparison to postwar interventionism even in a deregulated, neo-liberal political economy, due to a continued presence and perhaps even an increase in the amount of contract and regulatory law. A different question, and one that is not just a matter of definition, is whether a de-politicized, "Williamsonian" social order, one that is entirely at the voluntary disposition of self-interested economic actors, can ever be more than a liberal utopia, not just for reasons of political and social cohesion but also for economic reasons. The intuition here, inspired of course by Durkheim, would be that a world depending exclusively on voluntary Williamsonian contracts would be not only socially but also economically unsustainable. This raises the question whether and in what sense self-interested economic actors must for their own sake also be— or made to be—other-interested, and what conditions are needed for them to be able to act on that interest. Marx posed this question with unsurpassed precision in the chapter of the "working day" in the first volume of Capital (Marx 1966, Chapter 8). I will return to this subject later.

Liberalization, then, in the meaning of disorganization as specified upon inspection of our empirical material, may be described not as abolishment of institutions *tout court*, but as *a move from Durkheimian institutions to Williamsonian ones*. Sometimes, as in German industrial relations, that move may take place as a slow transformation of institutions of the former into institutions of the latter type, gradually de-emphasizing obligatory solidarity, perhaps by abolishing sanctions on non-solidaristic behavior, and increasingly emphasizing efficiency as the leading criterion for the appropriateness of social rules. Rather than an atomistic market, what results from liberalization so defined is an institutional substructure of economic action that is decentralized, fragmented, diversified, and privatized, and shaped by individual choice and local conditions instead of public-political design representing collective values and objectives. For example, as a political economy becomes progressively less organized, or more liberal and "pluralist," membership in intermediary organizations becomes less compulsory and more voluntary, and it becomes more difficult to impose interest accommodation from above. Also, public status and the compulsory powers of intermediary organizations erode, and interests represented become narrower while actors begin to experiment with new, more market-like methods of interest articulation.[11] Other dimensions of a move from obligatory Durkheimian to voluntary Williamsonian institutions, as found in our empirical material, include the insertion of markets and competition in the provision and regulation of social policy; the formation of less compact and less publicly instituted patterns of interest representation and political conflict in the social policy organizational field; the privatization of state functions, turning obligatory into voluntary provision and consumption; the transformation of the rules for corporate governance, away from an emphasis on management in the public interest to management at the pleasure of shareholders;[12] the replacement of obligatory rules and forms of corporate organization with codes of conduct granting a wide range of discretion for shareholders in organizing their business;[13] and the individualization of corporate strategies in the course of the disintegration of the German company network and of the disappearance of its capacity to enforce collective solidarity among its members.

Returning to our diagrammatic representation of the dimensions of organized capitalism, or postwar capitalism before its liberalization

(Table 11.1), disorganization, or liberalization, involves a retreat of public institutions, including the state, in favor of private ones (from row 1 to row 2), as well as a shift in the objectives of institutionalized coordination from solidarity to efficiency (from column 2 to column 1). As the state delegates efficiency to the private sphere, in effect to private business acting under the, presumably, salutary pressures of competition, traditional concerns for solidarity are merged into and made subservient to efficiency as a collective objective. What remains of organized capitalism, or the institutions of the postwar political economy, is the Williamsonian mobilization of transaction-specific trust for the "coordination" of production, by private ordering at the micro-level of idiosyncratic exchange (Table 11.1, column 1, row 2). Again, private institution-building of this kind is fully compatible with a liberal order as long as the institutions in question either make markets possible or are driven by them, promoting competition and presumably, as a result, competitiveness and efficiency.

Liberalization of organized capitalism, that is to say, need not dispense with what Tocqueville called the "art of associating together" (Tocqueville 1988 [1835–1840]) and its use in political economy at all. While liberalization sometimes does create atomistic markets, or aims to create them, it is not in principle hostile to institutions, provided their purpose is confined to making markets, or making them more efficient. (*Ipso facto*, the presence of a rich supply of institutions for economic coordination cannot be taken as indication of organized capitalism having successfully resisted pressures for liberalization.) Private ordering is not restricted to arms-length relations in perfect markets and may well draw on inherited cultural repertoires of social order (Williamson and Ouchi 1981), as long as their deployment remains voluntary and can be ended if economic expediency demands (which it may not always and need not in principle do). What disappears in liberalization is not institutions as such, but institutions designed for and capable of subjecting economic actors individually or collectively to social obligations and public responsibilities, beyond their residual obligation to observe the rules that make markets function, and apart from their responsibility for maximizing their profits within them. In short, the parallel processes of *disorganization* we have observed in five institutional settings of the German political economy, having started separately and independently to merge later into a stream of mutually re-enforcing institutional change, together do form a broad process of systemic *liberalization* even though they are far from resulting in *de-institutionalization*.

Notes

1. The following is much inspired by work of Martin Höpner.
2. But see Höpner (2007*a*).
3. Leaving open who was the dominant party—which was characteristically not easy to tell (Kocka 1974). See the debates in interwar Germany, with their replay in the 1970s, between Social Democrats and Communists on whether close coordination between the state and big business was *staatsmonopolistischer Kapitalismus* (state monopoly capitalism), a term coined by Lenin in 1917, which was to be eschewed, or harbored a promise of *Wirtschaftsdemokratie* (economic democracy) (Naphtali 1984 [1928]), which was regarded as desirable but also, by the radical Left, as impossible short of a change to communal forms of property. Rudolf Hilferding, as Höpner reminds us, in his lifetime moved from the former position to the latter, enabling him eventually to serve as Minister of Finance in the Weimar Republic.
4. Moving, as it were, from corporatism at the level of the national society to "corporationism" at the level of individual firms; from national to company loyalty; from public to private order; and from political authority to economic markets.
5. State ownership of large firms, cross-shareholding among firms, workforce representation on company boards, strong trade unions, and trade associations.
6. That distinction, in turn, would correspond fairly well to that between "governance" and "government," or between "system integration" and "social integration."
7. The distinction I am proposing must not be confused with that between competing "approaches" to institutional analysis like, famously, "rational choice," "historical," and "sociological institutionalism" (Hall and Taylor 1996). My subject is not what institutions *as such* "are" and how they are therefore best conceptualized, but how *different types of institutions* operate and relate to one another in the real world. By implication, I suggest that the different paradigms of institutional analysis refer to different types of institutions, although they pretend to deal with institutions in general. I consider the historical relationship and sequential emergence of these types an important dimension of institutional and indeed social change.
8. Of course this does not mean that their enactment is not subject to the same ambiguities and indeterminacies as that of institutions in general. Even the most authoritative institution may over time be discovered to have gaps, or to offer space for interpretation that allows inventive actors "in bad faith" to evade their obligations. That a normative constraint needs to applied to varying and specific conditions, and that it can be contested or violated, does not in itself make it less of a constraint as long as it is still sanctioned. For example, that there is tax evasion does not make paying taxes voluntary or a matter of contractual agreement.

9. For a random selection: "We cooperate because we have wished to do so, but our voluntary cooperation creates for us duties that we have not desired... The contract is not sufficient by itself, but is only possible because of the regulation of contracts, which is of social origin... There are rules of justice that social justice must prevent being violated, even if a clause has been agreed by the parties concerned... Every society is a moral society... Duties are imposed on us that we have not expressly wished" (Durkheim 1964 [1893], 161–3, 173, 174).

10. On legitimacy and sanctioning by third parties, see Streeck and Thelen (2005).

11. This corresponds, of course, to Schmitter's distinction between corporatism and pluralism (Schmitter 1974).

12. See the dissertation on the subject, in progress, of Philip Klages at the Max Planck Institute for the Study of Societies.

13. Note the recent attempts by German organized capital to get rid of the representation of workers and trade unions on the boards of large German firms (supervisory board codetermination). Like in similar cases, the demand was not to abolish workforce representation by legislation but to make it voluntary, to be agreed upon between management, shareholders, and the workforce. After all, if codetermination was as good for the competitiveness of the firm as its advocates claimed, shareholders and management would be the first to institute it on their own!

12

Convergence, nonconvergence, divergence

Do disorganization and liberalization, as found to have been under way in Germany since the 1980s, amount to convergence of the German pattern of capitalism on an Anglo-American pattern? Current debates in political economy on convergence and divergence, even where their units of reference are countries, mostly take place in terms of efficiency theories in which competitive market pressures figure as the root cause of institutional change.[1] At one end of the spectrum, "best practice" theories assume competition to force social formations to adapt the properties of their most successful competitors in world markets, which in the present period of economic "globalization" is supposed to be the US or British version of a free market economy.[2] At the other end, also invoking as the driving force a struggle for survival between national economic systems, competitive pressures are believed to lead, rather than to convergence and uniformity, to specialization and diversification, not just of products but also of the institutional regimes under which they are produced. This, of course, is fundamentally the view of the "varieties of capitalism" school.

It is impossible to present the modern debate on convergence exhaustively here, if only because it is beset with a host of conceptual difficulties that would have to be disentangled first. For example, if convergence of social configurations were to mean they were to become completely identical, it would be impossible, and convergence theory would never have a fair chance. If the debate is to make sense at all, convergence can refer only to select characteristics of societies, designated as essential for good theoretical reasons. Rather than pursuing this further, I will limit myself to four points. First, turning back to the narratives presented on the German case, I will show that the institutional change we have observed in the past three decades cannot possibly be explained as convergence on the model of superior competitors in search of higher performance. Specifically, I take on the claim by some theorists of "globalization" that the liberalization of political economies like the German one was caused by inferior performance compared to the Anglo-American economies. Second, I will go further and argue that the problem lies, not simply with a misjudgment of the—German—evidence, but with efficiency-theoretical accounts of institutional change in general. Moreover, I claim that this problem remains even if the theory, like that of capitalist "variety," were to predict continued divergence rather than convergence. Third, by drawing on the distinction between organization and coordination, I will suggest a conceptual template that allows for forces of convergence and divergence *operating simultaneously,* in different dimensions of institutional structure as well as, importantly, for different reasons. Specifically, where we do observe convergence, I hold that it must be explained, not by one "model" emulating another, but as part of a broad, "historical" stream of change occurring simultaneously and for identical, mostly endogenous reasons in all advanced capitalist countries, more or less at the same time. Fourth, and finally, I will introduce an explicitly temporal, process perspective on convergence and divergence, among other things to show how institutional regimes may remain different even if subject to identical historical trends.

First, there is no evidence to the effect that the processes of institutional change that we have observed in Germany originated in a collective attempt to create or restore competitive advantage, especially in relation to Anglo-American countries. This is indicated already by the fact that whatever it was that happened in the German political economy, it started long before the country came to be regarded, and to regard itself, as economically underperforming. In particular, there is no indication that, when the "German model" began to dissolve in the 1980s, it was less internationally competitive than, say, the British or the American "model." Actually, the opposite was and indeed continues to be the case, at least with respect to the United Kingdom, which was vastly outperformed on a wide range of indicators of economic competitiveness before German unification, and even thereafter (Table 12.1). Quite appropriately, as mentioned above, Germany was, together with Japan, considered well into the 1990s by leading academics as well as by the first Clinton administration as a model for the United States, for example with respect to matters such as workforce training and the organization of subcontracting and technology transfer in the manufacturing sector (Dertouzos et al. 1989).

Table 12.1. Economic performance: Germany, the United Kingdom, and the United States, 1980–2000

	Per capita income*			Rate of unemployment**			Rate of inflation***			Trade balance****			World market share*****		
	D	UK	US	D	UK	US	D	UK	US	D	UK	US	D	UK	US
1980	90	68	100	2.6	6.8	7.1	5.5	18.0	13.5	3.2	-2.4	-1.6	9.4	6.1	11.9
1985	90	68	100	7.2	11.2	7.2	2.1	6.1	3.5	7.7	-5.2	-4.5	9.9	5.8	11.8
1990	91	72	100	5.5	6.9	5.5	2.7	9.5	5.4	6.0	-8.1	-4.2	11.6	5.7	12.0
1995	78	71	100	7.1	8.5	5.6	1.7	3.4	2.8	2.8	-5.9	-3.8	10.4	5.2	12.4
2000	75	74	100	6.9	5.4	4.0	1.4	0.8	3.4	5.6	-6.7	-5.3	9.5	4.6	13.1

D: Germany, UK: United Kingdom; US: United States.

* Purchasing power parities; USA = 100. 1980–95: Scharpf and Schmidt (2000), Vol. I, 338; 2000: own calculation based on Eurostat Internet tables.

** Standardized. Internet-Auftritt des Sachverständigenrats, Internationale Zeitreihen, Table 4. UK 1980: ILO LABORSTA.

*** Consumer prices. 1980–95: Scharpf and Schmidt (2000), Vol. I, 340; 2000: Eurostat Internet tables.

**** In manufacturing; in percent of GDP. OECD National Accounts Database; own calculations. 1995: data is from 1994. 1980–95: Scharpf and Schmidt (2000), Vol. I, 371; 2000: World Bank, World Development Report 2002, as in Kitschelt and Streeck (2003).

***** In exports, in percent.

I maintain that German institutional change reflected the gradual historical exhaustion of the country's postwar political peace formula rather than a need to improve national economic performance relative to other countries. In fact, the "German model" became unsustainable *in spite* of its continuously high competitive performance in international markets.[3] The self-undermining dynamic of its centralized collective bargaining regime was endogenous, and actually its beginnings coincided with the rise of Germany to European economic hegemony in the 1980s. The same holds for the exhaustion of social policy and the overextension of the interventionist tax state, which had been in the making since the end of the "Golden Age." Also, the privatization of the German infrastructure in the 1990s was driven by a fiscal crisis, not by competitive market pressures; instead of being caused by these, it created them in the first place, in part to relieve the state of responsibilities it could or would no longer shoulder. Social policy, as long as the state could pay for it, had served to support not just social peace but also, *ipso facto*, the international competitiveness of the exposed sectors of the German economy, until the costs became too high. When social policy later had to be reformed, this was to protect, to the extent still possible, the state's remaining room for fiscal maneuver and prevent a further increase in publicly funded unemployment—which as such had always been entirely compatible with international competitiveness.

It is true that in the second half of the 1990s, when sectoral changes had accelerated and merged into mutually self-reinforcing systemic liberalization, the latter came to be supported and promoted in the name of economic competitiveness by a variety of actors hoping to benefit from it, including the government. However, political "reforms" began only after change had already come a long way, and while they were presented to the public, in the spirit of the age, or of capitalism in general, as measures to restore competitive efficiency, they served primarily a broad range of other objectives.[4] In some cases, such as capital market reform aimed at strengthening *Finanzplatz Deutschland*, political interventions were consciously designed to make German institutions more similar to and compatible with Anglo-American institutions, thereby undoubtedly contributing to some kind of "convergence." Most of the problems, however, that occupied political actors at the time, such as low job growth in domestically traded services, had little to nothing to do with international competitiveness. Other changes that took place in response to new market pressures, such as the emergence of a new regime of coordination with labor, were far from copying Anglo-American practices. In short, efficiency-theoretical explanations of the liberalization of the "German model" in terms of an attempt at emulating the supposedly superior Anglo-American economic regime are profoundly irreconcilable with the empirical facts.

Second, as we have seen, efficiency-theoretical concepts are used to predict not just convergence but also continuing divergence, the most prominent example being the "varieties of capitalism" literature. However, although that literature commendably rejects the "best practice" economistic simplicities of neo-liberal wishful thinking, I submit that it does so for the wrong reasons, explaining divergence by the same causal factors on which "globalization" theories draw to explain convergence: namely, pressures for efficiency originating in competitive markets. In the subsequent chapter, on "Economizing," I will show why efficiency-theoretical accounts of institutional change are *inherently* deficient, whatever they are called upon to prove. Here I simply note that any binomial typology of institutional systems, especially if the two types for which it provides are defined as alternative, self-stabilizing, and functionally equivalent equilibrium conditions, is conceptually biased against and tends to rule out convergence, not by theory but already by definition. This may be gleaned from the fact that, as mentioned, "varieties of capitalism" allows for just one possibility of convergence, which is capital market-driven convergence of "coordinated market economies" on the "liberal market economy" model, and which is, moreover, both only weakly theorized and declared a priori to be empirically improbable. Apart from what looks very much like a defensive ad hoc addition in response to uncomfortable empirical observations, the theory remains one of strict nonconvergence, with two alternative models of capitalism reproducing themselves in two functionally equivalent and equally efficient institutional equilibrium conditions, "coordinated" and "liberal."

Such a concept, however, hardly fits what we have learned about institutional change in the German case. Here we observed a process of broad, systemic change that made the German political economy much more market-responsive and "liberal" while preserving or creating anew significant nonmarket mechanisms of coordination, in the course of what we have identified as a gradual shift from Durkheimian to Williamsonian institutions. In a model with only two possible types representing alternative equilibria, however, real change can only be convergence, in the sense of migration from one type of equilibrium to the other, while everything short of convergence must be functional adjustment: the reestablishment of the kind of equilibrium that defines the kind of capitalism to which a given system belonged and continues to belong. Liberalization of the German kind, which preserved significant nonmarket coordination in at least one major sector of the political economy, is not adequately described as either of the above, *being neither convergence nor a return to equilibrium.* Nor is it really possible within the logic of "varieties of capitalism" to account for it in terms of a gradual move from a "coordinated" to a "liberal" end of a spectrum of different capitalisms. It is true that sometimes the attempt is made to represent the distinction between "liberal" and "coordinated" "market economies" as continuous rather than dichotomous. The reason why this is not very convincing, however, is that both types are defined as governed by categorically different institutional logics and complementarities. This must mean that mixed cases will be attracted by and as a result "converge" on the nearer of the two types, rather than freely moving along a continuum or remaining somewhere "in between."[5] Where equilibrium types are held together by complementarity, one expects polarization rather than gradualism.

By locating coordination in just one of its two types—one could also say, by not distinguishing between *political organization* and *productive coordination*—the "varieties of capitalism" literature treats as insignificant a distinction we have found to be of major importance: that between public government and private governance. This is not by accident, as within its paradigm, institutions seem to be generally and quasi-ontologically conceived as Williamsonian in kind and origin, folding Durkheimian institutions into Williamsonian ones by subsuming them under the primacy of efficiency. In fact for Hall and Soskice (2001*a*), in classically economistic fashion, all institutions seem ultimately consensually conceived and constructed for the shared purpose of enhancing economic performance and international competitiveness. No other purposes and motives matter, or clearly take second place by general agreement. Institutions are set up by rationally economizing actors, under the leadership of far-sighted firms interested in competitive survival and with the help of accommodating politicians and public bureaucracies—or they are later accepted as welfare-maximizing by those who may originally have opposed them due to a less enlightened view of their real interests. The process of disorganization-cum-liberalization, then, that we have found at work in the German "coordinated market economy"—a complex stream of interlocking developments making political-economic institutions less Durkheimian and more Williamsonian—was about something that, strictly speaking, cannot exist in the vocabulary of the "varieties of capitalism" school: the de-institutionalization of nonvoluntary public obligations. This is because in economistic functionalism, all obligations are voluntary since they exist only as rational commitments to the shared and uncontested objective of successful reproduction in competition.[6]

Third, properly addressing the issues of change, convergence, and reproduction requires a richer conceptual template than what is offered by efficiency theories of whatever stripe—one that, in short, allows politics and history back in. All functionalist social theories project the same sense of *posthistoire*, where nothing can really happen since everything has already happened in the past, when the best of all worlds was established once and for all. That "varieties of capitalism" provides not for one, but for two best worlds does not make much of a difference since no interaction is assumed to take place between them, except in international trade where their equal competitiveness assures their separate self-reproduction. With convergence ruled out, no place is left for change except for technocratic adjustments of parts of the national economic machine to fluctuating external conditions, and politics is strangely reduced to what both the Marxist tradition and the pluralist industrialism literature of the 1950s and 1960s (Kerr et al. 1960) expected it to become with the final completion of the transition to industrial society: the expert administration of—different but equal—modes of production.[7]

Complementing, as suggested by Höpner (2007a), the distinction between coordinated and liberal market economies by another, orthogonal distinction between organized and disorganized capitalism, we learn not only that national versions of capitalism may differ with respect to the degree to which they are organized, *but also that versions of disorganized, liberal capitalism may differ with regard to the extent to and in the way in which they make use of institutional coordination*. Obviously, there are many ways to govern liberal capitalism, just as there were many ways to manage the organized capitalism of the postwar era (Shonfield 1965). There is in particular enough space in disorganized capitalism for historical experience, accumulated social capital and "path-dependent" evolution to exercise influence on institutional arrangements. Williamsonian institutions created to cut transaction costs may, and probably will, be differently structured and be in different supply in different but equally liberal countries. The implication is that the German way of institutional coordination, and that of other countries as well, will for the foreseeable future remain distinguishable from British and American ways, even if the German economy will have finally ceased to be a politically organized one.

If efficiency pressures fail to produce convergence, however, the same need not be true for other factors. By distinguishing between coordination and organization, we can allow for nonconvergence with respect to coordination to coexist with convergence in organization, or disorganization, in the course of a global process of capitalism becoming "unleashed" (Glyn), freeing itself from constraining social obligations.[8] Post-Durkheimian convergence driven by politics, or better: by a secular decline of postwar national politics, may then exist side by side with Williamsonian divergence driven by considerations of efficiency and competitiveness in production. In other words, just as envisaged by "varieties of capitalism," certain kinds of diversity seem indeed to be caused by efficiency pressures, and unlike what is predicted by "best practice" functionalism, it may precisely be diversity and not convergence which efficiency pressures produce. Convergence, for its part, seems to be driven instead by politics, unlike what is suggested by best practice models of "globalization" in which it is caused by economics, and in contrast also to "varieties of capitalism" theories that rule out convergence altogether. As obligation-creating and solidarity-enforcing institutions fade away, a country like Germany, in which arms-length market relations were historically much less important than, say, in the United States,[9] may still be able to rely heavily on private institutions for economic coordination, such as those making up the country's emerging new industrial relations regime. But this would not interfere with rapid evolution in an American direction with respect to a decisive weakening of the capacity of the public order to impose Durkheimian obligations on self-interested economic actors.

Fourth, our understanding of convergence and nonconvergence may be additionally enhanced by placing it in a temporal dimension and considering, as suggested above, the social *systems* that are being compared as historical *processes*. This is because cross-sectional comparison, looking at different systems at the same point in time, may find lasting differences between them while in reality they are moving on the same historical trajectory but with a time lag keeping them apart. Conceiving of social systems as processes suggests the possibility that systems are more appropriately compared, and the stability of differences between them is more realistically assessed, in terms of stages in their evolution that *need not necessarily be attained simultaneously*. For a stylized illustration one might refer to the fact that the New Deal in the United States was rightly considered as a delayed effort at state formation emulating and catching up with—in other words: converging on—the European nation-state. But

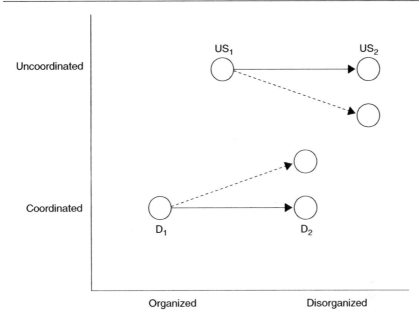

Figure 12.1. Convergence, nonconvergence, divergence

just as organized capitalism had come late to the United States, it went earlier than in Europe, beginning with the breakup of the New Deal coalition in the 1960s and 1970s when the United States took the lead in the disorganization of postwar capitalism worldwide. The fact that, all in all, Continental-European capitalism seems more "organized" than US capitalism, with the difference not about to disappear, need not, however, mean that disorganization was limited to the "liberal market economy" of the United States; all it might mean, in a process perspective, is that leader and follower, moving at the same pace along the same path, continue to remain one or two decades apart.

A more general presentation of the same idea is offered in Figure 12.1, which distinguishes countries in terms of different levels of both political organization and productive coordination. Two stylized cases are shown, "Germany" (D) and "United States" (US), the latter being both less coordinated and less organized at time t_1, which is now. Both countries are undergoing disorganization, moving the same distance in the same direction toward a future condition at t_2 (solid arrows). While they are becoming less organized, and by the same degree ("convergence"), they end up being as different at t_2 as they were at t_1 ("diversity"). Moreover, even if "Germany" became less coordinated in the process of disorganization and

169

the "United States" more, reducing divergence on this dimension (broken arrows), there would be no reason at all to expect the two countries to look alike as a result.

Summing up, even when the organized, nonliberal capitalism of the postwar era will finally be gone—which it likely already is—there will always be enough differences between countries, produced by time lags and tradition, for institutional theorists and policy researchers to make comparisons, suggest lesson-drawing, find path dependency and study hybridization. In fact, so many differences will remain that studying them close up will keep analysts busy enough to overlook the big commonality that lies behind the differences: the retreat in contemporary capitalism of institutions imposing and enforcing collective public obligations on economic actors, in favor of voluntary, privatized institutions of the Williamsonian kind. Here again, as so often before, careful study of the trees may blind one for the forest. Obsession with the diverse pathways of the transition to a more liberal phase of capitalist development, and with the differences between their results, may hide the transition itself—which is all the more likely as long as the mainstream of institutional analysis remains fixated on cross-sectional comparison to the neglect of historical development over time.

Notes

1. International competition as the presumed cause of institutional convergence has today taken the place of technological progress and political development in the now almost forgotten theories of "pluralist industrialism" (Kerr et al. 1960) and "modernization" (Rostow 1990 [1960]). Focusing on political economy, I disregard the sociological institutionalism as inspired by DiMaggio and Powell (1983), which explains the cross-national homogenization of institutions and organizations with normative rather than economic pressures.
2. This is the position of those who Campbell (2004) groups together under the label of "globalization theorists."
3. See also the chapter on "Internationalization," below.
4. On the complexity of collective objectives in a democratic-capitalist political economy, see the next chapter, on "Economizing," and Chapter 17, on "Capitalism."
5. I understand that it is precisely in this sense that Soskice (Soskice 1999) speaks of "bifurcated convergence."
6. Institutions that are not now voluntary are Hobbesian in character: even though they are coercive, they were created to be so by voluntary agreement in a far-distant past.

7. In the Communist Manifesto, in a rare reference to what society will be like after "the disappearance of class conflict" (*Wegfallen des Klassengegensatzes*), Marx and Engels predict "the transformation of the state into the mere administration of production" (*die Verwandlung des Staates in eine bloße Verwaltung der Produktion*) (Marx and Engels 1972 [1848], 491). This is in a nutshell how the new economistic functionalism in institutional theory conceives of politics: as submerged in (the logic of) production.

8. On historical trends see Chapter 16, on "History."

9. I am using the US for stylized comparison only, as an ideal type. Note that there is a long literature on US firms suffering from a lack of ingenuity in designing institutions for economic coordination, for example between assemblers and suppliers, that cut transaction costs by building trust.

13

"Economizing" and the evolution of political-economic institutions

The previous chapter has raised the issue whether institutional change in capitalist political economies, or in political economies in general, is to be explained as progress toward higher levels of economic efficiency. Can, or must, the development of social systems be conceived as "rationalization" or, in a more modern term, "economizing"?[1] Is it appropriate to assume the evolution of a political-economic order, an example of which we have presented in the empirical sections of this book, to be driven by economic imperatives for higher efficiency in the use of scarce resources?

Economic functionalism is defined by the fact that it answers these questions unambiguously in the affirmative. This is true for the various theories of "globalization" that predict convergence of national institutional regimes on one and only one "best practice," just as it holds for the "varieties of capitalism" paradigm, which draws on efficiency pressures to explain not change and convergence, but stability and non-convergence. Also functionalist are standard accounts of institutional change in the rational choice version of economic history. Here, historical development is described in principle as a long-drawn sequence of change in social orders making them ever more efficient, for example by replacing communal with private property, thereby avoiding the "tragedy of the commons" and creating incentives to use resources with maximal efficiency. Theories of this sort, like North's, may sometimes find it impossible to avoid paying tribute to the empirical fact of long-term survival of institutions that they believe to have good deductive reasons to consider inefficient (North 1990). But such survival, where it is grudgingly acknowledged, is and can only be regarded as a deplorable factual deficiency, a contingent imperfection compared to how the world could and should be if things could be set right.

Drawing on the German case, I will argue in the following that economic-functionalist explanations of institutional change are profoundly and incurably deficient, even if conceived and defended as simplified models of an admittedly much more complex social world. While abstraction from what is always a confusing abundance of empirical observations is indeed a fundamental necessity for any attempt to make sense of the world, what is "abstracted from" or "drawn out of" the world's endless supply of "facts" must include what is *essential* in the world, and leave out only what is nonessential. As it turns out upon empirical inspection, however, *non*economic actions or arrangements—those *not* directed at maximizing the returns on economic assets—are *not at all nonessential* for the way an economy, including a capitalist economy, works and changes, and are therefore omitted from theory only at the price of losing touch with reality.[2] Also, in order not to be misleading, models must avoid construing mechanisms and relations into their simplified representation of the world whose absence is one of its essential characteristics—not to mention making assumptions that suggest certainty and closure where the real world is beset with uncertainties and remains open for unexpected events and intentional intervention.

There are six points in particular where economistic-functionalist theories of social order and institutional change disregard essential elements of the world or, to the contrary, deductively "load" their models with agents or relations where it is precisely their nonexistence that is a defining property of empirical reality:

(1) Economic-functionalist theories of systemic institutional change or, for that matter, stability have as yet failed to specify convincingly a collective societal agent with sufficient intention, control, and foresight to design and build social institutions so that they maximize, or continuously increase, the return on economic resources. Sometimes, the role of agent is ascribed to a government stylized as a well-meaning, omniscient, and all-powerful custodian of what is assumed, on the grounds of presumably uncontestable plausibility, to be a general interest of society in efficiency. Since all the theory knows is how governments ought to behave in order to perform what ought to be their role, it can respond to governments behaving differently only by ad hoc explanations—normally drawing upon politicians' intellectual shortcomings, corrupt habits or ideological fanaticism. Alternatively, it can proffer "scientific" advice to politicians and citizens which, if taken, would make the world conform to the theory.

Looking at the German case, what is conspicuously absent in our story is an actual or potential *systemic rationalizer* governing institutional change over three decades to turn it into rational economizing. As has been frequently noted, West Germany's postwar economic constitution both limited and divided the economic powers of the country's "semi-sovereign" state (Katzenstein 1987). For most of the period surveyed, the federal government and the central bank were deeply at odds over what was the right economic policy. Moreover, if we take the Council of Economic Advisers, the *Sachverständigenrat,* to be the voice of economics as a "science," it untiringly criticized the government for failing to do what it ought to have done to ensure economic progress. Indeed, as we have seen, rather than maximizing allocative efficiency, German governments were concerned above all with social integration and political peace, and not least with their reelection. Social policy was expanded on what was early on denounced by economists as an irresponsible scale, and public debt was accumulated continuously until the postwar welfare state was politically bankrupt in the early 2000s. It is true, and in fact quite remarkable in a sense that transcends economistic reasoning, that social peace and political stability secured economic growth and the international competitiveness of a great number of firms, as reflected in impressive aggregate national statistics—or at least it did not stand in the way of satisfactory growth and competitiveness as firms learned to use social peace, while expensive, to their advantage.[3] Nevertheless, competitiveness was far from identical with allocative efficiency and as a matter of fact did not really require it: as *Modell Deutschland* developed beyond the 1970s, it involved, alongside impressive levels of competitive international performance, high and rising unemployment, publicly subsidized underutilization of resources, and steadily increasing public debt and private entitlements—until it ended, not in an act of "economizing" institutional reform, but in political bankruptcy and institutional exhaustion.

If government was unable to act as systemic rationalizer, perhaps business stepped in? Indeed, most of the functionalist "varieties of capitalism" literature assumes, more or less explicitly, that efficiency in national institutional regimes is the result of collective action of firms instructing the government of the state to do what they know to be in their interest in international competitiveness. But in the case of Germany, organized business initially cooperated whole-heartedly with a social policy that subsidized the retirement of productive resources. Later, the efforts of large firms to defend or increase the return on their assets undermined the unity of business associations in general and the commonality of purpose between large and small firms in particular. Thus, as the system disintegrated, organized business and its capacity to act collectively disintegrated as part of it. Rather than engaging in national institution-building, or rebuilding, large firms exited from the corporatist postwar regime where they could.

Withdrawal from *Deutschland AG* and from the German system of collective bargaining took place in pursuit of firms' individual profitability, not of efficient national institutions. In fact, as evidenced among other things by the collaboration of organized business in the "inefficient" practices of the corporatist period, there is no reason whatsoever to believe that business cares about efficiency as such, as distinguished from its own profitability and survival. Political protection and redistribution, monopolistic markets, oligopolistic collusion, and the like may be much preferable to efficiency from the perspective of established firms. This is why firms, including collectivities of firms, cannot be relied upon to act as responsible agents of national competitiveness, except where their own, individual competitiveness happens to depend on it.[4] For example, even where an aggressive national competition regime promotes the international competitiveness of the firms subject to it, these will as a rule not be enthusiastic about having it imposed on them, and will certainly abstain from deploying their political capital to have it instituted.[5] Even when ultraliberal economists like Friedrich Hayek, therefore, who consider everything political with extreme suspicion, search for an agent to ensure economic progress and economizing institutional reform, they find themselves turning away from business and calling upon an idealized "state" assumed—or better: desperately hoped—to be committed to and capable of a market-promoting *Ordnungspolitik* enforced against the resistance of capital, organized or not. Not surprisingly, Hayek's ideal state consists mostly of non-majoritarian institutions effectively shielded from political pressures of all kinds—a state that would hardly, if at all, qualify as democratic.[6]

(2) Alternatively, economic-functionalist theories of economic progress, or of "economizing" as a teleological historical process, could assume an "invisible hand" aggregating the irrational, uninformed, or corrupt activities of politicians or firms behind their backs in a way that makes them contribute to a more efficient economic order, without or even against their intention. In essence, this would expand the Mandevillean "private vice, public virtue" model from markets to institutions. The question is, however, how exactly the anonymous and unplanned process would

work that would have to configure self-interested actions and parochial institutions into a coherent and efficient institutional system. No mechanism of unintended rationalization of social orders, equivalent to the price mechanism in self-equilibrating markets, has as yet been specified plausibly in institutional theory, and certainly it has not revealed itself in our narratives of institutional change in the German political economy. Just as there is no *visible* agent of systemic economizing, there seems to be *no hidden hand*, either, to design efficient and redesign inefficient institutional configurations.

Sub specie aeternitatis, one might try to solve the problem by falling back on a survival-of-the-fittest model gleaned from evolutionary biology under which different institutional architectures would be assumed to arise by random mutation, compete against each other for economic advantage, and only the most efficient would survive. Rather than by circumspect and effective societal agency, systemic efficiency would be enhanced by an impersonal process of selection. The difficulty, however, is that alternative societal architectures are in short supply and their mutation, if this is what constitutes institutional change, is not only slow but also far from random. Moreover, even more importantly, there is, as has often been noted, no perfect market for institutions, so that competitive selection, where it does occur, is in no way certain to favor economic efficiency. For example, in the international arena, political power may compensate for lack of efficiency, as in the case of a hegemonic country biasing the rules of international exchange in favor of its national strengths or business practices. Or countries may thrive in an international market, like Germany and Japan did in much of the postwar period, with collusive national institutions sacrificing allocative efficiency for social peace and cooperation, thereby de facto subsidizing the internationally exposed sectors of their economies.[7]

(3) Implied in the above is that even where there was a societal agent capable of designing national institutions for survival in international competition, whether such survival would necessarily or optimally be achieved by institutional rationalization remains an open question. To a large part, the answer would depend on the rules of the competitive game and on the strategies adopted as well as the performance achieved by competitors. International struggles for economic advantage[8] take place in comparatively small settings with a limited number of players and even more limited "market access." In a context like this, national systemic agents, to the extent they exist, are likely to behave like the management of oligopolistic firms, aiming at satisfactory relative instead of maximized

absolute performance. Even in the biological world, species can live with a lot of "slack," that is, traits that are not conducive to reproductive success, and they become more "efficient" only in response and in relation to a real, "historical" threat offered by a competing species, or mutant, that happens to enter their environment (Gould 2002).

(4) Economic functionalism assumes that societies are and can be structured for the single purpose of efficient economic performance. To the extent that other interests or purposes are recognized, for example interests of a redistributive nature, they are assumed to be taken care of more or less automatically if the economy functions well. High economic performance is treated as a consensual goal providing the basis for consensus on all other goals; this is why it can serve as an uncontested and uncontestable principle for policy in line with which to structure a society's institutions.

In fact, of course, there is no agreement in the practical world on the indicators with which performance is to be measured. Is a low profit rate that is safe over a longer term to be preferred over high profits in the short term? Does 3 percent unemployment indicate superior or inferior performance compared to 3 percent inflation? Are high wages to be preferred over high labor market participation, or vice versa? Is a society with high employment at wages below the level of subsistence economically more successful than a society with a high minimum wage and an extensive welfare state to back it up? Moreover, policy and politics today puzzle over the question whether the goal of social policy should be commodification or de-commodification of labor; to what extent efficiency should be allowed to take precedence over social stability; and where and how a rich society can and should afford preventing the market from further penetrating into the lifeworld of individuals and their families. On issues like these, politics inevitably encounters interests and objectives that are not easily commensurable with economic performance and efficiency. While politicians may sometimes wish this to be otherwise, in the real world in which decisions have to be made, an economistic interpretation and reinterpretation of the pluralism of really existing interests is only rarely feasible, if at all.

Even in an economy, very likely also in an enterprise, and certainly in a republic, collective interests and objectives are not preestablished or self-evident but must be continuously defined and revised. Politics, which in an economistic worldview figures at the same time empirically as corrupt and ideally as the impartial application of technical expertise, is nothing other than an institutionalized practice by which the multiple and in principle irreconcilable goals that exist in a society are—inevitably temporarily and provisionally—accommodated. Subsuming them under a supposed general interest in high rates of return on capital remains a utopian dream of economists, economic technocrats and, of course, capitalists. Economic functionalism, as any theory of collective choice must, abstracts from the vast variety of objectives that coexist in a given society. It does so, however, by reducing that variety to one overarching superobjective: economic competitiveness-cum-efficiency, which is to subsume all others. This overlooks the fact that the existence of multiple and ultimately incommensurable interests is an essential rather than a contingent or ephemeral element of a society—and that efficiency as such is too empty to be anybody's objective except, perhaps, that of economists. Representing a political economy as an integrated single-purpose system is the kind of abstraction that is also a profound misrepresentation.[9]

(5) Assuming nevertheless for the sake of argument that societies could develop, or could be made to develop, a shared and unambiguous dominant interest in institutional efficiency, there would be another fundamental mismatch between economic functionalism and the real world, which concerns the extent to which a visible or invisible systemic rationalizer could know what to do in order to increase institutional efficiency. In fact, what is and what is not efficient is inevitably shrouded behind a veil of *uncertainty*. Uncertainty, rephrasing Beckert (2002, 36), is not an accidental deviation from an underlying relationship between theory and reality, or between observer and observed, in which sufficient investment in knowledge could be made to preclude unpleasant surprises. As suggested in the debate on institutional complementarity (Crouch et al. 2005, Streeck 2004*b*), predicting whether or not and in what respect a proposed institutional reform will "fit" with existing institutions, thereby supposedly enhancing systemic economic performance, vastly overtaxes the cognitive capacities of institution-builders and institutional theorists. Among other things, this seems to be because abstract specifications of desirable institutional properties, such as "flexibility," must be realized under historically unique and therefore only partly understood circumstances. Moreover, causal effects in complex systems are often unpredictable as such, and even more so where they depend on the uncertain strategic reactions of actors in a society ("double contingency") with an unpredictably changing external environment.

Cognitive uncertainty makes any policy proposed to advance institutional efficiency contestable, even if efficiency was a commonly agreed goal. This is so in spite of standard economics, which likes to intimate that single solutions to problems of optimization—assuming that it *is* problems of this kind that are at stake in political economy—can in principle be found and implemented if only its advice is heeded. Much like the multiplicity of interests in a society, cognitive uncertainty opens a space for politics where, and to the extent that, desirable solutions cannot be deductively identified even for agreed problems. Neither what is good performance or systemic survival, nor how it is best achieved can be known with sufficient certainty to preclude conflictual debate and eliminate the need for political power and the authoritative decisions it makes possible. For example, nobody can be sure what sort of social security is required to underpin flexible labor markets, given the needs, "objective" and "perceived," of firms and individuals, and the way they change under the impact of changing technologies, markets, family structures, power relations, and economic cultures.

What "flexicurity" actually *is*, that is to say, and what form of it is maximally economically efficient, is and must be a matter of continuing social, political, and economic experimentation, of successive trial and error, and of tentative approximation requiring not just deductive reasoning and experiential accounting, but also political persuasion and a legitimating societal discourse. In the German case, this applied even more to the policies suggested in the 1990s to update the postwar system of "social market economy," presumably to match changed conditions of global competition. Ends and means alike were sufficiently uncertain to make political conflict both inevitable and necessary. The same holds also for the more liberal economic regime that emerged in the 1990s. Will the established German system of skill formation, long a model for others to emulate, "work" alongside a more flexible labor market and under intensified international competition? Will market incentives be sufficient to contain the sectional conflicts that may come with decentralized wage setting and a growing wage spread? Can a state committed to fiscal austerity sustain the public infrastructure required for an advanced private economy, assuming such infrastructure is required at all? What are the drawbacks, as distinguished from the advantages, of shareholder-oriented management of large firms for the development of economic efficiency in the longer term? There is no way to answer questions like these with enough certainty a priori to rule out contentious political debate.

(6) Finally, designers and redesigners of economic institutions, assuming they had sufficient purpose, power, and knowledge to promote institutional reform for maximum efficiency, do not have a tabula rasa before them on which freely to implement the solutions they think best.

Institution-builders are always faced with an inherited social order which inevitably constrains what they can do. As Niklas Luhmann is reported to have noted, while everything can in principle be changed in a modern society, all cannot be changed at the same time, removing from the reach of reformers and leaving in place a multitude of inherited structures suited for present purposes, if at all, only by accident and less than perfectly. Time, because it is in short supply, is once again of the essence. The same holds in the sense of the past conditioning the present, which is how history makes itself felt not just in society but also in nature.[10] The idea that extant institutions should be instantly available for expedient rebuilding by rational actors pursuing a common goal—that institutional traditions can, as it were, be recalled and reformed anytime if one only wants—is a modern illusion that is particularly deeply engrained in economic and rational choice theories of action. In fact, the presence of history and tradition means, if anything, that *not everything* can be reformed to serve a purpose—implying that in every society, even the most "rational," institutional legacies will be present that are far from maximally efficient from the perspective of current objectives, and the more so the more rapidly the external conditions change that determine whether an institutional arrangement can still perform its designated function.

Theories of action and of institutional change that play down the resistance to rationalization of an inherited social order appear to reflect the experience of a unique society, that of North America, which in its formative period could imagine itself as founded out of nothing by a collective act of will of independent individuals starting, indeed, on a historical tabula rasa (see Offe 2006). This "American dream" became the dream also of liberal progressives in Europe in the nineteenth century and later, who projected their own modern desire for creative freedom in the arrangement of their social circumstances onto the "New World" on the other side of the Atlantic. It was this sentiment to which Goethe gave expression in a poem included in his "Zahme Xenien":

> America, you've got it better
> Than our old Continent. Exult!
> You have no decaying castles
> And no basalt.
> Your heart is not troubled,
> In lively pursuits,
> By useless old remembrance
> And empty disputes.[11]

Current theories trying to account for social order as a product of the rational choice of rational actors undertake to perpetuate in really existing societies the magic of an imagined founding moment by implying that it can be and indeed is being repeated any time:[12] that social order is easily and momentarily at the disposition of every new generation of institutional designers, or engineers, and indeed of anyone feeling a desire to change it, which by definition makes any extant social order freely and consensually chosen. In reality, of course, and especially in the "normal," non-exceptional world of "European" societies burdened with an irrepressible past, individuals, as Durkheim has taught us, are born into a social structure that invariably precedes them, which they encounter as a "hard" external reality that resists their efforts to change it, and with which they must mostly learn to live. This is not at all to imply that an inherited social order, even a "European" one, is necessarily static. For Durkheim, rapid capitalist rationalization—or, as he called it, a rapidly expanding "division of labor"—represented the overwhelming reality of his time, one that changed fundamentally the way people lived together. What he insisted on, however, was that any social change, even the most revolutionary one, is bound to take place inside an already existing society whose past affects what can happen in its present (Durkheim 1964 [1893], 275ff.).[13] Just as freedom exists only in the midst of constraints, change is always surrounded by continuity, and it is only as conditioned by a present shaped in turn by a past that a society can have a future.

It is at this point, where one recognizes the nonrational constraints imposed by historical legacies on the functional organization and reorganization of social structures, rendering the latter inevitably "suboptimal" from a rationalist-constructivist perspective, that we can return to the comparison, briefly touched upon above, between social change and biological evolution. There are many important differences between the two, must fundamental among them that biological species change primarily by random mutation of their genotype while societies change mostly by incorporating new properties in existing phenotypes ("cultural learning"). But there are also parallels such as, importantly, the fact that pressures for adaptation, or efficiency, are not absolute, but depend on historical events and conditions. In part this is why, in remarkable analogy to human societies, the properties of biological organisms cannot be fully accounted for in terms of optimally performed functions for individual reproduction and intergenerational survival.[14] As Mayr (2001, 199) notes: "No organism is perfect; indeed, as Darwin already emphasized, an organism only has to be good enough to compete successfully with its current competitors." Put otherwise, the extent to which an organism is optimized to serve, and can therefore be explained by, its function—the capacity on which it is selected—is historically contingent on the character of the competition that happens to have shown up in its niche. Darwin himself was entirely unambiguous about this:

> As natural selection acts by competition, it adapts the inhabitants of each country only in relation to the degree of perfection of their associates... Nor ought we to marvel if all the contrivances in nature, be not, as far as we can judge, absolutely perfect; and if some of them be abhorrent to our ideas of fitness... The wonder indeed is, on the theory of natural selection, that more cases of the want of absolute perfection have not been observed...   (Darwin 2004 [1859], 507–8)

In fact, biological organisms seem to be peculiar amalgamations of functional and historical properties, where the former are not freely designed—if the word is permitted in this context—but are, and have to be, carved out of or grafted onto inherited historical material with which evolution must make do, even if the eventual result leaves much to be desired.[15] A good example might be the anatomy of the human body (Gould and Lewontin 1979, 594). If biological engineers had to build an optimally efficient bipedal organism, they would surely come up with a skeleton less likely to give its owner backaches; with a position of the skull less prone to causing headaches; and with a spine less conducive to slipped disks. They would also better separate the air pipe from the gullet, saving a considerable number of individuals from suffocation, not to mention separating the reproductive from the digestive system. But "nature" in "creating" a new species is compelled to work with what it has created in the past ("phyletic constraint"). Instead of radical innovation through rational engineering,[16] evolution produces piecemeal modifications on an inherited *"Bauplan"* (Gould and Lewontin 1979), one that might be radically different had natural history taken a different course at critical junctures in a distant past. Evolution, that is to say, comes down to a sequence of ever new improvisations on a theme, or to perpetual conversion of more or less accidentally available structures, such as the basic anatomical traits of the first fish-like vertebrates with their horizontal spine, the straight "wiring" of their nervous system, and their single digestive-cum-reproductive channel inherited, in turn, from more primitive predecessors. Inevitably, the results of evolution taking place within the constraints of natural history remain suboptimal compared to what would be an ideally efficient performance of functions still unknown in the far-away past when the dominant design was established. There is, however, no natural history for nature to work with apart from the history that happens to have happened, and there is no material for evolution to adapt to changing conditions other than the material that evolution itself has generated.

Evolutionary biology may help historical institutionalism develop a concept of a history that is open but not indeterminate; intelligible without being teleological; and full of both critical junctures and path-setting constraints. Among other things, it also suggests highly productive intuitions as to how rational economizing fits into historically existing societies. Economic functionalism constructs stylized efficiency-theoretical genetic mythologies on the origins of social institutions that were in reality never meant to be efficient, such as the welfare state, worker participation, electoral systems, or centralized collective bargaining, systematically misrepresenting them as machinery purposively engineered to increase economic efficiency or match economic needs. For a while, evolutionary biology followed a similar paradigm, until it had to convince itself that not everything in life is adaptive, and what is adaptive is embedded in a contingent historical context that firmly circumscribes what kind of adaptation is possible (Mayr 1988). The surprising lesson from evolutionary biology for social theory and, in particular, political economy is not to confuse causal explanations with retrospectively constructed Panglossian functionalist narratives ("adaptive stories") under a theoretical program that expects to find for each social institution an identifiable rational purpose if only enough time is devoted to searching for it. Instead, the task for political economy is to understand how economizing, including capitalist economizing, is embedded in and shaped by preexisting noneconomic social structures; how capitalist rationalization, driven by a multitude of actors pursuing particularistic interests and acting under incomplete information, proceeds in conflict with a variety of social objectives other than the maximization of efficiency; and how efficiency is generated and encapsulated in the broader context of society.[17]

What drives economizing in a historical context, and how does it proceed in it? As far as the German political economy is concerned, it may or may not be the case that its newly liberalized version—with its decentralized collective bargaining regime, higher wage spread, weakened class associations, market-enhancing social policy, fiscal austerity, privatized public services, and more market-driven corporate governance—is more economically "efficient" than was its corporatist predecessor. If it is, however, this is not, as would be implied in an economistic-functionalist worldview, a result of consensual reform in pursuit of shared economic interests, or the product of some market-like invisible coordination mechanism moving social systems into a stable equilibrium in which they are maximally efficient. The erosion of Durkheimian institutions in Germany and the demise of German organized capitalism proceeded not by design, but through self-contradiction, self-erosion, exhaustion, desertion, and the like. There is no retelling the story told in Part I as a political history of rational institutional redesign and purposive, reformist *Steuerung,*[18] or as a steady process of self-equilibration. Proper appreciation of the embedding of capitalist liberalization in noneconomic historical conditions reveals its contested, contingent, constrained, in a word: historical nature, suggesting among other things that it may best be understood as a phase in a longer, multidimensional evolutionary process in which capitalist rationalization-through-liberalization, effective as it may have been in the period of observation, was and continues to be just one competing social force among others.

Notes

1. I take "economizing" to be the equivalent in institutional economics of the concept of "rationalization" in Weberian sociology.
2. This is the fundamental insight of the "new economic sociology." See Granovetter (1991) and, for a more sophisticated recent version, Beckert (1996, 2003, 2007b).
3. The way this may happen is spelled out in general terms in Streeck (1997a) and (2004a). Also see the section on "Bounded Economizing," in Chapter 17.
4. Which, as Herrmann has shown, is less and less the case in a global economy (Herrmann 2006).
5. The *locus classicus* here is, of course, Adam Smith's astute observation that "people of the same trade seldom meet together, even for merriment and diversion, but the conversation ends in a conspiracy against the public, or in some contrivance to raise prices. It is impossible indeed to prevent such meetings, by any law which either could be executed, or would be consistent with liberty and justice" (Smith 1993 [1776], 129).
6. I refrain here from discussing the possibility of labor rather than capital or the government assuming the role of rationalizing agent in a national economy. Like business, the economic interests of labor lie not in efficiency as such, but in a high (and steady) income, "earned" or "unearned." Efficiency and

international competitiveness may help, but there are also other means to the same objective. Moreover, as will be pointed out later in more detail, labor is interested in social stability even more than capital is. Rationalization in pursuit of economic efficiency, however, inevitably undermines the stability of existing social structures (Polanyi 1957 [1944]).

7. This is not to say that analogies between institutional change and biological evolution are entirely inappropriate. I will suggest, below, a few lessons political economy can learn from evolutionary biology.

8. I leave aside the important issue of whether systems of economic institutions, and in particular national variants of capitalism, may be conceived at all as having to fight for their "survival." Unlike firms, social systems rarely die—which is another reason why a strict selection model of evolution seems less than appropriate.

9. See also Chapter 17, especially the section on the "double movement."

10. The relevant concept in evolutionary biology is "phyletic inertia," or "phyletic constraint" (Gould and Lewontin 1979).

11. Amerika, du hast es besser
als unser Kontinent, der alte,
hast keine verfallenen Schlösser
und keine Basalte.
Dich stört nicht im Innern
zu lebendiger Zeit
unnützes Erinnern
und vergeblicher Streit (1818).

The poem is cited by Offe (2006, 6) as well as by Hirschman (1992, 132).

12. See the interpretation in American labor law in the early twentieth century, as reported by John R. Commons, of the contract of employment as being continuously implicitly renewed: "The labor contract is not a contract, it is a continuing implied renewal of contract at every minute and hour…" (Commons 1924, 285).

13. More specifically, in his polemic against Spencer, Durkheim was adamant in his claim that contractualism did not and could not gradually replace the emergent properties of society, but remained firmly embedded in them (Durkheim 1964 [1893], 200ff.).

14. Not claiming to be an expert in biology, I obviously take sides here with that branch of evolutionism, self-identified as "Darwinian pluralism," that refrains from imposing on itself the obligation to tell an "adaptationist," Panglossian-functionalist efficiency story about everything observed in the biological world, allowing instead for widespread satisficing and suboptimality in natural history (Gould and Lewontin 1979).

15. In his article on "Darwinian Fundamentalism," Gould (1997) quotes a fellow evolutionary biologist to the effect that "Evolutionists are essentially

unanimous that—where there is 'intelligent design'—it is caused by natural selection...Our problem is that, in many adaptive stories, the protagonist does not show dead-obvious signs of Design..."

16. I disregard the question, which is interesting but irrelevant to my argument, whether rational engineering does not in fact work much like natural evolution.

17. See Chapter 17.

18. The German concept of the 1970s for the politically controlled purposive restructuring of social institutions and society in general.

14

Internationalization

But was the liberalization of German capitalism, and especially its acceleration in the 1990s, not simply an effect of economic internationalization, or "globalization"? Rather than looking at the complex interactions between different processes of sectoral change over time, could one not content oneself with standard variable sociology and a simple causal-analytical model in which internationalization—of product, capital, and labor markets—figures as the independent and liberalization as the dependent variable, connected by functionalist assumptions about a positive relationship between domestic liberalization and international competitiveness, with increasing internationalization accounting for a satisfactory percentage of increase in liberalization and disorganization?

Perhaps such a model, based on cross-national comparison or on time series or both, could in fact be constructed, given that some of the changes that we have observed were obviously related, in some way, to changing relations of the German economy with its international environment. The closer one would look, however, the more qualifications one would have to introduce. Above all, any such model would have to be reconciled with the fact that internationalization was nothing new to the German political economy in the 1980s and 1990s, and certainly was far advanced long before its disorganization and liberalization began. In fact, postwar Germany was *organized and internationalized at the same time,* and it was strongly competitive internationally while being highly corporatist domestically. Among other things, this raises the question of why and how the original compatibility and even, perhaps, complementarity between corporatist organization and competitive internationalization in the German case should have been succeeded at the end of the twentieth century by a relationship in which internationalization appears to have undermined organization.

In the following, I will show that internationalization in the 1980s and 1990s did not come as a shock to the German political economy. Nor did it represent an adaptive response to changing economic conditions, engineered by a designing hand in fiduciary pursuit of German national competitiveness. Rather, the new wave of internationalization in the 1990s in particular was no more than another phase in a long historical process of capitalist market expansion which had reached a point where it could continue only by a massive crossing of national borders, also in sectors that had hitherto remained by and large nationally based. This, I claim, was why and how internationalization became linked up with the—also—ongoing process of disorganization and liberalization of national capitalism, which it both reinforced and required. As to its underlying mechanism, internationalization was driven above all by entrepreneurial firms concerned about their competitive position and acting under the impact of the push and pull of evolving domestic constraints and newly arising international opportunities. It was also promoted by state policies responding to growing problems of domestic governability and nationally centered capital accumulation.

As Peter Katzenstein has pointed out in his seminal work (Katzenstein 1987), postwar Germany was from its beginnings more than other countries at the time firmly embedded in an international order that sharply curtailed its sovereignty and in particular precluded any return to economic protectionism or, worse, autarky. The end of postwar occupation was conditional on Germany's integration in a variety of international organizations, among them the European Economic Community and its successors. When reconstruction came to a close, West Germany had become by far the most internationally exposed of the large European economies. For example, even at the beginning of the 1960s, West Germany had accepted a degree of financial openness that was to be attained by other nations, including ones strongly committed to international free trade, only by the mid-1980s (Table 14.1). Also, Germany from early on piled up record trade surpluses year by year. This continued even after the D-Mark was revalued in 1969, and further under the floating exchange rates of the 1970s (Table 12.1).[1] As noted, in the 1980s, Germany's economic success in world markets was such that the country came to be considered, together with Japan, as both a competitor and a model even for a country as powerful as the United States.

Not only was West Germany highly internationally exposed, its political economy was also structured in many ways like that of a small country compensating for its inevitably high international vulnerability

Table 14.1. Index of financial openness,* seven large and small countries, 1960–90

	D	F	UK	US	A	NL	DK
1960	13	8.5	6.5	13	5.5	10.5	7
1965	14	11	6.5	13	9.0	10.5	7.5
1970	14	11	8	12.5	10.0	12	8.5
1975	14	11	8.5	13	10.5	12	10
1980	14	11	14	13	11.5	13	10
1985	14	11	14	13	11.5	14	11
1990	14	11.5	14	14	12.5	14	14

*The index varies from 0 to 14. The highest value means absence of restrictions on payments, on receipts of goods and invisibles and of capital, as well as maximum adherence to international agreements that constrain a nation's ability to restrict exchange and capital flows.

Source: Klaus Armingeon et al., Comparative Political Data Set, 1960–2004.

D: Germany, F: France, UK: United Kingdom; US: United States; A: Austria; NL: Netherlands; DK: Denmark.

by cohesive internal organization.[2] Again according to Katzenstein, West German corporatist organization resembled countries like Austria, the Netherlands, Sweden, Denmark, and others (Katzenstein 1985):[3] it offered protection from international uncertainties while supporting cross-class cooperation in the joint exploitation of international opportunities. For this reason, German nonliberal capitalism was amenable to being interpreted as a strategic response to high international exposure and economic vulnerability, with governments, firms, and trade unions holding each other responsible for joint success in international markets, for example, through wage moderation and high investment in training. National politics appeared focused on organizing the domestic economy so that all of its constituents, in particular capital and labor, could benefit from deep engagement with the international economy.[4]

Why, then, did the disorganization of German capitalism become associated with its internationalization in the 1990s? Rather than in pressures for or policies aimed at systemic competitiveness, the answer must be sought in the nature of the actors involved and their changing position in a changing domestic and international environment. Jumping ahead, I argue that it is a defining disposition of actors in a capitalist economy, in particular of capitalist firms, that they can never be satisfied with a given state of affairs,[5] like a given market share or an institutional shell like that offered by the former *Deutschland AG*, however supportive it may be. Firms competing under capitalism must, if only to hedge against competitors taking the first step and reaping the benefits of the "first mover," and even if they are fully content with their current situation, ultimately seek out whatever new opportunities for expansion may potentially arise. "Internationalization" in the 1980s and 1990s, that is to say, was above all another phase in a continuing pursuit of economic advantage resulting in ever further expansion of market relations, constrained only by the limits of technological capability and no more than modified and, perhaps, temporarily delayed by national borders.

This, however, is only half the story. Internationalization of economic relations and the institutional change it wrought inside the "German model" were clearly also propelled by rising dissatisfaction on the part of business with the accumulating obligations imposed on it inside the corporatist political economy of the 1970s into which the postwar settlement had evolved. This reflects the fact that, unlike what is assumed in functionalist theories, the domestic institutions of the postwar political economy were not just useful Williamsonian instruments for the competitive pursuit of shared economic interests, but also sources of social constraints that firms would not have subjected themselves to voluntarily. Exit is therefore as basic a response of firms to social institutions as is their utilization, primary or secondary, in the perennial capitalist pursuit of competitive expansion. Rather than a break-in of unknown extraneous forces into a well-settled social order, therefore, internationalization resembles at least as much a break-out of powerful domestic actors seeking new opportunities for growth outside the confines of the national political economy, also to shed burdensome obligations imposed on them as a price for being allowed to utilize for private purposes the common pool of their society's good will. Push and pull came together to drive the process of internationalization, which unfolded in an interaction between the internal organization of the national political economy and its changing international context, mediated by the strategic decisions of actors responding to evolving constraints and opportunities in their two environments, international and domestic. It is only with a conceptual template like this that historical "process tracing" will allow us to understand how the changing insertion of the German into the international political economy[6] left its mark on its institutional structure, which was already changing by itself for reasons of its own.

14.1. The Decay of Embedded Liberalism

Putting the above in less abstract terms, postwar capitalism was characterized by a specific configuration between national and international economic governance, for which John Ruggie had coined the influential concept of "embedded liberalism" (Ruggie 1982). German "semi-sovereignty,"

the construction Katzenstein had described, had been one national variant of that general model. Ruggie's concept recognized that capitalism
had for long been a global system, and indeed already Marx and Engels
in the Communist Manifesto of 1848 had declared the "world market"
to have been finally completed.[7] As a consequence, both capitalism and
international politics became beset with a fundamental tension between
the evolving system of nation-states establishing and defending their
sovereignty and assuming responsibility for the welfare of their citizens,
and rising international interdependence due to expanding flows of goods
and capital across national borders.[8] After the Great Depression and the
catastrophic international conflicts caused by nationalist efforts to insure
countries against economic volatility at the expense of other countries,
the postwar settlement represented an ingenious—although, as it turned
out, no more than temporary—solution to the Wilsonian problem, so
spectacularly unsolved in the wake of the First World War, of combining
international free trade with national democracy and at least a modicum
of national sovereignty. In particular, pegged but adjustable exchange
rates made for rapid expansion of international trade, which was urgently
needed for reconstruction. At the same time, they allowed for some sort
of national governance of national economies, both sufficiently circumscribed to avoid international distortions and sufficiently autonomous to
make national sovereignty and democratic politics meaningful and secure
the legitimacy of the reconstructed nation-state, of liberal democracy, and
of a capitalist market economy.

As John Ruggie had been one of the first to note (Ruggie 1998), the
postwar regime of embedded liberalism depended on two highly frag-
ile conditions: moderation in the domestic politics and economics of
included countries and responsible American hegemony in the international arena.[9] Both had ceased to exist in the late 1960s.[10] Worker militancy in Europe and the unilateral American closure of the Bretton Woods
"gold window" had undermined the institutional form invented after the
Second World War for the intersection between the national and international economies. While national governments could no longer deliver
stability, the United States was no longer able or willing to absorb the costs
of instability. After the breakdown of the international economic order
in the early 1970s, the turbulences of the subsequent decade, reinforced
by the "oil crises" of 1973 and 1979, had to be addressed by countries
individually and with whatever national political resources they had at
their disposal. The corporatist experiments of the 1970s in particular
were attempts to deal with the new economic instabilities with national

means, without sacrificing liberal democracy. At first, some countries, including Germany, were more successful at this than others. But in the end, national governments, unable to rely on international discipline for assistance, began to lose control over the spiraling aspirations of their constituents, making the price of domestic peace explode, for governments as well as for capitalist enterprises. The ensuing profit squeeze (Glyn 2006) prepared the ground for a new push for economic internationalization in the 1980s and 1990s when the corporatist institutions, or relations of production, that had emerged as a provisional response to the demise of embedded liberalism, had turned out to be too constraining for further evolution of the productive forces of capitalism. As it happened, this coincided with growing attraction of international markets, made possible by new technologies facilitating internationalization of trade, finance, and production, as well as by the end of Communism and the opening of China, which offered practically endless new opportunities for capitalist expansion and accumulation.

In the 1980s and 1990s, that is to say, what is commonly referred to as internationalization was just another stage in a dynamic historical process in which different configurations between the national and the international followed upon each other. "Model Germany"—the escape of the German high-wage economy into world market niches for specialized premium products in the 1970s and 1980s—was but a short stretch in a long sequence of ever new modes of interpenetration between national capitalism and international markets—and was inevitably short-lived since competing countries, foremost among them Japan, were sure at some point to catch up and restore price competition in German firms' high-quality product markets.[11] Other factors contributed as well to ending the short era of harmonious fit between the evolving structures of international opportunities and German institutional capabilities and constraints. Changing technologies enabled production systems to become more far-flung than ever, in effect extending the labor market of German firms beyond German borders. Simultaneously, the continuing expansion of international free trade regimes, strongly supported by Germany's export-oriented manufacturing industries, as a side effect opened the German domestic market to foreign competition, to an extent entirely unforeseeable in the 1970s. Later, evolving international capital markets changed the conditions for the procurement of finance and set new standards of acceptable and appropriate profitability. These and similar developments coincided with endogenous change inside domestic institutions, among them the growing labor costs caused by the high-equality, low-activity employment regime and the progressive fiscal exhaustion of the state as insurer of last resort of the postwar class compromise. Just as the evolution of German institutions conditioned the strategic uses German actors made of their evolving international environment, changing international constraints and opportunities affected the way German actors behaved in relation to their domestic environment.

Internationalization, then, interacted with and influenced domestic institutional change through the choices of domestic actors responding to how they perceived the range of domestic and international constraints and opportunities confronting them. Internationalization of sales, production, finance, and ownership progressed differently in different firms and sectors (Hassel et al. 2003), depending on where managements saw the least risks, the greatest opportunities, or the most burdensome constraints (Beyer 2001). For some, engagement in newly emerging international markets offered a long-sought chance to escape from the stranglehold of national institutional obligations on business strategies and profitability. It was forced on others by rising competitive pressures, and in particular by a return of price competition, either in foreign or in domestic markets. Yet others again, like Deutsche Bank, became active contributors to internationalization by taking the first steps, later copied by their competitors, into as yet uncharted international markets still in the process of being formed, reaping first-mover profits until competing firms mustered the courage or had no choice but to follow. Far from being a sudden external shock, internationalization of markets and business strategies was active choice and inescapable fate at the same time, and which of the two it was in concrete cases depended to a great deal on how the changing contingencies of German domestic institutions defined the relative costs and benefits of increased exposure to the world economy. The aggregate result was a new stage in the evolving relationship between national and international markets, one characterized by much more liberalism and much less embeddedness than the postwar configuration that Ruggie had described.

A few examples from our five sectoral trajectories of institutional change might be in order. As to *industrial relations,* in the 1990s relocation of production to foreign countries became technologically and politically[12] possible for a growing number of German firms, including small- and medium-sized ones. Apart from the entrepreneurial opportunities offered by low wages and accommodating tax regimes, relocation suggested itself as a response to increasing competition and price pressures in both domestic and international markets. It also was a possible answer to the endogenous rise of German labor costs, whose economic significance was increased by the simultaneous rise in both international competition and opportunities for exit. Even if firms ultimately chose to remain in Germany, which most of course did, they found it more and more tempting to use the effective expansion of their labor markets across national borders to shift the balance of power inside German industrial relations in their favor. In particular, by threatening to relocate their production to other countries in part or in whole, firms could effectively promote decentralization of collective bargaining and contribute to the ascendancy of works councils as surrogate trade unions—something that many of them had always wanted but had never dared to try. Changes in the insertion of the German into the world economy, including more competitive product markets and more demanding financial markets, enabled and sometimes constrained firms to push for a gradual transformation of German industrial relations, toward a new pattern that was not only more favorable to their interests but also more pleasing to their passions: the regulation of employment conditions under market pressures at the workplace (*Verbetrieblichung*), under the cover of a thinned-out industrial agreement protecting firms from strikes while imposing fewer and fewer binding obligations on them.

The changing insertion of the German political economy in its international environment also affected the stability of *intermediary organizations,* especially of employers, and in essentially the same way as industrial relations: by unsettling long-standing settlements between divergent interests, unbalancing historical compromises, and reviving cleavages that had long been kept latent. The ensuing disorganization gave enterprising firms an opportunity to try for more than what for them had always been only a second-best solution: being protected by associations that had for years burdened them with more and more negotiated obligations while offering less and less protection. Growing competitive pressures in international product markets widened the rift, suppressed for a long time but made ever more salient by the accumulating effects of the egalitarian wage regime, between large and small firms organized in the same employer associations. Decentralization of industrial relations, where it ensued, weakened employer associations and, unless they learn to respond by changing their strategy and structure, will weaken trade unions as well.[13] Internationalization thus contributed and continues to contribute to the pivoting of the relationship between encompassing collective bargaining and intermediary organization from mutual support to mutual erosion. Simultaneously, internationalizing production systems and corporate structures made large firms lose interest in corporatist representation at national level, allowing them to hand over national business associations to disgruntled small firms, as a means for satisfying their growing expressive-ideological desires to publicly denounce the cooperative regime of postwar organized capitalism and demand its thorough liberalization.

Not only did internationalization have many facets, but it also affected different institutional spheres differently. *Social policy* had long been supportive of large German firms' forays into the world market, among other things by enabling them to benefit from early retirement of redundant or less productive workers. Later, however, the government presented its desperate attempts to extricate its finances from the stranglehold of rising social entitlements as a necessary measure to defend or restore the international competitiveness of the German economy, although German exporting firms had never ceased to earn huge surpluses in international trade. For the state, internationalization was as much an ideology, or a political strategy to discipline ungovernable domestic interests, as it was an economic fact of life to be accommodated through institutional reform. Above and beyond the rhetoric of international competitiveness, state policies of privatization actively contributed to internationalization as they involved the creation and expansion of markets which, in advanced capitalism, could no longer be confined within national borders. Indeed, wherever disorganization through market expansion became the strategy of choice for a state squeezed between domestic demands for protection and the electoral and economic limits to taxation, it always and inevitably involved opening up national borders.

As to the *German company network*, internationalization undermined its cohesion when changing international markets offered its core members new opportunities that for them tipped the postwar balance between mutual security and individual risk-taking in favor of the latter, offering both higher profits and the prospect of transforming binding into voluntary obligations. Before that, German firms had more often than not relied on each other's support in their quest for world market share and in defending their independence. Exit from national solidarity, as we have seen, was started by the attractions of a sort of entrepreneurship in financial markets that had simply not been envisaged in the founding years of postwar organized capitalism. The first to leave were those who felt strong enough to deal with a more risky economic environment on their own. But once the strong had emigrated from the national risk pool, exit became, not just a choice, but almost a necessity for the rest.[14]

In the same way, *government policies* of market expansion, especially European integration, while initially no more than paving the way for new forms of engagement in the international economy, later effectively forced firms to take this route. When the European Union transformed from an international extension of national Social Democracy, which it was about to become in the 1970s, into the liberalization machine that it finally did become under the Delors presidencies, a broad range of strategic opportunities were opened for both firms and governments no longer willing or able to live with the constraints imposed on them by postwar organized capitalism. Today, for example, the European Court of Justice is undertaking, with increasing self-confidence and in the name of the "four freedoms" of the integrated European market, to undo central institutional legacies, inevitably national in character, of the postwar compromise between capital and labor, like codetermination of worker representatives on the supervisory boards of large German firms (Höpner and Schäfer 2007). The attraction of this to capital and, perhaps, governments is that it shows a way out of organized capitalism and its institutions that bypasses national politics, formally weakening the national state but in reality enabling it to pursue successfully an agenda of economic liberalization, and thereby escape from political commitments on which it can no longer deliver. As international market-making by juridical decree takes legal, and indeed constitutional, precedence over national politics and national legislation, internationalization effectively voids national institutions whose demolition would be extremely difficult if not impossible to achieve if it had to be done by means of national legislation (Scharpf 2007).

Seen from here, the more generic term for the political-economic internationalization that we observe today would be market expansion. While internationalization refers to institutional form, market expansion highlights its content: the fundamental dynamic of capitalism and capitalist development. Indeed, if capitalist development means anything, it is about the inherent need for a capitalist economy to grow by transforming ever more nonmarket relations into market ones.[15] Today, the domestic economies of advanced capitalist countries are already thoroughly subsumed under capitalist relations of production, after the capitalization of agriculture and, in the past two decades, the inclusion of women in wage labor. As a result, further expansion of capitalist market relations can take place only across national borders. In fact, in the countries of the postwar settlement, where capitalism came to be organized into a tight regime of institutionalized social obligations that have proven remarkably sticky and capable of path-dependent reproduction in spite of profoundly changing circumstances, expansion of economic activities and relations beyond national borders is the most obvious way out of the constraining conditions of the postwar past and toward a renewal of the dynamism of capitalist entrepreneurship. This is all the more so since international markets are not only less constrained by social obligations but are also, at least at present, largely immune to attempts to impose such obligations on them, due to the absence of collective actors with sufficient power and legitimacy (Scharpf 1996, 1998a, 1998b).

For German firms, becoming more international when this became possible offered a promising way out of some of the increasingly uncomfortable constraints forced on them within Germany. With domestic institutions becoming ever more restrictive and, at the same time, the new international opportunities becoming more tempting, internationalization of strategies and structures opened a door into a much less regulated environment allowing for inventive new approaches, not least in relation to labor and national tax authorities. Expansion of markets, especially for labor and capital, meant an increase in firms' alternatives and choices. While it did not immediately force firms to exit from national corporatism, it offered them the choice to do so or not, on their own conditions. Unlike what is suggested by a static model like that of a "coordinated market economy," temptations to defect from national risk pools have never been alien to the entrepreneurial instincts of capitalist firms, including German ones. As entanglement in social obligations depresses the market value of economic assets, cutting loose from them may generate irresistible opportunities for profit. For example, some shareholders in German companies under worker codetermination seem to expect, rightly or wrongly, the price of their assets to increase if codetermination were to be abolished by the German government or the European Court of Justice. Rather than workers delaying necessary adjustments in production—which they hardly ever did—this seems to be the real economic explanation for the recent demands of German national business associations for the codetermination legislation of the 1970s to be rescinded.[16]

14.2. Internationalization as Strategy and Opportunity

Using the example of the automobile manufacturer Daimler, Saskia Freye has demonstrated in a fascinating case study how the dissolution of the German company network and the declining organizing capacity of the German nation-state interacted in the 1980s and 1990s with changing international economic opportunities to shift the strategy of German firms—in her case: the model firm of *"Modell Deutschland"*— in the direction of internationalization (Freye 2007). Freye reports how by the mid-1980s, Daimler's top management began to lose confidence in the willingness of Deutsche Bank to defend the firm's stable structure of ownership. Having protected Daimler in the 1970s, at the request of the German government, from an attempt by the Shah of Iran to purchase from the Flick family a large chunk of Daimler stock, the bank now seemed increasingly intent on divesting itself of its shares and handing responsibility for the firm's fortunes to the management or whoever was willing to take it. At about the same time, facing what it believed to be a secular stagnation in the market for automobiles, the management board came to the conclusion that further growth was possible only externally through acquisitions in other sectors. With hostile takeovers becoming a daily practice in the United States, the strategic decision was made to grow by diversification into related industries, such as electronics and aerospace, in order to achieve internal synergies that would make the company as a whole worth more than its parts, thereby deterring potential raiders.[17] The CEO at the time, Edzard Reuter, a card-carrying Social Democrat and son of a prominent postwar political leader, accepted as a matter of personal conviction the idea that a large firm had a responsibility vis-à-vis society as a whole. Not least for this reason, his strategy of sectoral diversification—the building of an *"integrierter Technologiekonzern"*—concentrated on Germany, where he was among other things willing to pick up and reorganize the ailing electronics firm AEG.

Very soon, however, Reuter's national strategy began to falter. Acquisitions turned out to be less easy to integrate or to turn around than expected, and some of the new activities competed with other firms in *Deutschland AG*, resulting in tensions with suppliers such as Bosch as well as with the banks which, apparently, were no longer able to keep competition among their clients in check. Meanwhile, economic pressures mounted for Daimler to develop its international presence, at first in the distribution and assembly of automobiles, then with respect to capital markets and the firm's listing on foreign stock exchanges. In 1993, Daimler became the first German company to be traded at the New York Stock Exchange, a step the management seems to have taken basically for reasons of prestige, not caring or knowing much about the economic consequences. At the same time, difficulties in Germany were on the rise, not just economically, but also politically. Having just assembled one of the largest armaments manufacturers in Europe, clearly not without encouragement by the government, Daimler suffered severely from the sharp cutback in arms spending after 1989. In other respects as well, politics proved unable to pay back the favors the company had done the government, for example when, ultimately in vain, it had tried at huge losses to save AEG. Conflicts on environmental issues, for instance over an attempt to get permission for building a large test track, damaged the company's public reputation and made it obvious that the German state, now under the influence of a rising Green party, could no longer be relied upon as much as in the past to come to Daimler's rescue. Moreover, the European commission intervened to prevent the government subsidizing a new Daimler plant in Germany, forcing the firm to cover the costs on its own and teaching it a lesson on the diminishing power of the national government as organizer of the "German model." Another aspect of the political system becoming more unreliable was growing concerns on the part of the Federal Cartel Office over the firm's nationally focused merger and acquisition policy, which also made for bad public relations and once more signaled the fragility and declining usefulness of the firm's formerly close alliance with the German political system.

In 1995, then, Reuter had to turn over the post of CEO to Jürgen Schrempp, who had previously served as the CEO of Daimler's South African daughter company. Within a few months, Schrempp completely dissociated himself and the firm from Reuter's *integrierter Technologiekonzern*. Under a new political formula—Daimler as a *"Welt AG"* (a "world corporation")—Schrempp closed down or got rid of most of Reuter's German acquisitions, instead expanding internationally within the automobile sector in pursuit of sectoral-international instead of intersectoral-national growth. In 1998 Schrempp announced the takeover of Chrysler, first advertised as a "merger of equals." No longer mentioning what Reuter had regarded a firm's public responsibility, Schrempp became the first and foremost proponent in Germany industry of "shareholder value," making clear that the only constituency to which Daimler would from now on feel obliged was its shareholders. Shortly after the Chrysler merger, English was made the firm's official language, and in line with its new shareholder value ideology, German management was paid American salaries, a large part of which were in stock options. Moreover, in 2000, Schrempp began to acquire Mitsubishi, to put the *Welt AG* on proper trilateral footing.

As to Germany, under Schrempp Daimler began to use all possible ways to avoid paying taxes in its country of origin, including ones that his predecessor had explicitly rejected.[18] Also, an internet platform was developed as a marketplace for suppliers in order to put German supply firms under international price pressures. In 2001, Daimler unilaterally cut the prices it paid to suppliers by 5 percent, introducing practices into German supplier–assembler relations that had until then been mostly confined to the United States. As mentioned earlier, in 1996, the new management cut sick pay entitlements, without having sought agreement with the works council, in line with government and employer association policy after the failure of the Kohl "Alliance." When workers struck in retaliation shortly thereafter, however, Daimler, having put at risk the "social partnership" the firm had built up over decades and afraid of losing market share, was the first to defect from Gesamtmetall's hard line, inflicting damage on the association from which it never recovered. *Gesamtmetall*, of course, was the same association that Daimler's Hanns Martin Schleyer had made the most powerful employer association in Germany and the most important pillar on the employers' side of corporatism in German industrial relations.

It is well known, and need not be elaborated, that the *Welt AG* failed as dismally as did the *integrierter Technologiekonzern*. The issue here is not to second-guess the Daimler management of the day. What matters, rather, is to understand how, in the case of the most important manufacturing firm in what used to be the German company network, constraints and opportunities both within the German system and in its international environment came together in the 1980s and 1990s to cause strategic changes that, more or less intentionally and inevitably, amounted to a departure from the traditional national context in favor of increasing involvement in the global economy. Daimler having led the way, German capitalism has for almost two decades now been breaking out of the national institutional forms it had been given after 1945, expanding into new international arenas in an effort to recover its dynamism and free itself from uncomfortable social obligations that had restricted entrepreneurial initiative and profitability. In the 1980s and 1990s, escape from the social-democratic legacies of democratic capitalism, as reinforced in the turbulent 1970s, came to be bound up with the emancipation, more possible than ever due to technological change and the maturation of markets, from the protective control, or the controlling protection, of the national state. In this situation, defending the postwar embedding of markets in political control would have required defending the political-economic capacity of the nation-state—something, however, in which nation-states themselves had become less and less interested.

In fact, as the history of European integration as an international project pursued by national states shows, it was not just capitalist firms that found nationally organized capitalism increasingly constraining. In the 1970s, European integration had still been sought by governments as a backup for the "social dimension" of postwar capitalism. However, with the capacity of democratic governments to subsidize peaceful cooperation between capital and labor withering away, integration of the European economies began to take the form of international market-making, facilitated by the absence of Durkheimian institutional restraints in the international arena. As internationalization of markets for products, capital, and labor set enterprises free from the restrictive terms of national political-economic settlements, it also opened an opportunity for the nation-state to cast aside obligations such as the provision of full employment that it had been able to discharge only for a historically limited time, if at all. This is why "globalization" today, in Germany as elsewhere, is both a political and an economic project, a project of the state as well as of entrepreneurial firms seeking new opportunities for growth and profit. While it weakens the state in that it reduces its power and limits its traditional functions in the capitalist economy, it also liberates it from burdens it can no longer carry, and in this sense strengthens it. This apparent contradiction, which ceases to be one if placed in the historical perspective of capitalist development in the twentieth century, is at the heart of the many misunderstandings about the role of politics and the nation-state in "globalization" that tend to lead contemporary debates in the social sciences astray.

To conclude, the internationalization of the German political economy was not the result of an external shock imparted in the 1980s upon a static regime of "coordinated" capitalism. Rather, it reflects a historical period in which the mode of governance of global capitalism—or, which is the same: the institutional form of the insertion of national economies in the world economy—was and continues to be changing after the end of the postwar settlement. Unlike the postwar era, capital today no longer needs the protective shell of the democratic nation-state, neither for political nor for economic reasons. In fact, having for some time found it increasingly constraining, it has also gradually acquired the capacity to extricate itself from it. The national state, for its part, has progressively lost its capacity to govern a capitalist political economy that can expand only by crossing national borders. As capital wants out, the state can no longer keep it in, and therefore no longer wants to try. Internal accumulation of tensions and dysfunctions over time in domestic regimes of organized capitalism coincide with favorable external political and technological developments to promote another wave of liberalization in the history of capitalism, in the form of further advancement of economic internationalization in new directions and in new forms.

14.3. A Note on Endogeneity

Was not 1989, the end of Communism, all that one needs to mention in order to account for the dissolution of Germany Inc.? Historically it is important to remember that "1992"—the project to complete the European "Internal Market"—dated from 1985, preceding 1989 by four years. Moreover, as early as 1984 the French turn to a hard currency economic policy had ended the era, first, of national protectionism in Europe, and second, of any credible attempt at a European industrial policy building Europe into an economic fortress. Shortly thereafter, the European Commission under Jacques Delors managed to reconcile large European firms with European integration—which until then they had still suspected to be a social-democratic project for labor-inclusive corporatist governance at supranational level—by promising them a new wave of economic internationalization, not just within Europe but also beyond its borders.

1989 was undoubtedly a turning point, and indeed a moment of great economic opportunity as would become apparent in subsequent years. But what it was ultimately used for depended on and was conditioned by the then existing predispositions and intentions of those able and willing to take advantage of it. By the end of the 1980s large capital had already been on the jump, more than prepared to extend finally and for good its activities beyond national borders. That this was so was due, in short, to the historical accumulation of profit-squeezing social obligations in national political systems since the 1970s, which had reached a point where the innate tendency of capitalism to expand its markets was less than ever diluted by whatever political benefits of industrial patriotism were still to be had.

As the politically embedded capitalism of the postwar era lost its remaining attraction to capital in the 1980s, the breakdown of Communism was one event among others that triggered and accelerated a new push forward in the secular process of capitalist land-grabbing. Generally, while external conditions do matter in that they either impede or facilitate change, in social systems change as such is always in an important sense endogenous, for at least two reasons. One, for a stimulus in the environment of a system of action to be met with a response it must be interpreted and processed internally, and to what effect this is done depends as much on the system's internal state as on the stimulus as such. Put otherwise, whatever the stimulus there is always more than one response on the part of a social system, that is, one with agentic capacities, and which response is selected is determined not by the stimulus but by the actor, whoever it may be. Two, following Schumpeter (Schumpeter 2006 [1912]), if change is to mean transformation of existing structures, or the replacement of old structures with new ones—in other words, innovation—it cannot come about as a normal response of the existing system as determined by its established routines and operating procedures. Instead it requires actors willing and able to make risky decisions under high uncertainty that are precisely not determined and predicted by the past. After its experience with the European welfare state in the 1970s and 1980s, European capital, including German large firms, was ready to use any window of opportunity to break out into new and larger fields in which they could experiment with new structures and strategies, abroad and at home. The end of Communism was certainly welcome. Had it not happened, however, other opportunities would have been encountered, or better: other events would have offered themselves to be perceived and creatively used as opportunities for ending the era of capitalism in its nationally organized form.

Notes

1. According to the International Monetary Fund's World Economic Outlook Database, after the second oil crisis, the German current account balance went positive in 1982 and remained so until unification. For one decade, from 1991 to 2000, it showed a deficit before it turned positive again in 2001. In 2005, the surplus amounted to 4.6% of GDP. By comparison, the current account of the United Kingdom became negative in 1982, in spite of North Sea oil, and has remained so ever since (at −2.4% of GDP in 2005). The US account went

negative also in 1982 and, with the exception of one year (1991), remained in a permanent deficit (at −6.4 in 2005).

2. The smaller a country, the greater its international exposure, measured by quantitative political science as the sum of imports and exports in percent of GDP. Country size and vulnerability are always found to be strongly negatively related. Germany is an outlier in that its vulnerability is higher than it would be expected to be given its size. Thus in 2004, the vulnerability coefficient for the United States was 25.4 and for Japan, 20.0. For united Germany, with roughly half the population of Japan and a quarter of the population of the United States, it was 71.1. For France, Italy, and the United Kingdom, all large countries but smaller than Germany, it was clearly *below* the German level, at 51.7, 52.5, and 53.4, respectively. Smaller countries' coefficients of vulnerability were, as expected, higher than Germany's, but not much higher: Austria had a score of 97.3 in 2004, Denmark of 86.4, Sweden of 83.8, and Switzerland of 85.1 (Armingeon et al., Comparative Political Data Set, 1960–2004).

3. "Germany provides perhaps the closest approximation to the political practices characteristic of the small states. West Germany's corporatism derives as much from openness, dependence, and a sense of vulnerability brought about by the diminished size of the Bonn Republic after 1945 as from the implementation of its political parties in fresh democratic soil" (Katzenstein 1985, 200f.).

4. This, of course, leaves aside the crucial question how far a functionalist explanation of national solidarity as a response to external economic vulnerability can in fact carry. See Chapter 13, on "Economizing." Rather than causally explaining corporatist organization by pressures for competitiveness, it is sufficient here to note that it was apparently amenable to being used as insurance against economic uncertainty, in the mode referred to by Gould and Lewontin (1979) as "epiphenomenal adaptation," or "secondary utilization" of elements not originally produced for adaptation.

5. More precisely, an ideal-typical disposition that evolves to become increasingly real and dominant, growing in and on capitalist actors as capitalism becomes more capitalist over time. The main mechanism responsible for this is competition. See Chapter 17.

6. International insertion is one of five "institutional forms" by which French regulation theory characterizes national political economies. The four others are the monetary regime, the wage-labor nexus, the citizen-state nexus (the welfare state), and the competition regime (Boyer and Saillard 2002).

7. "Modern industry has established the world market, for which the discovery of America paved the way ... " (Section I).

8. This, of course, is the central theme of Polanyi's "Great Transformation" (Polanyi 1957 [1944]), and a theme to which we will return in the final chapter.

9. To be sure, the relation between the two was far from straightforward. Countries with strong Communist Parties, France and Italy in particular, were more often than others allowed to tolerate domestic inflation and devalue their currencies at other countries' expense, so as to enable their pro-Western governments to keep them in the Western camp.

10. Here again, one could make the case that they could not have lasted forever as they were bound to consume themselves or wither away over time.

11. As Joseph Schumpeter famously pointed out, product advantage in capitalism can never be more than temporary as it lasts only until the next competitor manages to catch up.

12. This refers to the historical defeat of Communism in Eastern Europe, which opened the region up for foreign investment. Because of the spatial proximity, Eastern Europe is a particularly attractive production location for German firms.

13. *IG Metall*, for one, is considering decentralizing its operations in response, enabling workplace organizations to negotiate firm-specific amendments to the industrial agreement, thereby preventing works councils from taking the place of the union.

14. Here, too, the principle applies that competitive markets are opportunity and constraint at the same time: as soon as enough firms behave competitively, or have pressured the state to remove restrictions on competition, other firms are forced to compete as well, even if they would have preferred to do without the additional opportunities and be protected from the risks associated with them.

15. This is something on which early analysts of the emerging capitalist order always agreed, from Left to Right, from Marx and Engels to Weber and Schumpeter. Rosa Luxemburg's metaphor of capitalism depending for its very survival on continuously progressing *Landnahme* (colonization of the "land") would have been approved by all of them without hesitation (Luxemburg 1913). In the pacified world of the postwar democratic compromise, the inherent dynamism and restlessness of capitalism was temporarily forgotten, or memory of it was suppressed.

16. "Wer es zulässt, dass die mitbestimmte Deutschland AG den Kurs der Aktien drückt, soll jetzt nicht auch noch um diese Unternehmen Schutzzäune bauen." The *éminence grise* of German neo-liberalism, Otto Graf Lambsdorff, responding to a question on whether Germany should legally restrict the possibility of foreign investors to buy up German companies. *Frankfurter Allgemeine Sonntagszeitung*, January 6, 2008, 31.

17. Interestingly, the rationale was the opposite of the current belief that a conglomerate tends to be worth less than its parts sold individually. The difference is made by the expectation of technology-based synergies.

18. *Frankfurter Allgemeine Zeitung*, March 12 and June 27, 1998. Not least because of its high losses, Daimler paid no taxes at all in Germany for several years.

See also *Tageszeitung*, May 11, 2005: "After the Chrysler takeover in December 1998, the then CEO, Schrempp, announced that the (German) Minister of Finance would for a considerable period of time receive not a penny from his corporation since the costs of the expensive takeover of the tumbling US auto manufacturer were tax-deductible in Germany. It took until 2003 for the firm, again according to Schrempp, to resume paying German taxes." A public scandal was caused when after the Chrysler merger, the German management chose to pay their personal taxes no longer in Germany but in the United States.

15

German unification

If internationalization was not a one-time event that affected the "German model" from the outside, the unification of the country in 1990 certainly was. Unlike the almost continuous gradual change during the postwar period in the way Germany was linked into the world economy, unification hit German politics and the German economy unexpectedly and required them to address, from one day to the next, problems of a kind and magnitude that were entirely unprecedented. In most theories of institutional change, historical accidents of this sort—exogenous to the social order they affect, in that they cannot be predicted from internal causes—are expected to do one of two things: they may either set in motion a process of systemic self-stabilization that ultimately results in the restoration of a former stable state, perhaps after a prolonged period of crisis and recovery, or they may transform the system fundamentally by shifting it to a new equilibrium. Which of the two alternatives applies in a particular case would depend on the magnitude of the shock. In much of current theorizing on institutions and social order, it is only through powerful exogenous events such as wars, conquest, revolution, the redrawing of national boundaries or the like, that social systems may be pushed at "critical junctures" and in "formative moments" from one equilibrium condition to another,[1] while normally they are assumed to maintain their stability through balancing responses to whatever fluctuations may occur in their environment.

Applying this template to the case at hand, discussion of the impact of unification on the German political economy would require inspection of the empirical evidence in order to do two things. First, it would have to establish whether the change observed in Germany since unification was in fact caused by the events of 1989 and 1990 and would not have occurred without them. Then, second, if unification was found to have been of consequence, a decision would have to be reached between two possibilities: that the changes observed subsequently were reactions to the challenges of unification that will restore the old system with time (in this case, the shock of unification might have been strong enough to cause temporary disturbances, but ultimately would have been too weak to do away with the old order and force transition to a new one), or, alternatively, that the present, or emerging, political-economic institutions in Germany represent a new equilibrium different from what it would be had unification not occurred.

The problem with this approach is that it assumes a basically static social order that can change meaningfully only if disrupted by a powerful shock while normally it will return to its original condition, although sometimes only after an interlude of critical turbulence. Not only is this at odds with a view of social systems as processes—as strongly suggested by inspection of the German case, among other things. In such a view, whatever may be "restored" decades after an event cannot possibly be identical with what existed before it, shaped as it would be by a different past and the experiences and expectations these would have indelibly produced. It also would seem to make little sense to speak of a crisis of an *existing* system if the time during which that system would de facto *not* be existing may last a generation or longer.[2] Moreover, equating change with disruption by catastrophic events precludes the possibility of gradual transformative change of the sort described in our account of parallel disorganization in five sectors of the German political economy. While it is true that disruptive change should never be ruled out, neither as we have seen should slow and gradual change. Assuming both to be possible, it becomes an empirical question whether a single event such as unification was powerful enough to change profoundly and from the outside a social order conceived, as it should be, as inherently dynamic and in flux.

In the case of Germany and the evolution of the German political economy, that question does not seem difficult to answer. Considering unification in the context of the longer-term trajectories of change over three decades that we have constructed, there appears to be ample evidence that, rather than setting in motion something radically new, unification primarily reinforced and bundled together, and thereby perhaps accelerated, gradual processes of transformative institutional change that had long been going on. In part, ironically, it did so by bringing to a halt political efforts in the late 1980s at institutional reform that conceivably might have slowed, modified, or even stopped these processes.[3] As a result, unification was carried out as a transfer to the former GDR of exactly the same West German institutions (Lehmbruch 1991, 1993, 1994, 1995) that by the late 1980s had already begun to show critical signs of exhaustion and dysfunction. Since in the judgment of the government of the day, institutional reform of the West German system and the incorporation of the former GDR in it were impossible to achieve simultaneously—which they probably were (Ritter 2006, 161)—the problems associated with unification came to be added to the already accumulating problems of a "German model" whose logic of action, as enshrined in its institutions, had been made sacrosanct by unification, at least for the time being. Already in this sense, the institutional crisis that became manifest following unification in the 1990s cannot really be considered exogenous, as its substance and extent were importantly affected by the endogenously formed and historically conditioned behavior of actors beholden to the political and institutional traditions of the West German system.

Reviewing the processes of change that preceded German unification, the exodus of small firms from employer associations in the metal industry and elsewhere began already in the early 1980s (Table 3.1), and this was when union membership, after the intermediate peak in the early 1970s, also began to fall. It is true that in the 1990s, the attrition of organized industrial relations proceeded much faster in the East than in the West, but there is nothing to suggest that without unification it would have progressed significantly less rapidly in the West than it did. Social security contributions had started to increase in the early 1970s, and their rise after 1990 simply continued an established trend (Figure 4.1). What changed after unification was that federal subsidies to the social security funds had to rise as well in order to prevent contribution rates from becoming economically even more unsustainable than they already were when they had reached 40 percent. It seems clear that without reform, subsidies would have had to rise in any case, even in the absence of unification, to slow down and arrest the increase in contributions, but the breaking point would have been attained several years later. Public debt had been rising steeply since 1974, and the same holds for debt service (Figure 5.1). Public borrowing may have been lower in the 1990s without unification, but it is also quite conceivable that the ceilings imposed by the run-up to Monetary Union would have been exhausted by West Germany alone, given the general political attraction of using future instead of present resources to satisfy present demands. Privatization started as early as the late 1980s, in a first attempt to cut fiscal deficits (Figure 5.2). The idea was made more familiar by unification, when early on the government envisaged covering its entire costs, and indeed making a profit, by selling off East German firms to the private sector. Later, it turned out that privatization of East German industry was possible only with hundreds of billions of subsidies for buyers, which made privatization of West German assets for fiscal reasons even more necessary than it had already been in the 1980s.[4] But then, privatization would have proceeded even without unification in the course of the completion of the European Internal Market, with the pressures it put on governments to open up national infrastructures to international competition. Also, the disintegration of the German company network began before unification and had nothing to do with it at all when it continued thereafter, and the same applies to the growing turbulences in large German firms in the 1990s (Figures 6.2 and 6.3).[5]

Where unification did resemble internationalization was that the way it played out was shaped by the strategic decisions of actors steeped in West German habits and institutions. As mentioned, reforms of the West German system, including early retirement and pensions, that were being debated in the late 1980s were halted when unification became a possibility, partly because there was no space any more on an overcrowded political agenda. But other factors also seem to have played a role, among them fear that tinkering with the West German system in the course of incorporating a former Communist country might set in motion uncontrollable developments unwelcome to powerful domestic interests, for example, in health care or education (Lehmbruch 1994). There was also the concern that opening up the West German system for general revision could critically undermine support for unification in the West while inviting political retaliation by a new electorate in the East eager to join the West Germany they knew, or believed to know, and likely to become suspicious if it was suddenly revised upon their arrival.

Note that unification, when it happened, took the legal form of accession to the Federal Republic of five successor federal states to the former GDR—the *"neue Länder"*—and explicitly not of the creation of a new state succeeding both of the two states into which postwar Germany had been divided. This was the logical consequence, among other things, of economic and monetary union having preceded unification in early 1990, when the East German currency was exchanged one-to-one for the West German D-Mark. While many, including the head of the Bundesbank who resigned over the matter, were certain that this spelled economic disaster—which it did—it took into account that East Germans would have migrated to the West in massive numbers had their former country been turned into a low-wage enclave of the unified German economy. The one-to-one exchange rate was also, obviously, good politics since it assured the return of the Kohl government in the first general election of the unified country in the fall of 1990.

The introduction of the D-Mark in East Germany at a politically expedient but economically catastrophic exchange rate was only the first step in what Lehmbruch and others have described as a unique historical experiment in the wholesale transfer of a complete national institutional system from one country to another (Lehmbruch 1993, 1996). Especially interesting from the perspective of this study are the extension to East Germany, already before or shortly after unification, of the West German collective bargaining regime; of West German intermediary organizations; and of West Germany's entire social security system. There were numerous good reasons for this in the political and institutional logic of the West German system, which for the actors at the time obviously prevailed over or eclipsed the profound economic risks associated with the course that was eventually taken. Organized capital and labor were both convinced that they could not allow a low-wage area to emerge in the East to undermine both the wages of Western workers and the market share of Western firms while at the same time posing an unpredictable risk of political radicalization. Transferring in one big step all valid collective agreements to Eastern workplaces, combined with joint efforts to set up regional bargaining machinery and a functioning works council system and followed shortly by "escalator" agreements to equalize East and West German wages within a few years,[6] seemed to have been without alternative in an established system of consensual industrial relations that was, for one last time, successfully mobilized to address a national problem perceived to require responsible cooperation from all parties.[7]

With respect to intermediary organization, West German unions had in the decades before unification almost eliminated their Communist factions and were determined to avoid seeing them reinvigorated, or reemerge as separate organizations, first in the East and then, perhaps, in the country as a whole. East German unions therefore had to be absorbed into the West German system of politically encompassing *Einheitsgewerkschaften*, but only after they had been purged, one way or other, of their Communist officials.[8] While employer associations could start from scratch, they had to be aware of former Communist managers, now running their former establishments as privatized firms, setting up competing associations (Ritter 2006, 312). Just as would have been the case with separate regionally or politically based unions, this would have undermined a corporatist industrial relations system that depended on effective representational monopolies on both sides of the industrial divide.

As to social policy, the *Sozialpolitiker* of all parties recognized unification as a unique opportunity to protect the West German welfare state from mounting pressures for reform by extending it to the country as a whole and thereby vastly increasing its social base.[9] Moreover, for trade unions and the Social Democratic Party, full inclusion of East Germany into the West German social welfare system, including old-age pensions and early retirement—that is, "Social Union" complementing Monetary and Economic Union—was a fundamental condition of their eventual support for unification on the government's terms. That the government did not seriously object had obvious electoral reasons, but it was probably also motivated by the expectation that privatization and restructuring would impose considerable hardship on East Germans that must not be allowed to generate disaffection with unification or with liberal democracy and capitalism. In an interesting sense, this amounted to the definitely last instance of social policy largesse motivated by the postwar "system conflict" with Communism.

More generally, widespread optimism at the time with respect to the economic prospects of the united country[10] prevented almost everybody, including organized employers, from realizing that together with the politically expedient but economically unrealistic rate of exchange and the jointly agreed high-wage policy of trade unions and employer associations, the wholesale transfer of the West German solidarity apparatus to the *Neue Länder* prepared the ground for the extraordinarily high unemployment rates and the declining rates of economic activity that were to become emblematic of East Germany in subsequent years (Wiesenthal 2003). In fact it did not take much time for exactly the same mechanism to begin to operate, only on a larger scale, that had already been at work for roughly a decade in the old West Germany: the use of social protection to support economic restructuring and social peace under an egalitarian wage setting regime by taking surplus labor out of the market. With one integrated welfare state for the entire country, growing side effects on West Germany, where the bulk of social security contributions had to be raised, were inevitable, causing unemployment throughout Germany to spiral upward together with ever-growing social security contributions.

The way unification was implemented was designed to protect the West German status quo, although in fact it had the opposite effect since it made the West German system even less sustainable than it already was. West German actors were motivated by self-interest, but there was also a strong normative commitment on the part of many, including the representatives of employers, to one of the most important institutionalized values, or political imperatives, of the old West German system, which was keeping social inequality within narrow limits. "*Modell Deutschland*" had little if any tolerance for regional differences in incomes and living standards, as expressed not just in the central coordination of wage bargaining within unions and employer associations but also in the constitutional provision for the federal government to ensure "equal living conditions" in the *Länder*.[11] Mass migration as a solution to regional disparities was never really considered and was indeed abhorred throughout the unification process and the decade that followed it. Tellingly, it took several years for the employers of the metal industry to realize that their escalator agreement with the union to bring East German wages up to the West German level not only ruined East German industry but also threatened to destroy their own organization.

Another old West German habit that was allowed to shape the course of unification was increasing social security contributions in order to avoid tax increases. To make unification palatable to the West German electorate, the Kohl government had promised that it would be achieved without raising taxes. Inevitably, this implied that the social costs of restructuring in the East, however high, would have to be borne by the social security funds, which meant that they were paid, in effect, by workers in employment out of payroll taxes. Full extension of the West German welfare state to East Germany was, of course, an essential condition for this to be possible. Although the "social partners" must have at least vaguely known the risks for the social security system inherent in Kohl's refusal to raise taxes, they seem to have accepted them as a quid pro quo for the continuation and extension of the welfare state in its established form. They also seem to have looked forward, as they always had in the past, to another increase in the size of the parafiscal budgets that they at least partly controlled. Later, it turned out that rising contributions meant declining employment, not just in the East but also in the West, and in addition had disastrous consequences for the cohesion of West German employer associations, the stability of corporatist cooperation at the national level and the sustainability of the welfare state as such, including its institutional infrastructure. In the end, when contributions had reached their economic limit, tax subsidies to the social security system had to grow rapidly. With tax increases ruled out, also because of rising tax competition in the integrated European economy, and with budget deficits above the Maastricht limit and debt service consuming a rapidly rising share of federal expenditure, the mold finally broke, and the West German welfare state came to be transformed profoundly in the Schröder reforms.

It took a few years, until after the end of the short economic boom caused by unification, for the self-destructive effects of the extension of the West German system to the East to become fully visible. Unification increased the heterogeneity of the national economy governed by the de facto centralized West German wage setting regime, reinforcing developments that had for some time been under way and exacerbating the tensions they had produced. Symptomatic of this was the fate of *Gesamtmetall*, the national federation of employer associations in the metal engineering industry, during the 1990s. Having fully endorsed the escalator policy at the time of unification, it later, after the subsequent collapse of the East German economy and under pressure from its new Eastern member associations, tried to have the agreement rescinded (Turner 1998, 1–16). When the union refused, *Gesamtmetall* unilaterally canceled the agreement, followed by a strike in May, 1993, that the union won.[12] Having had to give in, *Gesamtmetall* not only saw its losses of members in the East accelerate, but it also had from then on to live with a regional association, the one in Saxony, that was fundamentally opposed to the West German approach to industrial relations and social partnership. A few years later, when *IG Metall* called another strike in the East, this time to bring working hours down to the West German level, the low density of employer association membership in the region and the militant antiunionism of regional employer associations combined with the self-interest of the workforces of West German manufacturers in a steady flow of East German supplies to inflict the worst defeat yet on what used to be a trade union proud of its industrial muscle. The resulting factional infighting in *IG Metall* almost tore the union apart.

As to trade unions in general, the takeover of their Communist counterparts in East Germany after unification, in whatever form, caused a sharp increase in membership which, however, was followed by successive years of catastrophic losses. At first, West German unions had expected unification to put an end to their evolving membership crisis, and all of them invested heavily in building up regional organizational units in the *Neue Länder*, also because these provided a welcome receptacle for a growing surplus of middle-level officials in the West. When the initial membership boom in the East turned out to have been little less than a statistical artifact, the financial crisis that many West German unions had begun to experience in the 1980s worsened rapidly from year to year. One consequence was that the trend toward merger between industrial trade unions that had started in the preceding decade accelerated. Importantly, as pointed out, the mergers that occurred followed a financial and political rather than an industrial logic (Fichter 1993; Müller and Wilke 2003). Among other things, this resulted in more rather than less interunion competition for members—a rivalry that industrial unionism and affiliation to a common federation had been designed to preclude (Ritter 2006, 311). The "Wild East," as it came to be called among union officials, with its rapidly narrowing membership potential, became a testing ground for new competitive strategies which were then transferred to the West. Moreover, as the financial base of East German regional union organizations eroded, many trade union offices could be maintained only by attaching them closely to the local bureaus of the Federal Labor Administration, the *Bundesanstalt für Arbeit*, or to the plethora of semi-public organizations offering training courses for the unemployed paid for by the *Bundesanstalt*. Like in the late nineteenth and the early twentieth century (Heidenheimer 1980; Manow 2007; Steinmetz 1991), the parastate institutions of self-government of the Bismarckian social security system were used by weak trade unions for organizational support, in a sometimes almost parasitic fashion and more often than not in a form that bordered on the illegal. For example, it seems to have been quite frequent for full-time local union officials in East Germany to draw their salary, not from their union, but from a perfunctory second job as manager of an organization carrying out active labor market policy measures on behalf of and paid by the Federal Labor Administration.

It has already been recounted how unification and the way it was conducted accelerated the financial crisis of the social security system and the fiscal crisis of the postwar German state. In the end, the postponement of reform on the eve of unification preserved not the system, but only its self-undermining dynamic. The upshot is that as social systems are in fact processes, the real choice is not between change and stability, but between different directions of change, within the parameters of given historical constraints. Unification reinforced a process of transformation that had already been in progress and that, without it, might perhaps have proceeded less rapidly and in a less politically costly fashion. The Schröder reforms in 2003 and 2004 did what could and perhaps would have been done already at the time of unification, after problems had accumulated to cause much stronger resistance and far higher political costs. However, at the time of unification the political interests in sustaining what was already then an unsustainable system had become so strong that policy probably had no choice but to let the system's self-undermining forces run their course for yet another decade.

Unification was a one-time exogenous event, but the way it played itself out was mostly determined by endogenous factors. While not caused internally, it was processed internally. Unification itself was not predictable from the inside of the German system, although its consequences might have been. Actors, however, were too immersed in their acquired habits and conventions, and perhaps too constrained in their practical alternatives to worry about them. Studied optimism may have been the most rational response to an overwhelming set of uncertainties and a very narrow strategic corridor. The shock of unification neither moved the German political economy to a new equilibrium, nor was it absorbed by a self-stabilizing response restoring the old order. Rather, it reinforced and accelerated an endogenous process of disorganization that had long been under way. By preserving what existed at the time, including its self-undermining dynamics, unification contributed to continuing systemic transformation through gradual institutional change.[13]

Notes

1. Like, for example, after the defeat of the Nazi regime in Germany or at the end of the Second World War in Europe, when the transition was made under American hegemony to a reconciliation between capitalism and democracy. Note, however, that even in moments like this there may be more continuity than meets the eye, as pointed out for example by Thelen (2004) for the German vocational training system.
2. Cf. the following chapter, on "History."
3. In his history of social policy during unification, Ritter quotes a letter written in August, 1990, by the then Minister of Labor and Social Affairs Norbert Blüm, indicating that the governing parties had agreed early on "not to use the opportunity of unification to try to resolve old points of contention by means of the legislation regulating the transition." Blüm's undersecretary Jagoda, one of the most influential social policymakers at the time, referred all demands for reform to a later legislature representing all of Germany (Ritter 2006, 294).
4. When the *Treuhandanstalt*, created in 1990 as a holding company for the state-owned industries of the former GDR, was dissolved in 1994, its total revenue had been about DM 60 billion from the privatization of its assets, compared to about DM 300 billion it had to pay to buyers as subsidies. Its estimated debt of about DM 200 billion (€100bn) had to be absorbed ultimately by the (West) German taxpayer.

5. For the large firms of the German company network of old, East Germany continues to be a *quantité négligeable*. None of them has moved there—or, for that matter, to Berlin—and there is not a single East German firm that would matter at the national level in terms of its size or market share.

6. As, for example, in the metalworking industry where *IG Metall* and *Gesamtmetall* agreed in March, 1991, to increase East German wages gradually over three years, by 1994, from 65 to 100% of the West German level (Ritter 2006, 315; Turner 1998, 3).

7. This assessment is based on interviews, conducted in 2001 and 2002, with leading representatives of trade unions and employer associations at the time of unification.

8. A union like *IG Metall*, which still had a Communist minority faction, insisted on its East German counterpart dissolving itself before it took over its members. By comparison, the Union of Chemical Workers, which had been more effectively purged in the 1970s, could afford to incorporate the respective East German union as a whole, together with those of its officials who were prepared to declare in writing their allegiance to the new system. On these and other aspects of West German unions during unification, see Fichter (1997), Fichter and Kurbjuhn (1992), and Wilke and Müller (1991).

9. As reported in several interviews with leading participants.

10. An optimism that, in large part, seemed to have been purposefully adopted since politically there may have been no real alternative to the extension of the welfare state to the East. Certainly there was none in the perception of almost all relevant political actors.

11. Article 72 (1) speaks of *"Herstellung gleichwertiger Lebensverhältnisse im Bundesgebiet"* ("establishment of equal living conditions"); Article 106 (3) of *"Einheitlichkeit der Lebensverhältnisse im Bundesgebiet"* ("uniformity of living standards throughout the federal territory").

12. In part the strong support for the union in the strike of 1993 was motivated by the peculiarities of the West German welfare state. Many workers in the East had apparently already resigned themselves to the prospect that they would lose their jobs sooner or later. Since the amount of unemployment benefit, unemployment assistance and old-age pensions under early retirement rules depended on what a worker had been paid in his or her last job, many workers were willing to insist on full implementation of the escalator clause although they knew that this might accelerate their—presumably inevitable—march into unemployment.

13. *"Das von der Sozialdemokratie im Wahlkampf 1976 propagierte 'Modell Deutschland', das zunächst international als Synonym für die relativ reibungslose Bewältigung der Probleme des wirtschaftlichen Strukturwandels durch die Einbindung von Gewerkschaften und Wirtschaftsverbänden in ein neokorporatistisches System der Interessenvermittlung viel Anerkennung fand, geriet schon vor 1990, u.a. durch strukturelle Arbeitslosigkeit . . . , unter Druck"* ("Propagated by the Social Democrats in

the 1976 electoral campaign, *Modell Deutschland* initially met with widespread recognition internationally as a synonym for overcoming relatively smoothly the problems of economic structural change by involving unions and trade associations in a neocorporatist system of mediating interests, but became subject to pressure even before 1990 because of structural unemployment, among other reasons..." (Ritter 2006, 133). Elsewhere, Ritter notes that unification and the realization of "social union" had absorbed the attention of social policymakers for several years and marginalized discussions on reform. "The postponement (of reform—WS) and the enormous financial burdens of unification rendered the structural problems of the German welfare state more severe in the longer term ..." (Ritter 2006, 298).

16

History

In interpreting our account of slow transformational change in the German political economy over the past three decades, we have now had recourse in a variety of contexts to the notion of history. German unification was a unique, "historical" event, unexpected, entirely exogenous, and incomparable to whatever happened in other countries of the advanced capitalist world in the postwar period. Similarly, economic internationalization in the 1980s and 1990s was found to represent a new stage in a long-term, "historical" process of expansion of capitalist markets and firms finally and irreversibly crossing national borders. In an obvious although yet to be explored way, a historical perspective was also inherent in our emphasis on the dynamics over time, as opposed to the timeless statics, of social institutions ("The System as Process"), as well as in our reference to nondeterministic models of evolution, taken from "natural history," as an alternative to efficiency-theoretical, "economistic" concepts of institutional change. Before we return to and finish with our main theme, the institutionalist analysis of capitalist development, it seems appropriate briefly to clarify the different meanings of "history" and "historical" at this point as they may figure in a historical-institutionalist explanation of change.

To many modern social scientists, history is anathema in the precise Greek meaning of the word: it is a theme outside of the domain of legitimate themes, an accursed object from which a reasonable person can only stay away. Observing that social events or social structures are "historical" is highly irritating to much of the mainstream of today's social science, and enormous intellectual effort is spent on somehow enabling theory to work around the historicity of its subjects. Social scientists often perceive history as a huge pile of unsorted facts that, prepared by their "know-it-all" professional advocates, the historians, stubbornly resist the "economizing on information" which, after all, is said to be the essence and indeed the very purpose of the scientific enterprise. To those believing in parsimonious subsumption of empirical data under "covering laws," the endless supply of idiosyncratic facts, or "stories," delivered by history and historians threatens to blunt Occam's razor, building up before the theorist a gothic or baroque wilderness of themes and idiosyncratic variations immune to being conquered by the elegant, ultimately mathematical, Newtonian simplification that is at the heart of science, and supposedly not just of natural but also of social science.

Invoking history in the analysis of social phenomena is irritating to social scientists also because it conjures up a wide variety of meanings that do not always and necessarily appear compatible with each other, not to mention with major tenets of contemporary social science. Six such meanings may be distinguished at first blush, without entering too deeply into a methodological or ontological debate that is far too vast for the nonspecialist to survey. That something is "historical" may signify, first, that it is *unique and contingent,* like German unification was in relation to the "German model"; second, that it is *irreversible*; third, that it is *given,* in the sense that present actors have to take off from and work with it; fourth, that it is *dynamic and processual* rather than static; fifth, that it is *unpredictable,* and especially not controlled by some equilibrium-producing causal mechanism; and sixth, that it is part of a long-term trend, embedded in a "course of history" over the famous *longue durée.*

(1) To the kind of social theory that models itself on traditional physics and modern economics, a *unique and contingent* event is one that it is beyond its reach—one that it cannot explain. This is no problem for the theory as long as an event of this sort can be declared to be nonessential, or irrelevant within the world that is to be explained and to the explanation that is being proposed. Indeed the natural world, and even the world of physics, is full of unique events: no two real objects behave exactly alike when accelerating under the impact of the law of gravity, and none behaves exactly the way it should under Galilei's mathematical formula ($s = \frac{1}{2}at^2$, where s is the speed, a is the acceleration due to gravity, and t is the time: meaning that the distance traveled by a falling body is proportional to the square of the time of descent). But this does not matter to the theory, and in fact abstracting from the diversity of empirical observations and replacing the multitude of observed objects with one imagined, ideal object is exactly what science is supposed to do.

History, by contrast, insists on events and structures remaining indexed with reference to their location in time and space, making them unique and preserving their uniqueness. Max Weber's discussion of the bursting boulder[1] showed how physics—*nota bene,* the physics of his time—can entirely disregard the process how an individual boulder, falling off the edge of a mountain, shatters into a vast number of fragments that the theory can treat as "innumerable" although of course they are not. In the same way it can afford to treat as irrelevant the exact location of the fragments, as long as it can identify the general principles that governed the effect on the boulder of its hitting the ground. Weber knew that unlike physics, history is and social science may be interested precisely in the unique event rather than the general principle underlying it, since in the social world the concrete location of the fragments, as it were—the specific expression of the general principles at work in a given historical situation—may be exactly what one wants and needs to understand. Many feel that Weber ultimately failed to resolve the tension he described so well between a historical and a nomothetic approach to the social world, and of course, no attempt can be made here to fill this gap. Modern variable sociology, for its part, has tried to avoid the puzzle posed by the historicity of the social by eliminating uniqueness and contingency from the realm of theory and cutting the intelligible world down to a set of invariable relations between variable properties. It is this program that, although it has increasingly come under pressure, still dominates much of the practice of research, theory, training, and publication in the social sciences.[2]

(2) Historicity means not just uniqueness, but also *irreversibility.* History takes place over time, and time, as movie-goers know all too well, "goes by." What happens happens in time, and what happened in the past filled a space in time that cannot be filled with something else afterwards since it has forever closed. In a historical perspective on political economy, 20 years of high unemployment in a country cannot be disregarded as a no-man's land between two conditions of economic equilibrium, as they will have irreversibly shaped the experiences, life chances, identities, and opportunities of an entire generation who cannot live their lives a second time. Once time has passed, it cannot be restored, and while "in theory" things might have been different, in practice the one out of many other possibilities that happened to have been selected "by history" has crowded out all others "for the time being." Moreover, the Heraclitian principle applies that even if a past condition could somehow be restored in the present, the world around it will have become irreversibly different "in the meantime," if only because of the experience first of the condition's disappearance and then of its recovery, which turns even the

most faithful recreation of the old into something new and different. Normally, of course, recreation is not even tried, or it turns out simply to be impossible. With the dinosaurs extinct, nature had embarked on a path that firmly precluded their return, incomparably "fit" as they may have been "in their time." Similarly, when Roman civilization in the West finally ended in the fifth century, two or three generations of social turmoil later no architects were left and none had been newly trained who knew how to maintain the huge aqueducts of Spain, France, or Germany, and for more than a millennium it was impossible to put them back into use. Irreversibility presents a perennial irritant to those devoted, in the name of science, to timeless, ahistoric theories with a static property space and invariable causal relations, in which the production of a condition depends only on the presence of conducive causes, and not on the location of the producing event in a historical process.

(3) Historical *givenness* may be seen as a facet of irreversibility. That something has a history, or is "historical" in nature, is sometimes invoked to convey that it is sticky—a legacy that is not at the disposition of present actors but which they must take for granted, to be worked with or worked around, or to be incorporated in a more or less improvised, and more or less suboptimal, way into current structures and new designs. Such historical stickiness is, as we have seen, an irritant to theories that undertake to reconstruct the social world as the rational result of the rational choices, either of an elite of all-powerful and usually benevolent institutional designers, or of an atomistic multitude of individuals whose actions are instantly aggregated behind their backs into an emergent condition reflective of their collective will and interest. Rational choice theories know no "emergence" as it is known in classical sociology, where social interaction generates behind the back of human agency a compact, "strange," alienated, and alienating social reality: what emerges under "rational choice," if at all, is an equilibrium condition that is highly responsive to changing preferences or reformist intervention. Emphasizing that society has a sticky history collides with the optimistic-democratic constructivism of much of today's social science in that it presents social reality as an inheritance that one cannot reject even if one happens not to like it, as distinguished from an instant product of present actors' individual or collective volition. A "historical perspective," in this sense, is incompatible with what one could call a "hyper-active" theory of society (Etzioni 1968), one that systematically understates the constraints faced by social actors; just as it corresponds, as we have noted, to a "European" view of the "facts of life," a view liable to be accused

by rational constructivists of being historically deterministic or politically defeatist.[3]

(4) The fourth meaning of history emphasizes the dynamic nature of a world conceived as a *process*, as opposed to a static condition. That something is "historical" means, in this aspect, that it is *in motion*: that it was not always the way it is now, and will not remain that way in the future. The present is seen as a transient condition between a past and a future, as a moment in an ongoing "course of history" during which things change more or less continuously. That historical reality is a process need not be in conflict with its givenness: what is given, inherited, to be taken into account is the dynamic movement of the world, not its properties extant at a particular moment in time. That movement, as noted above, must be sharply distinguished from a system's predetermined, mechanistic return to equilibrium after a "historical" shock.[4] Such return may take time, but that time is not essential to the system or, for that matter, the theory; it is, as it were, ahistorical or timeless time, and is treated as ephemeral from the perspective of the self-enforcement of systemic equilibrium. It is on the background of a concept of time of this kind that Joan Robinson could claim that "Keynes brought back time into economic theory" by waking "the Sleeping Princess from the long oblivion to which 'equilibrium' and 'perfect foresight' had condemned her and led her out into the world here and now" (Robinson 1962, 76).

Together with irreversibility, the conception of history as process suggests the possibility of directedness, of history as development governed by a general tendency, perhaps of "progress," allowing for and even inviting the teleological imputation to historical change of a guiding purpose, which might even entail the notion of a potential "end of history" once that purpose has been fulfilled. We are obviously entering the field of historical philosophy here, which is much eschewed by social scientists today, most of whom believe "Hegelianism" or "historical materialism" to be a dirty word. Paradoxically, this makes quite a few of them liable to subscribing, without being aware of it, to a tacit teleology more acceptable to contemporary common sense and the powers that be under capitalism, which is the economistic teleology inherent in efficiency theorizing in political economy. We will return to the question of directionality shortly.

(5) Conceiving of history as a kind of dynamic change that is categorically different from a mere return to a preestablished equilibrium allows for a concept of society as facing an *open, unpredictable future,* and of human action taking place in a horizon of choices whose event is *uncertain.* Of course such a view tends to be the polar opposite of

teleology, implying as it does an agentic theory of social action serving as a "micro-foundation" of macro-sociology in general and of historical institutionalism in particular. The idea of an open and unpredictable future also makes space for a contest between different and conflicting collective purposes and decisions, ruling out among other things efficiency-theoretical predictions of universal convergence on a single "best practice" (see above, on "Convergence"). By implication this introduces, or reintroduces, into social theory what Joan Robinson, in the essay quoted *supra*, called "the problem of choice and judgment" (Robinson 1962, 75)—which, of course, is nothing if not the core problem of politics.[5] We have noted that Darwinian evolutionism may serve as a model for a theory of historical development that, while not being teleological, is nevertheless intelligible, that is, amenable to interpretative reconstruction in terms of underlying general principles. Unlike orthodox Marxism, as it has been received and passed on by Marx's followers, Darwinism suggests a nature evolving in an open horizon in which the future can be known and explained only with hindsight, when it will have become the past. Whether social science will be able to model itself on evolutionary biology properly understood depends on whether it will manage to discover and theorize a sociological equivalent to the biochemical mechanism of mutation, which was found by Darwin's successors to be the driving engine of change in natural life. Clearly, such an equivalent would require a theory of action which, among other things, would accommodate the fundamental fact of uncertainty—of limited foresight due to an incurable shortfall of human computational capacity as compared to the inherent complexity of the social world—as well as both the general and the historically specific limits on the reproducibility of social institutions through social controls.[6] Openness of the future and uncertainty may in fact generate one another: there would be no uncertainty if history made itself predictable by repeating itself, moving in circles, or following a recognizable singular purpose; and the future would not be unknown if the aggregate effects of the choices made by human actors could be predicted.

(6) Finally, the notion of history calls up the idea of a long course of events following or constituting a trend, linear, circular, or oscillating around a regression line, overriding and enveloping contingent events and prevailing over accidental differences between different entities located, or better: changing, in different places. History, in this sense and as noted above, carries a meaning of evolution and development, of more or less irresistible "laws" that govern how the world evolves over

time, regardless of what actors do to stem what would in this perspective appear to be an independent, self-driven "flow" of history. For example, Weberian "rationalization" or postwar American "modernization" and "convergence" theories suggested trends of this sort that were assumed to be invincible, especially "in the long run." Reference to "historical forces" of this kind may appear to be at odds with the notions, also and equally deeply attached to historicism, of contingency and an open future, whereas it clearly fits with irreversibility, stickiness, and a view of the social world as a process.[7]

Rather than trying to address the perennial question of historical determinism in the abstract,[8] I propose returning to the German case, where the tension between *history as accident* and *history as trend* is conveniently and dramatically highlighted by the coincidence of unification and internationalization in the 1990s. If ever there was in the period under consideration a contingent event that should have been capable of upsetting history's "business as usual," it was the end of the two postwar German states and their amalgamation into a common political and economic entity. As we have seen, however, *the causal power* of unification was remarkably minimal. All of the self-destabilizing processes of institutional change that would by the end of the century come together to undo the "German model" had already been in place at the time of unification, and after a short period of shock, if at all, they continued as though nothing much had happened—some with a small delay, some slightly accelerated, but on the whole along exactly the same lines that they had already been following when the German Democratic Republic still seemed to be there to stay.

In particular, momentous as the event of national unification certainly was, it did not in the slightest interfere with the ongoing internationalization, first of the West German and then of the *gesamtdeutsche* political economy, and with the profound liberalization of the West German postwar economic regime that came with it. Like the dialectics of self-driven domestic institutional change, event met trend only to be subsumed under it, with internationalization continuing in Germany just as everywhere else in the capitalist world, in some countries earlier and faster than in others, but ultimately in all of them without exception. Indeed that no national political economy became more national during the 1980s and 1990s appears so much a matter of course that many will find it unnecessary even to mention it. No country better illustrates how powerful and indeed irresistible were the social and economic forces that drove the general historical process of capitalist internationalization in

225

the last two decades of the twentieth century than Germany, a country that by historical accident was allowed to restore its nation-state in the 1990s but never even considered departing from the path on which it had long embarked toward the de-nationalization of its economy and the institutions that govern it.

To repeat, unification, enormous as it was as a political event, completely lacked any causal power to interfere with the historical trend of the time toward the internationalization, and simultaneously the disorganization and liberalization, of the postwar political economy. That this trend was indeed a historical trend in the sense of a general one is, again, confirmed by even the most superficial comparison with other, similar countries. Everywhere in the capitalist world of the time, organized labor and business were losing members and influence; collective bargaining was becoming more decentralized and fragmented (Katz and Darbishire 2000); social policy was cut back and became increasingly privatized; government spending hit a limit, until a turn to fiscal austerity became inevitable; large chunks of the public infrastructure were sold off to the private sector; and markets, firms, and production systems rapidly and irreversibly extended beyond national borders. Clearly, there were differences between countries, and they were and continue to be meticulously measured and analyzed by standard comparative social science. Meritorious as this was and is, however, it tends to hide the commonalities that also existed, even where these may arguably be much more important. Among them was, with very few exceptions if at all, that there was no country or sector with an *increase* in the membership and the power of corporatist associations; that no country, except perhaps for Ireland and Australia, *centralized* its wage-setting regime during the period in question, or *increased* its social policy spending; that the secular rise of the public share in the economy had come to an end *everywhere*, except perhaps in Denmark; and that the nationalization of industry, including infrastructural services, had *entirely* disappeared from the political agenda of countries. In short, none of the many "independent variables" of standard social science had proved independent enough to generate effects that would have gone against what appears to have been the grain of history in the period in question.

In what way, then, can and should "history matter" in the social sciences? One important, as it were: methodological insight seems to be that a truly historical perspective that emphasizes *dynamic process over static property* may tell us something about what different units of observation have *in common*. In the static comparison that is the basic analytical tool of standard sociology, common properties are constants that can neither be explained, nor can they explain something. This is one reason why the "varieties of capitalism" literature can see only the varieties but has literally nothing to say about capitalism, although *and* because this is the defining feature its units of analysis share.[9] It is only in a diachronic as opposed to a merely cross-sectional view—in a flow as distinguished from a stock perspective—that the causal significance of a property may be detected that is universally present in all units of comparison, assuming that it leaves traces of its effect in time and history. If, as in our case, all countries that are being compared are found to be changing in the same way and in the same direction, the cause is likely to be something they share—something that, however, remains hidden as long as only cross-sectional differences are observed to the exclusion of differences over time. There is no reason to believe that differences of the latter kind, caused by the dynamic effects of common properties, are always and necessarily more important or more interesting than the lateral differences captured by cross-sectional comparative snapshots; but certainly the opposite is also true, and very likely even more so.

If social science is to do full justice to the historicity of social life, it must simultaneously seek to understand both the uniqueness, contingency, stickiness, and irreversibility of its object world, as well as its processual dynamism, its openness, and the long-term, periodic tendencies that drive its transformation through time. In political economy, this requires as a minimum a radical departure from the timeless formalities of equilibrium economics, and indeed from analysis of the "economy" as such and as an equilibrium efficiency machine, to the study of *capitalism as a historical social formation,* or from a *general theory of institutional change* to a *historical theory of capitalist development.* The contours of such a program should by now be visible by and large, even though this is far from making the program any easier to carry through. Capitalism would have to be defined parametrically by specific, historically constituted dispositions of actors, distinctive institutional norms and sanctions, and a characteristic logic of action. Its theory would have to allow for agency and historical openness without rendering outcomes arbitrary, while it would simultaneously have to avoid mistaking the specificities of capitalist time, place, and social formation for general properties of all social orders. Capitalism would have to be considered as a contested and contradictory social system, with historically changing lines of conflict and contradiction and a multiplicity of interests and objectives which are reconcilable only intermittently. Historical-institutional analysis of capitalism, as distinguished from analyses of "the economy," would have to identify driving forces of historical change without falling victim to historical determinism or, again, structural-functionalist assumptions of equilibrium—locating action in an open horizon without making the past appear illogical, the present arbitrary, or the future free to choose.

Notes

1. To be found in the essay, "Roscher und Knies und die logischen Probleme der historischen Nationalökonomie," written 1903 to 1906. The essay is one of Weber's central methodological statements (Weber 1988 [1903–1906], 65ff.).
2. The program of variable sociology is not saved by exogenizing unique events into the environment of social systems, with nomothetic theory focusing on the way the latter deal with unpredictable challenges. As indicated, any deterministic approach faces the problem of the number of comparable cases being inevitably far smaller than that of relevant variables. In a technical sense, this leaves open too many degrees of freedom for a deterministic explanation to be sustainable. Ontologically, the fact that the number of variables exceeds the number of cases renders the cases that are being compared "historical individuals" in the Weberian sense, while opening up a wide space for agency and, as a consequence, creating a need for hermeneutic *Verstehen* of the meaning of social action.
3. Remember the old adage, attributed by James S. Duesenberry to himself (Duesenberry 1960, 233), "that the difference between economics and sociology" is that "economics is all about how people make choices" whereas "sociology is all about why they don't have any choices to make."
4. Just as historical time must be sharply distinguished from the time needed for the independent variables to reset the dependent variable in a static property space. Even where "lag time" is written into the equation, a system thus conceived is not really dynamic as the relations between its elements, including the time required for them to work themselves out, are considered invariant in time.
5. The full passage reads as follows: "By making it impossible to believe any longer in an automatic reconciliation of conflicting interests into a harmonious whole, the General Theory brought out into the open the problem of choice and judgment that the neo-classicals had managed to smother. The ideology to end all ideologies broke down. Economics once more became 'Political Economy'" (Robinson 1962, 75). It is ironic that much of the institutionalist political economy of today has fallen back behind Keynes by importing economistic equilibrium models into, of all disciplines, political science. This can hardly be anything other than a surrender to the *Zeitgeist* of the present period of

capitalist development, the period of the liberation of capital accumulation from the fetters of the postwar relations of production.

6. As tentatively sketched out in Streeck and Thelen (2005). See Chapter 17 on the "enactment" of capitalism.

7. In a recent paper, Sewell (2008) grapples with the tension between his own concept of history as "eventful temporality" (Sewell 2005) and the existence of evolutionary regularities in the development of capitalism. Like the present essay, Sewell comes down in favor of a historical theory of capitalism providing a conceptual structure for a narration of institutional change. Sewell's solution to the conflict between an event-driven and an evolutionary perspective on the social world has inspired much of what will be presented in the final chapter.

8. Or, for that matter, the possible combinations and permutations of the different meanings of "history" and "historical" that I have tentatively distinguished.

9. I cannot agree more with Jonas Pontusson: "The 'Varieties of Capitalism' litera-ture has a great deal to say about 'varieties', but surprisingly little to say about 'capitalism'" (2005, 164).

17

Bringing capitalism back in

Why capitalism? If the gradual disorganization and liberalization of a postwar "coordinated market economy" like Germany is to be explained, as I believe it must, as a secular historical process driven by endogenous, dialectical forces, conceptions of "the economy" as a system in, or on the way to, static equilibrium, however defined, are not really of use. Speaking of capitalism instead has the advantage that it conceptualizes the economy as inherently dynamic—as a historical social formation defined by a specific, characteristic dynamism, and as an evolving social reality in real time. Speaking of capitalism, in other words, avoids the *fallacies of misplaced abstractness* that plague mainstream economics as well as rational choice social science and prevent them from engaging the world *as it really happens to be.* Specifically, the concept of capitalism draws our attention to a core process of market expansion and accumulation that, it suggests, makes up the substance and defines the identity of what is now the hegemonic and indeed the only form of economic organization in the modern world. Moreover, it also and at the same time moves into the center of analysis the fundamental issue of the compatibility of expanding markets with basic requirements of social integration, thereby providing a coherent analytical framework in which to consider the manifold social conflicts associated with the "capitalist constant" (Sewell 2008) of progressive commodification.

The present chapter, somewhat longer than the others, will proceed as follows. It will begin with a brief discussion of why it was a mistake for institutionalist theory and comparative political economy to lose sight of what once was the central subject of modern social science, capitalism, and replace it with a functionalist construct called "the economy" even where, as today, the issue is to be its presumed "variety." As liberalization is once again bringing to the fore the capitalist nature of the modern economy, removing the veil under which it was hidden by postwar social pacification, the argument is that it is time to bring capitalism back also to the theory of political economy. Next, and second, the model of institutional enactment proposed by Streeck and Thelen (2005) will be expanded to provide what one might consider a micro-foundation for understanding the specific dynamic of gradual and dialectical institutional change *under capitalism*. In particular, by introducing a number of stylized characteristics of actors socialized in and endowed by a capitalist economic order, a conceptual toolkit will be offered for a historically grounded account of the slow, entropic erosion of postwar organized capitalism in a long-drawn process of disorganization and liberalization. Following this, it will be argued, third, that at the macro-level of society as a whole, the conceptual apparatus of Polanyi's "double movement" of market expansion and market containment allows for a much superior interpretation of institutions and institutional change in contemporary capitalism, and of the tensions and contradictions that underlie them, than does functionalist economism. To develop the Polanyian framework further, and to show how well it connects to micro-level institutional analysis, it will be linked to the distinction between Durkheimian and Williamsonian institutions, specifying Polanyi's account of the historical dynamic of capitalist development in terms of a theory of action in and with an institutionalized social order. Fourth, building on Polanyian institutionalism, a way will be suggested to accommodate economizing and rationalization—the subjects of "efficiency theory"—in a historical-institutionalist model of capitalism. The chapter, and the book, will close, fifth, with speculation on the future of German capitalism, returning to a subject first raised more than a decade ago (Streeck 1997*b*) and placing it in the broader context of capitalist development as a whole.

17.1. It's Capitalism, Stupid![1]

In order to connect to economic history as it unfolds in contemporary society, institutionalist political economy must drop its pretensions at timeless and placeless general theory and focus instead, not on *institutions as such,* and not even on *economic institutions,* but on *the economic institutions of capitalism* as they have evolved in the nineteenth and twentieth centuries. Unlike what many would believe, such movement from the abstract to the concrete, and from the general to the specific, does not really involve sacrifice (Mayntz 2004, 253). Universalism in the social sciences is almost always tainted with ethnocentrism and an unwitting dependence on what seems self-evident at a given time but very soon will have become obsolete or forgotten. For an illustration think of one of the great books of the past, Machiavelli's *Prince* (Machiavelli 1976 [1513)], which was written with the intention to provide a general praxeology of successful government based exclusively on empirical evidence. Most readers who look at the book today, hoping to find in it exactly that, are disappointed when they realize that at least two-thirds of it deal with highly period-specific questions, such as whether a ruler should invest in fortifications, move his residence to a conquered city, or rely on merce-naries rather than citizens as soldiers. For Machiavelli, who was drawing on the best historical and contemporary material available to him, from the Roman Empire to his own experience in Northern Italian politics, these were universal issues that would always have to be addressed by political rulers, regardless of time and space. To us, they are no more than reminders of how rapidly the world changes and how radically history may make societies forget old concerns and replace them with new ones wholly unpredictable even for the best and brightest of a former age.

I have already indicated in Chapter 13, on "Economizing," that by focusing on capitalism as a really existing social and economic order in historical time, institutionalist analysis avoids the pitfalls of conceiving of its subject as of "the economy" in general. In particular, speaking of an abstract "economy" as a distinct sphere of social life invites the misunderstanding that economic action is about uncontested and incon-testable common objectives that are optimally attained by observing and respecting general principles of prudent management, to be identified by scientific analysis and incorporated in specifically designed institutions. As we have seen, the way from here to the functionalist fallacy that economic institutions are to be explained as a result of successful or, for that matter, unsuccessful "economizing" aimed at improving a commu-nity's efficiency and competitiveness—implying the further fallacy that institutional change is driven by a consensual pursuit of ever higher levels of "economic rationality"—is very short.

Speaking not of an abstract "economy" but of capitalism as a concrete social formation draws attention to conflicts and tensions that are more than just misunderstandings concerning the right way toward optimal economic efficiency. By referring to a historically evolved and evolving social order, the concept of capitalism evokes the memory and makes

232

visible the enduring presence of conflicts, not just between classes in different market positions battling over the distribution of economic benefits, but also over the extent to which social life should be controlled by competitive markets and by imperatives of economic efficiency. It furthermore points to potential tensions between different institutions governed by different principles, such as firms and families, and to problems for both social life and economic management that do not just derive from shortsightedness or opportunism but reflect the ambiguous effects of markets expanding into social relations hitherto subject to noneconomic modes of social order. Where capitalism is the topic, the progressive rationalization of social life, the advance of private property and free markets, and the use of politics for market-making and the enhancement of "competitiveness" are not taken to be the natural direction of social development, but are as much in need of explanation as the social forces that resist rationalization and sustain principles of allocation other than competitive pricing in free markets.

As our account of institutional change in the German political economy indicates, the need to bring capitalism back into theory *results from the fact that capitalism has forcefully brought itself back into reality.* Three decades ago this would have seemed implausible at best. It has already been mentioned that as early as the first half of the twentieth century, all of the major theorists of capitalism, from Luxemburg to Weber and from Schumpeter to Keynes, firmly expected capitalist development to issue in secular stagnation, with markets and entrepreneurship giving way to bureaucratic administration of prices and production by the state or large corporations or both. The driving force behind this supposedly irresistible tendency was believed to be a general search for security and stability, not just by workers and governments, but also and no less by firms and second-generation capitalists. The almost universal expectation was that tight political supervision and a long-term exhaustion of entrepreneurial energy would put an end to capitalist dynamism and the economic progress it had wrought.

The postwar settlement after 1945, then, seemed to be the moment when the social-democratic utopia of a domesticated capitalism turned into a public utility for a pacified industrial society was to come true. With the bourgeoisie weakened and the working class strengthened in all countries of the West, whether victorious or defeated, and with the memory still vivid of the catastrophic economic and political consequences of what was perceived to have been a profound lack of economic governance nationally and internationally, claims of broad political majorities

233

for both a fair share in the proceeds of capitalist industrialism and for protection from the ups and downs of free markets appeared uncontestable. Moreover, it seemed that by a stroke of historical luck, Keynesian economics had in time delivered a set of effective tools to direct the dynamism of a capitalist economy, at the national and international levels, into safe channels where it could do useful work producing ever-increasing prosperity, without threatening the social lives of those hoping for an end, once and for all, to the tyranny of economic need and social uncertainty.

The socialization of capitalism, as it were, and its social-democratic organization were made possible not least by the enormous task of reconstruction after the devastations of the Second World War. For roughly two decades, capitalist accumulation could proceed without the "creative destruction" on which it normally depends, given the massive *destructive destruction* afflicted on the core capitalist regions by the war. Busy rebuilding the world, capitalism was able for a time to respect the desire of the period for predictably increasing prosperity for all, combined with security and stability. As early as the mid-1960s, however, open-ended demands for political protection and redistribution encouraged by progressive de-commodification of labor markets—in the form, above all, of a political guarantee of full employment—resulted in rising inflation (Fellner et al. 1961) hiding profound distributional conflicts (Hirsch and Goldthorpe 1978) and a widening mismatch between popular expectations and what a capitalist economy was able and willing to deliver. Temporarily strengthened by the worker revolts of the late 1960s, social democracy in the subsequent decade undertook to push to its limits and beyond a policy that regarded capitalism as a shared resource, a common pasture for society as a whole to be administered by expert technicians elected on a promise to provide for eternally growing prosperity-in-security.

Today, we know that the problem of mainstream social democracy in the 1970s, with its strong belief in the power of democratic legitimacy and the efficacy of the modern state as an instrument of social control, was that it mistook capitalism for a neutral apparatus for the joint production of shared prosperity. Indeed, it did not take long for technocratic fantasies of capitalism as a politically governable "economy" to turn out to have been just that. Capitalist firms and those that own and run them can only for so long be treated as patient cogs in a collectively serviceable machine. Then, their true nature must come to the fore again, revealing them to be the live predators that they are, for which politically imposed social obligations are nothing but bars of a cage bound to become too small for them and for their insatiable desire for the hunt. In fact, by the end-1970s at the latest, capitalism had become determined to break out of the social-democratic stable into which it had been pressed after the war, being no longer willing and able to make do with the sensible but small servings of profit allowed to them by their political masters. Safe as life may have been under social-democratic tutelage, it also was boring, calling forth increasingly resolute efforts by capital to liberate itself and start a new cycle of accumulation, by expanding beyond the narrow confines of the neo-traditionalism of a social-democratic economy dedicated to the supply of fixed social needs.

Against all expectations, capitalism in the 1980s and 1990s recaptured its dynamic and once again became an unwieldy stochastic source of unplanned social and institutional change. As we have seen in the German case, the new dynamism, which for a variety of reasons soon gained the support of the very states and governments that only a short time before had aspired to be capitalism's keepers, gradually began to undo the Durkheimian institutions that had been set up to tie capitalist accumulation to the discharge of social obligations. Capitalism redux began to absorb the slack that had been tolerated by the protected production regimes of the postwar period; migrated to new markets outside national control, pushed by domestic constraints and pulled by foreign opportunities; and did its utmost to empty the modern village of the welfare state, in its relentless search for new land to be subsumed under capitalist relations of production. *Thus capitalism returned even though it had never really been gone.* After this, I suggest, the issue for institutionalist political economy can no longer be how an economy that happens to be "coordinated" either by markets or by institutions is governed as a national resource. Rather, it must be how the rejuvenation of capitalism and the renewed expansion of capitalist market relations slowly wreaks havoc on established regimes of social order and forces societies to restructure themselves, both to satisfy new and unpredictable demands of the market and to bring such demands, again, under some sort of social control.

In the following, I will outline what I consider to be three important building blocks of an institutionalist analysis, not of "the economy," but of capitalism as a concrete political-economic social formation.[2] First, I will sketch a model of the behavior of "typically capitalist" actors in an institutional context, treating the peculiar creativity and indeed unruliness of capitalist "rule-takers" in Durkheimian regimes as a defining element of capitalism as a social system. Second, I will draw on the Polanyian concepts of embeddedness, properly understood, and of the "double movement" to identify the not just plural but inherently contradictory forces responsible for the specific dynamism of capitalist development, making it move, not linearly but in fits and spurts, and in cyclical waves of institutionalization and de-institutionalization. And third, expanding on earlier ideas on the relationship between institutional constraints and the pursuit of efficiency (Streeck 1997*a*, 2004*a*), I will suggest how economizing as a practical entrepreneurial activity may fit into an institutional theory of capitalist social action.

17.2. Capitalism: Enacted and Reenacted

> Capitalism . . . is by nature a form or method of economic change and not only never is but never can be stationary. And this evolutionary character of the capitalist process is not merely due to the fact that economic life goes on in a social and natural environment which changes and by its change alters the data of economic action . . . Nor is this evolutionary character due to a quasi-automatic increase in population or capital or to the vagaries of monetary systems . . . The fundamental impulse that sets and keeps the capitalist engine in motion comes from the new consumers' goods, the new methods of production or transportation, the new markets, the new forms of industrial organization that capitalist enterprise creates . . . (Schumpeter 1975 [1942], 82–3).

Change, according to Sewell (2008), is the only thing that is constant about capitalism. But there is also a constant *within* capitalist change that gives it direction. "At the core of capital at its most abstract level," from where capitalism's uniquely dynamic "eventful temporality" issues, Sewell finds "an extraordinary stillness," an unchanging mechanism generating perpetual change, with "capital . . . always churning, always self-valorizing, moving endlessly in Marx's sequence of M-C-M' (from its money form, to its commodity form, and back again to its money form with the amount enhanced by profit)." The direction is expansion and its mechanism, as we learn above all from Schumpeter, is innovation. Innovation is by definition unpredictable as one knows the new only when one sees it; what can be safely predicted in a capitalist economy, however, is that the unpredictable will not only happen but also change the world in a predictable direction. Capitalism, that is to say, is a social order that changes in an orderly way by systematically encouraging disorder, giving rise to unpredictable events.

Capitalist dynamism, as defined in the tradition of the classics, is specific to a particular historical period and geographical space. It is, in other words, not a characteristic of social systems in general. The trend of development to which it gives rise—which may proceed continuously or intermittently—is formed by a sequence of events that are both unpredictable and recognizable as elements of a broader pattern, similar to natural history as reconstructed by Darwinian theory of evolution. Event is integrated in trend, not by the latter somehow controlling the former, but by the nature of the latter, which is defined by a specific kind of indeterminacy. That indeterminacy is caused by constitutively devious actors who are driven by both competition and a particular ethos of seeking economic advantage by strategically subverting or working around established norms and traditional practices. While what such actors will be doing cannot be predicted, which makes it a stochastic source of imperfect reproduction of the social and economic order, its general character is such that it will always add up to conversion of traditional social relations into market relations—unless progress of the trend is kept in check by constraining institutions that have not yet fallen apart under continuous attempts to break through them.

A social order is governed by rules, created by social actors, with which the same or other actors are expected to comply. Understanding how social orders change, predictably or unpredictably, just occasionally within a static property space or historically through evolution, ultimately requires a theory of social action within and in relation to institutions, one that opens up for analysis the multi-faceted interactive relationship between what may be referred to in shorthand as rule-making and rule-taking. An action-theoretical micro-foundation for an *institutionalist theory of capitalism as a social system* would have to spell out what is peculiar about social action in relation to social institutions *under capitalism,* to account for the latter's specific mode of predictably unpredictable change moving in the predictable direction of expansion of capitalist relations of production. As stated above, I suggest that a historical-institutionalist theory of capitalism and capitalist development of this sort should be able to explain processes like the parallel, endogenous, dialectical, and mutually reinforcing institutional change observed over 30 years in five sectors of the disorganizing and liberalizing German political economy—processes that, as I have argued, *cannot* be explained as a return to economic or institutional equilibrium, a response to a historical shock, the result of economizing convergence on a superior model of "best practice," as secular progress in rationalization, or the like.

In the following, I will outline a few core elements of a model of social action under capitalism that, while clearly requiring further elaboration, is to illustrate the sort of approach by which historical institutionalism could, as I believe it must, recapture capitalism as its subject.

In a previously cited paper, Kathleen Thelen and I (Streeck and Thelen 2005) explored some of the micro-dynamics, at the level of actors and social action, of gradual change in institutions, in response to widespread dissatisfaction with models of change that leave only a choice between stasis and catastrophe. Basically what we did was introduce into historical institutionalism a model of *imperfect reproduction*, similar to received models of change in evolutionary biology. In our exposition, we located slow but continuous gradual change in the, as it were, ontological gap between the general and the specific—here, between a rule and its application, or between an ideal order and its *enactment*.[3] In terms of social structure, we modeled this gap as inherent in a complex relationship of domination, or social control, between elites and nonelites (Etzioni 1961).[4] To indicate that we were dealing in particular with authoritative, that is, legitimate institutions—institutions not based on contract but preceding it—we embedded what we conceived as a Weberian *Herrschaftsverband* of rule-makers and rule-takers in a surrounding society of "third parties" that those seeking compliance can call upon for support (Figure 17.1). Nonetheless, we argued that even in optimal circumstances, compliance with and enactment of a given order, or institution, can never be perfect, for general logical if not for other, more historically specific and contingent reasons. In particular, we emphasized that those designing an institution at a given time cannot fully foresee all future situations to which it will have to be applied, so that even where rule-takers act in the best of faith the results of their enactment of the rule will often and inevitably be surprising to those who created it. The same, we pointed out, applies to variations in place as distinguished from time, in that each situation in which a rule is to be followed will be strictly speaking unique, requiring creative interpretation of the rule's exact meaning and, inevitably, its discretionary and potentially unique enactment.

In the paper cited, Thelen and I suggested that imperfect reproduction over time and in space may somehow congeal in nonrandom patterns, making not just for differences between different instances of institutional enactment, but also for change in enacted institutions themselves. In this vein, we developed a typology, more or less phenomenological and not meant in any way to be complete, of five distinct modes of

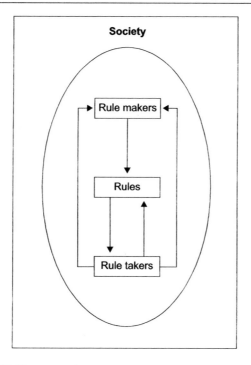

Figure 17.1. Institutions as regimes

gradual institutional transformation which, we implied, may in principle be observed in any institutional setting anywhere (Streeck and Thelen 2005). Fundamentally unrelated to this and, perhaps, in a sort of leap of faith, we connected our notion of slow transformative change to what we perceived to be a common process in all contemporary capitalist societies, political-economic liberalization. This was based on not much more than the observation, made by many others as well, that the most important tendency of gradual change in contemporary capitalism is liberalization, and that liberalization today happens to proceed, not by a revolutionary break with the postwar past, but mostly slowly and gradually. What we neglected was to connect this observation with an elaborated concept of the economy in which liberalization is currently making such powerful progress. Busy with our taxonomy of morphological properties of institutional change, we abstained from asking why it is that the gradual change we observe in the interaction between rule-takers and rule-makers in today's political economy—in the niches between general rules and their specific application—is almost always tantamount to liberalization: to increasing significance of markets and competition and to decentralization and disorganization.

Why is gradual institutional change *in contemporary capitalism* not random but patterned, proceeding toward liberalization rather than in no particular or in some other direction? The notion of imperfect reproduction implies that change is continuous, but it implies nothing about the character or direction of change. To understand why the "natural" tendency of institutional change in capitalism seems to be disorganization whereas organization seems to require rare "political moments" (Streeck 2001*b*), I suggest lowering the level of abstraction of the Streeck and Thelen model of institutional change to allow for parametric specifications that represent what is peculiar to capitalist actors and the functioning of institutions under capitalism, ultimately leading to *an institutional theory of capitalism as a specific type of social order.* For such a theory, the general idea of imperfect reproduction would remain highly useful even though the source and kind of imperfect reproduction would be assumed to vary with the type of society. To account for gradual institutional change under capitalism, capitalist social actors[5] would be specifically defined by two characteristics, a particular resource endowment (*resourcefulness*) and a special behavioral disposition in relation to social rules (*unruly opportunism*). The hypothesis would be that together the two give rise to continuous pressures on and within institutions that slowly and gradually subvert Durkheimian social obligations while expanding the realm of voluntary, utility-maximizing action and of Williamsonian social arrangements, unless constrained by political restoration of social obligations—which, however, will soon be subject to the same corrosive forces as the obligations that had preceded them.

As to resource endowments, the uneven distribution of property under capitalism makes for differential capacities of social actors to circumvent social rules or challenge their received interpretation. Large firms in particular have practically unlimited means at their disposal to lobby governments for revision of rules they find inconvenient, or to pay for legal expertise to find gaps or uncover inconsistencies in the law, or fight in courts for new interpretations of old rules. Tax lawyers (Streeck and Thelen 2005) are just one category of specialists in creative reinterpretation of formal social obligations for the purpose of avoiding them in a legally unassailable way. Creativity in such a context typically involves a studied absence of "good faith," in the sense of a determined rejection of shared informal understandings on the meaning of the norm in question, combined with, paraphrasing Dennis Wrong (1961), an "under-socialized" attitude of skillful instrumentalism in relation to social rules in general. Unlike in premodern social orders, this attitude is explicitly considered legal and indeed legitimate in a contemporary "state of law," where the only obligations with which actors have to comply are those that are formally instituted, which implies that their meaning can always be legitimately disputed provided one commands the necessary legal expertise.[6]

Differential resource endowment under capitalism works in favor of interests in the liberalization of social obligations, imparting on gradual institutional change a bias toward disorganization unless counteracted by political intervention. This bias is reinforced by a specific disposition of capital-commanding actors, both individuals and, even more so, firms, who may be stylized as entrepreneurial utility-maximizers and constitutively restless advantage-seekers, with a trained habit of continuously scrutinizing the social world for new, hitherto undiscovered opportunities for profit-making—what Marx called *"Plus-Macherei"* (Marx 1966 [1867], 189). Capitalists as social characters may be modeled as lacking any normative-expressive attachment to social institutions enforcing collective solidarity, in the sense of restraint on the pursuit of individual interests; they may be stylized as either not socialized at all, or socialized in a culture, or subculture, in which the deliberate outwitting of social rules is an approved and indeed prestige-carrying behavior. Ideal capitalists, in other words, are born opportunists when it comes to social order, and indeed "opportunists with guile."[7] Moreover, they are always dissatisfied with their current state of affairs, insatiable and unendingly greedy regardless of past achievements in accumulation, which makes them invent ever new ways of converting social arrangements into opportunities for profit, or subverting them where this turns out to be impossible. Capitalists, in other words, are the modern, nontraditionalist economic actors par excellence: they never rest in their perennial rush to new frontiers. This is why they are *fundamentally unruly*: a permanent source of disorder from the perspective of social institutions, relentlessly whacking away at social rules, continuously forcing rulers to rewrite them, and undoing them again by creatively exploiting the inevitable gap between general rules and their local enactment.[8]

It should be pointed out that the above is a stylized model of a social character, or persona, not necessarily a psychological profile of the average individual capitalist. It is probably true that those making a living as professional capitalists are personally greedier and will exhibit greater opportunistic inventiveness than others,[9] given that a market economy may realistically be expected to select in favor of individuals with strongly "capitalist" dispositions. Still, making human actors into capitalists must be a complex and conflicted process of moral, or amoral, education, under powerful cross-pressures from social communities trying to make future capitalists less capitalist by insisting on their "social responsibility," be it corporate or individual. The extent to which this can be successful differs between contexts and actors; owners of medium-sized family firms are likely to be more susceptible to moral pressures than managers of private equity funds. What matters in the end, however, is that in a contemporary social context, making a living by specializing in the subversion of social constraints is not just legal but also legitimate, as is the adoption generally of a detached, probing attitude of instrumental advantage-seeking toward social relations. Those who find and exploit a new, originally unintended meaning, or a hole, in a social institution—such as a tax code—tend to attract the admiration rather than the contempt of others, and on demand will always be given reassurance that what they have done was "entirely their right." This holds in particular where actors are organizations, or representatives of organizations, as these are expected even less than modern individuals are to develop sentimental attachments to social values preventing them from maximizing the return on whatever their capital may be.

Most importantly, however, the presence and the institutional effects of entrepreneurial restlessness and capitalist guile do not in the end depend on normative internalization, de-socialization, or habit formation, even though these of course help. Capitalist societies command a unique means to wake up and keep alert the capitalist animal spirits, which is *competition*. Real capitalists, including capitalist firms, may be quite willing sometimes to take a rest, content themselves with a "reasonable" rate of profit, get used to being stall-fed by Social-Democratic governments, or accept the discipline imposed on them by all sorts of cartels. A lapse back into traditionalism is always a possibility, even in the most advanced form of capitalism. In fact, entire capitalist classes in the course of history have been known to prefer enjoying their riches once they had safely taken possession of them, and use them to underwrite a semi-aristocratic way of life. Competition, however—or, more precisely, the institutionally protected possibility for enterprising individuals to pursue even higher profit in an innovative manner at the expense of other producers— can end the peace *at any moment,* and has proven to be capable of doing so even in the most unlikely circumstances, such as the mature capitalism of the postwar era when even Schumpeter expected capitalist dynamism to come to a permanent end. The reason why competition is so effective as a mechanism of economic change is that where it is legitimate in principle, as it must be almost by definition in a capitalist economy, what is needed to mobilize the energy of innovative entrepreneurship is not collective deliberation or a majority vote but, ideally, just one player who, by deviating from the established way of "doing things," can force all others to follow, at the ultimate penalty of extinction. Any creative individual can become the leader and reap the advantage of the first mover. Since all others are aware of this, they must in principle constantly anticipate being attacked, and may therefore decide to attack first, in a preemptive strike. This is why it may take no more than the *possibility* of competition for competition to become a *reality*.

Competing with others for economic advantage may, of course, be outlawed, as it was in many sectors of the postwar economy. Institutionalization of monopoly, in a wide variety of forms, was quite successful for a long time, often because it was strongly supported by sectoral producer groups, including organized professions and capitalist firms in addition to trade unions. Political protection and collective organization, however, do not necessarily put to rest the capitalist drive for profit maximization. State agencies shielding economic sectors from competition often found producers abusing their resulting market power for self-enrichment far beyond what the public was willing to consider a "reasonable rate of profit," or what may have appeared as an "appropriate standard of living." Invidious comparison with sectors governed by free markets did its part to drive up expectations and make ever-increasing claims for higher benefits seem justified. Typically after a while, with growing productivity gaps, rising demands and accumulated experience on the part of protected sectors in extracting resources from the public, governments in desperation took to competition of all things as their ultimate instrument to discipline publicly protected producers whose greed they could no longer feed or, alternatively, control. In this way, in a world imbued with a capitalist ethos of maximization of private advantage, free markets became, ironically, the public policy instrument of choice to domesticate strategically placed private interests. Of course, the local enactment of competition regimes is subject to exactly the same distortion by resourceful and unruly utility-maximizing actors as is any other political-economic regime.

How the capitalist habit of self-interested circumvention and modification of rules works to produce institutional change, in connection with competition, may be briefly illustrated by the examples of the erosion of centralized wage formation in Germany and of the disorganization of the German company network. As we have seen, German firms held on to industry-wide collective bargaining well into the 1980s, disciplined by strong employer associations and trade unions as well as by ruling interpretations of collective labor law that made defection appear difficult if not impossible. But this should not be taken to mean that firms were normatively socialized in or content with the system, only that discontent needed time to mature and an opportunity to manifest itself in practice. With wage structures becoming more compressed over the years, as they were bound to, and competition in product markets increasing with internationalization, wage setting institutions were enacted by firms with growing inventiveness and entrepreneurial acumen, especially in the 1990s. More consciously than before, firms tested the constraints and explored the opportunities inherent in the old regime, searching with rising confidence for individual advantage through local redefinition or avoidance of collective institutions, for example by using works councils as substitutes for company unions. The result was a wave of dispersed discoveries issuing in gradual decentralization, specification, and fragmentation of the wage-setting regime as a whole, which was hardly noticed at first. Firms that had originally continued in the traditional ways saw their competitors bow out of collective solidarity and go unpunished, and felt encouraged to avail themselves of the same advantages, if they were not simply forced to do so by the need to catch up with the others. Simultaneously, new interpretations of applicable law, in line with changing entrepreneurial practice, were peddled in legal theory and before the courts, and found their way into proposals for legislative reform. Relentless and increasingly widespread local experimentation, including exit from employer associations and collective bargaining altogether, combined with political pressure to make trade unions and employer associations liberalize the postwar collective bargaining system, by offering firms more space for local modification of central settlements in line with individual needs and entrepreneurial strategies. As it turned out, even this failed to prevent a continuous shrinking of the core of the industrial relations system and the rise of a variety of new forms of wage setting outside of it.

A similar dynamic was at work in the disintegration of the German company network in the course of economic internationalization. As told, the story illustrates the fundamental fragility of social cohesion among capitalist firms, being habitually disposed to improve their position at the expense of their peers, as well as being habitually afraid of having done unto them what they would gladly do unto others if an opportunity arose. In a social field formed by actors like this, it takes in principle only one defection to start a stampede with all others following, pulled by the prospect of extra profit and pushed by the fear of falling behind. While solidaristic social relations among cooperating firms may under special conditions be instituted and maintained, they remain unstable due to powerful tensions beneath their surface that, like the spring of a clock, may be set off any time by only the slightest disturbance. Solidarity and the safety and stability it provides may be highly valued by capitalist firms, as the case of postwar Germany demonstrates. But looming over what can in fact be no more than a temporary cease-fire is always the possibility of an innovative entrepreneurial competitor finding the benefits of breaking away from the old ways and going it alone to exceed the gains from playing by the rules by so much that it seems worth taking the risk of losing the wages of peace in an attempt to gain the profits from aggression. This, as we have seen, is the moment when potential competitors are bound to get nervous—or more precisely, when their capitalist nervousness tends to trigger an almost automatic reaction that makes them follow in fear of missing something important. Solidarity, again, is not unknown to capitalists, and neither are the advantages of economic traditionalism; but the moment a potential winner exits in entrepreneurial pursuit of new ways, as capitalists can always legitimately do in a capitalist world, nobody can afford to be left behind in a solidaristic community of losers.

Summing up, capitalist actor dispositions specifically shape the enactment of institutions in the political economy, imparting on them a particular bias, or dynamic, that makes for continuous incremental change toward privatization of social order in general and the expansion of market relations in particular. The result is a more capitalist economy, a reenactment of capitalism through the imperfect enactment of institutions set up to constrain the expansion of markets. Liberalization is the most likely direction of gradual institutional change in a capitalist world left to itself, absent effective political effort at social containment, with capitalistically disposed actors, a culture sanctioning the maximization of private gain, and competition as a mechanism excusing and enforcing "opportunism with guile." Expected to control constitutionally restless actors in their relentless search for new ways of maximizing the commodity value of their money and the money value of their commodities, institutionalized social obligations in a capitalist society are permanently in danger of being subverted, if not at once, then slowly and incrementally. Endogenous exhaustion and exogenous internationalization are not much different if conceived in terms of the necessarily dynamic enactment of a constraining social order by resourceful and unruly capitalists. From a Durkheimian perspective, capitalism appears as a social field with strong inherent tendencies toward entropy, due to the characteristic cunningness of actors in socially sanctioned pursuit of unlimited profit and exempted from expectations of both solidarity with others and goodwill with respect to the enactment of social rules that stand in the way of their material interests. Institutional analysis of capitalism must expect, therefore, not order in equilibrium, but what Beckert has called a "dynamic disequilibrium" (Beckert 2008): a continuous contest between creative destruction of social rules by enterprising innovators interested, at best, in expedient voluntary arrangements for efficient coordination from below, and political projects to defend or regain a modicum of social stability. In short, what needs to be explained are order and stability, while gradual change toward public disorder may be expected as normal.

17.3. Polanyi: Embeddedness, the Satanic Mill, and the Double Movement

I now move on to the second of my three building blocks of an institutional theory of capitalism, or of a theory of institutions and institutional change under capitalism. In the preceding chapter, I have outlined the contours of a model of social action, driven by a stylized capitalist urge for liberty and profit, that is to give action-theoretical definition to the "Sewellian constant" of perpetual expansion of capitalist relations of production. Specifically, the purpose of the model was to identify the general direction of market pressures for institutional change under capitalism, as emanating from the micro level of social action in institutional contexts, with change moving—as it were, by default—toward progressive erosion of social obligations in favor of voluntary, individually "rational," contractual social relations. In particular, I have suggested that the liberalization of the social order to which this amounts may be conceived as a steady softening or undermining of what I have called Durkheimian institutions, leading in some instances to their replacement with Williamsonian ones (Table 11.2). Now I will look at the macro level of society as a whole to explore the functions of the institutions that constrain capitalist actors and provoke their resistance or evasion, in order to specify further the nature and direction of the evolutionary dynamism set in motion by imperfect institutional reproduction in a capitalist social order. In particular, I will undertake to outline a theoretical framework capable of accommodating conflictual, cyclical, dialectical, and contradic-tory moments of institutional change, one that avoids projecting a linear, one-dimensional, technocratic image of social development as implied, for example, by efficiency-theoretical accounts.

As already indicated, I believe that the best starting point for this is Karl Polanyi's narrative of the rise of liberalism on the one hand and of the social countermovements it provoked and continues to provoke on the other (Polanyi 1957 [1944]). Note that Polanyi was above all an economic historian who understood that the institutionalization of economic life in society was subject to both an evolutionary dynamic and purposeful human intervention. Note also that he belonged to a generation that had experienced first-hand the drama of modern capitalism from the beginning of the twentieth century—with the rise of the nation-state and the end of the gold standard, the chaos of the Great Depression and the catastrophic breakdown of a disorderly world economic system—to the postwar settlement after 1945. To make Polanyi's work productive for the study of institutional change in present-day capitalism, however, one must avoid reading it the way it is often read in American economic sociology and, in particular, at American business schools (Beckert 2007b; Krippner 2001; Streeck 1997a). Polanyi's message is decidedly *not* that a market economy works better, or works only, if it is underpinned by a network of noneconomic, community-type social relations. That he tends to be presented as a theorist of the "soft factors" in economic success—to have a profitable capitalist economy, you require a good society—is a misunderstanding that happens to be very similar to the reception, also in the United States, or in California, of another famous Viennese of the period, Sigmund Freud. As famously insisted upon by Adorno and Horkheimer in their criticism of Erich Fromm (Jay 1973), Freud's theory was never intended to be a general praxeology of human happiness, teaching people how to become less depressed by allowing their desires a little more satisfaction. Far from hedonistic optimism, Freud saw a deep and basically irreconcilable conflict between the demands of an ever more complex civilization for discipline and self-restraint on the one hand and the natural anarchy of human desires on the other, a conflict which was bound to be painful regardless of whatever institutions a society devised to deal with it (Freud 2004 [1929]). Quite analogously, rather than treating society as a functional infrastructure, however indispensable, for an efficient market economy, Polanyi emphasized what he regarded as a *fundamental tension* between stable social integration and the operation of self-regulating markets, the latter inevitably eating away at the former unless society mustered the capacity and the will to put markets in their place and keep them there. It is this view of the relationship between the liberal market economy and society that is behind Polanyi's powerful metaphor of the market as a "satanic mill" (Polanyi 1957 [1944], 33ff., passim) grinding away at the social fabric unless it is somehow safely contained by appropriate social institutions.

What exactly is it in the functioning of a market economy that, according to Polanyi, endangers social stability and social cohesion? There are places in Polanyi's work where the corrosive mechanism that we are looking for seems to be specified as a negative effect on the moral constitution of social actors of being regularly involved in calculative and competitive exchange relations, making individuals unable to build up and maintain altruistic relations of human community and solidarity (Polanyi 1992 [1957]). Fortunately, however, there is no need to resort to this kind of social psychology as Polanyi offers much more convincing structural imagery of the attack of markets on social structures. This is when he speaks of the "vagaries" of markets that are "self-regulating," that is, in which relative prices are allowed to fluctuate freely (Polanyi 1957 [1944], Chapter 6, passim). Such fluctuations are by definition unpredictable, and they may occur in rapid succession—faster than socialized human beings may be able or willing to adjust. What makes this so significant in Polanyi's view is that relative prices more or less directly determine social status orders and the life chances of groups and individuals. Groups that suffer a decline in the relative price of the product or the kind of labor they have to offer will lose resources by which to support their accustomed way of life; ultimately, they may have to accept or seek a new social identity adapted to their changed market position. If markets are truly free, such changes, being the unintended aggregate outcome of a myriad of individual decisions, may happen any time, making it impossible for those affected by them ever to feel secure, and imposing on human actors continuously new pressures for adjustment—pressures that Polanyi considered ultimately incompatible with social integration. The reason, that is to say, why Polanyi believed self-regulating markets to be grinding mills in relation to human society is that, if left to themselves, they tend to reset the relative prices of human productions—the terms of exchange between individuals and social groups—so rapidly and unpredictably that no reliable social order and no stable social identity can have enough time to crystallize, unless collective political intervention fixes at least some relative prices by exempting them from the "free play of market forces."[10]

There are of course sound efficiency-theoretical defenses for stabilized relative prices, for example, when collective industrial agreements or employment statutes guarantee a certain minimum wage to individuals who have invested in advanced qualifications, making such investment less risky and thereby more likely. While Polanyi would probably not have denied this, however, explaining institutions by their efficiency effects *alone*, and thereby eliminating what he regarded as a *systemic tension* between social structures and economic markets, was clearly not his program. Rather, Polanyi insisted on the inevitability of a fundamental conflict between the functioning of a free market and the needs for and of a stable social lifeworld—a concept he would have been happy to adopt from Habermas or from phenomenological philosophy. For Polanyi, that conflict manifested itself in permanent pressures by market forces on social actors to reorganize their lives constantly as dictated by unpredictably changing rates of exchange; in a continuous probing by "the market" of the adaptive capacity of human life-ways and social organization; and in subsequent collective-political efforts at stabilizing existing social structures against the dynamism of the market, in defense of a reliable social order in which individuals may have a chance to develop lasting social and personal identities.[11]

Institutions fixing relative prices may serve not just conservative, but also reactionary functions:[12] think of Weber's analysis of agrarian protectionism in Prussia at the end of the nineteenth century, whose purpose it was to keep the ruling caste of the *Junker* economically alive so they could continue to control the government of the state. Suspension of self-regulating markets also, however, underlay the postwar welfare state—for example, when labor markets were governed by comprehensive multi-firm industrial agreements, resulting in workers with low productivity earning more and workers with high productivity earning less than they would have earned if wage formation had been more market-driven. In both cases, relative prices, rather than blindly following supply and demand, were institutionally administered according to prevailing notions of social justice, favoring the "old rich" or the poor, depending on the distribution of political power and ideological influence in the respective society. Political price-fixing offered security and stability to those it was intended to protect, by circumscribing property rights and curtailing individual liberties of employers, workers, potential competitors, or whoever else might have threatened the stability of what those in the possession of political power considered a "good society."

Market-constraining institutions are bound to be politically contested; while they protect some groups and their ways of life, they deprive others of opportunities to compete and improve their social status. Capitalists may be as divided over them as workers, some seeking protection from competition, others clamoring for the right to compete. This applies at the elite level where institutions are negotiated and enforced, but it holds also at the micro-level of everyday enactment of institutionalized rules. Here, as pointed out, we may observe a wide range of behaviors, from value-led compliance to cunning circumvention to exit and rebellion. We also observe attempts to turn constraints into opportunities, when actors that have resigned themselves to the reality of a given institution, uncomfortable as it may be, learn to use it creatively to their advantage.[13] Moreover, there is the possibility of a given institution, originally created to prevent the erosion of a particular social status or practice, being colonized and "converted" to secondary use as an efficiency-enhancing device for low-cost coordination, by opportunistic rational actors on the lookout for shortcuts to more profitable ways of doing business. None of this, however, eradicates the tension that, according to Polanyi, underlies all major political struggles over institutional design between, as it were, the *social bedding* of a capitalist economy and *what is embedded in it*— between social order and self-seeking rational action—with the resulting tendency toward social entropy eliciting continuous efforts to work out, with no guarantee of success, ever new compromises between free markets and the quest of socialized human beings for security and stability.

With this in mind, we can now move on to what I regard as the core concept of Polanyi's work, that of a social "countermovement" called forth by the expansion of the market, and of the resulting "double movement" of market expansion and social protection that Polanyi considered to be the engine of capitalist historical development.[14] The reason why the notion of capitalist development as a "double movement" appears so fruitful today as we try to understand institutional change in an age of liberalization is not only that it specifies, in a historically concrete way, the forces that drive it, telling us what is materially at work if national institutions are not and cannot be exclusively efficiency-oriented and resist being explained in efficiency-theoretical terms. It also conceives of these forces as being in systematic conflict with one another, allowing for theory to be dialectical, and for change to result from contradiction and to be accounted for as the uncertain event of an ongoing contest between mutually incompatible social tendencies, or social needs.[15] It furthermore projects an image of change as potentially cyclical, moving "in leaps and bounds" (Polanyi 1957 [1944], 130), where one tendency may prevail during one period while the other may take its place during the next. With market expansion and social protection from the market acting on each other, the theory also suggests a specific directionality of institutional and social change, in the sense of Sewell, without becoming monocausal or monistic and deterministic as a result. Most importantly, it provides a space for building a genuinely political element into political economy, in that it accommodates and incorporates relevant interests that are not economic but social, assigning a prominent place to them in which they are far from systematically subservient to or derivative of interests in economic efficiency.

Unlike much of the "varieties of capitalism" literature, in other words, politics appears in Polanyi as an independent, autonomous force, and decisively not as a mechanism designed or devoted to bringing capitalist markets and transactions into equilibrium, or advance national "competitiveness." Where markets expand, politics, according to Polanyi, is always liable to be put at the service of interests in the self-protection of society from the destructive potential of self-regulating relative prices. It is true that in contingent conditions, a society's political system, in what may be called a deficient mode, may temporarily become subordinate to the progress of markets and allocative efficiency. Polanyi assumes, however, that this cannot last as social movements, especially in modern societies, can never be entirely deprived of the opportunity to express publicly, and gather a following for, concepts of justice that emphasize needs for normative stability and material security, two aspects of social structure that Polanyi believed to be indispensable for human beings. This is why he considered the political dimension of social life as irrepressible, exceptional moments of collective forgetfulness notwithstanding, given that even the most capitalist of societies had to decide collectively what role they were willing to assign to social as opposed to economic interests, and more specifically whether and how they would defend the "fictive commodities" of labor and nature against ever-present pressures for ever-increasing commodification.

Polanyi's main work was completed in 1944. While he anticipated the modern welfare state, as did many other writers at the time, he did not and could not foresee its potential pathologies. This is not to say, however, that these could not be accommodated in his general framework in principle. Actually there is nothing in Polanyi suggesting that societal reactions to the grinding "satanic mill" of the market may not sometimes be fundamentally misconceived, or insufficient, or sufficient only for a limited period of time. In fact, the famous Speenhamland chapter of the "Great Transformation" is a still highly instructive analysis of policy failure resulting from a misunderstanding of the logic of markets and the limits and conditions of their "embedding" in social institutions (Polanyi 1957 [1944], Chapter 7).[16] I believe that the image suggested in the present book of a state that draws on future resources to compensate the losers of a market that it has only limited means to control would not in principle have appeared surprising to Polanyi, and the same would apply to the breakdown of Germany Inc. under the pull of international markets and the push of competition. I also believe that Polanyi would have had sufficient sense of dialectics to appreciate the postwar state of organized capitalism finding at some point its resources for social protection exhausted and turning toward policies of liberalization, that is, politically promoted market expansion, to relieve itself of responsibilities it no longer has the capacity to carry. Not only capitalism, but also the results of the countermovement are dynamic and historical. Political protections from markets may last only so long in a market society, and are likely to become obsolete as the Durkheimian institutions in which they are enshrined lose their grip on changing social and economic realities. For Polanyi, the only conclusion that this would justify would probably have been that in a world subject to the double movement, human society will continuously have to reinvent its politics or find other instruments to ensure itself against unpredictable fluctuations of markets and relative prices and the abrupt changes they threaten to inflict on the lives of their members.[17]

Polanyi's concept of the double movement connects easily with institutional analysis along the lines developed in this essay. Social countermovements against marketization are essentially about the defense or the creation of Durkheimian institutions imposing social obligations on economic actors. While there are Durkheimian institutions devoted to making markets work effectively—such as contract law (Durkheim 1964 [1893])—they may to a large extent be replaced with private, Williamsonian regulation at the disposition of those immediately concerned. In any case, *Polanyian institutions* that are market-breaking rather than market-making probably need to be Durkheimian in character: public rather than private, obligatory rather than expedient, and political instead of economic. The struggle between market expansion and market containment—between a capitalist economy and the society in which capitalism is "embedded"—that is at the heart of the double movement may be construed, by and large, as one between different types of institutions, or types of social order. The metaphor of the double move-ment projects to the level of society as a whole, and lends substan-tive meaning to, the micro-level distinction and the everyday tensions between institutions of the Durkheimian and Williamsonian kind. It also connects to the related distinction, as developed above in our analysis of the German case, between organized and disorganized capitalism, and specifies what it is from which the proponents of market expansion must struggle to free themselves.

Institutional analysis that emphasizes enactment and compliance, or noncompliance, gives action-theoretical definition to the forces that drive the dialectics of the double movement. Together with a Polanyian concept of the relationship between economy and society, it reveals the structural sources of the historical perishability of market-containing institutions in capitalism, and thereby justifies considering institutional regimes, or sys-tems, as processes. Moreover, enriching historical-institutionalist analysis with Polanyi's basic concepts helps us specify the nature and the systemic direction of the inevitable "historical" deviations from perfect reproduc-tion of obligatory institutions under capitalism, by calling attention to the characteristic cunningness of capitalist actors under competitive pressures and in a society that culturally approves of innovative enactment or non-enactment of institutions that stand in the way of the maximization of private utility, or of the maximally efficient utilization of economic resources.

17.4. Bounded Economizing

Hoes does the pursuit of economic efficiency fit in a historical-institutionalist model of capitalism? If efficiency is not the *telos* of history, what, then, is its place, and how does it come about, if at all, in capitalism conceived as a dynamic social order? In preceding chapters, we learned that even in a capitalist society, rational economizing aimed at maximiz-ing the utility of resources is embedded in social institutions that are not, or not exclusively, designed to support it; that making the world more effi-cient is not an uncontested collective objective but is inevitably in conflict with other, competing objectives; that economizing can take place only in the context of a historical social order that serves many other functions as well and resists monistic rationalization; that that context is defined, basically, by the Polanyian "double movement" of market expansion and social reconstruction, as well as by Durkheimian institutions imposing, or trying to impose, noneconomic obligations on economic actors that limit their options in their search for profit; and that, unlike what efficiency theories suggest, institutional change and institutional development are not governed by a designing hand, visible or invisible, that could be relied upon continuously to improve institutional efficiency.

In the following I will suggest, as the third of my three select building blocks of a historical-institutionalist theory of capitalism, that to determine the status of economizing as a social activity, one must pay at least as much attention to the micro as to the macro level of social action. I am aware that this goes against the grain of much of today's historical-institutionalist political economy literature, which prefers to deal with organized and unorganized collectivities. These it sometimes endows implicitly with supernatural power and foresight—free of passion, full of mathematics—in their untiring design and redesign of social institutions to fit the needs especially of business, as conditioned by the respective "variety of capitalism." All too often, political economy has been content with tracing, if not inventing and imputing, grand institutional bargains supposedly struck between entire social categories, or between large firms and the government, presumably in joint pursuit of comparative advantage. Instead, or in any case in addition, I suggest looking for more realistic accounts at the micro level of social action within and in relation to social institutions—in other words, at the interaction between rule-makers and rule-takers—where resourceful and restless entrepreneurs encounter a social order that they have not created and with which they must make do if they want to survive and improve their rate of profit.

Of course this is not to mean that politics is irrelevant for capitalist economizing—only that its significance is *both systematically limited and historically contingent.* Capitalist actors may and clearly do lobby governments, individually or collectively, for flexible labor markets, industrial subsidies, and the like. Even the largest firms and the most powerful business associations, however, cannot realistically be assumed to fully control the design of the social order of which they are part, or to be able to instruct the government unambiguously on policies and institutions optimally conducive to economic efficiency. Nor can the state be expected to have the power to implement everything that capitalists collectively believe to be in the interest of improved competitiveness—if capitalists hold collective beliefs on this at all. Political scientists, probably due to a peculiar *déformation professionnelle*, are at risk of overestimating the significance of politics, just as they tend to overestimate the capacity of capitalist firms for individual foresight and collective action. In any case, it seems to me that, as indicated by its predominant "strategy-speak," much of contemporary political science habitually overstates the intended and understates the unintended effects of social action, the more so the less attention it pays to the foundation of collective action in micro-level individual action.

As we have seen in our account of the German case, attention to the micro level is indispensable already when it comes to understanding the extent to which capitalist economizers become collectively involved in politics, presumably to advance their interests in competitiveness and efficiency. In a pluralist world, political action typically results not in technocratic execution of functionalist institutional design, but in agreement on compromised second-best solutions. Elsewhere, in an analysis of interest groups, we have described the mechanism that brings this about as a "logic of influence" governing collective action in political-institutional settings (Schmitter and Streeck 1999). Unlike what is suggested, for example, in theories of business-driven welfare state development, whether capitalist actors, resourceful and unruly as they are, will put up with the sacrifices their collective representatives are likely to agree to on their behalf, is not a foregone conclusion. Collective action, that is to say, is subject, not just to a logic of influence, but also to a "logic of membership," and the way the two play out in a given situation is historically strongly contingent. Thus, in German industrial relations, we have seen that as the system moved through time, a growing number of firms refused to follow the rules created for them by their associations, with many defecting from membership altogether. Likewise, with respect to general business strategies, large firms especially began to prefer pursuing their interests individually rather than collectively, with rising numbers exiting from the national economy in general and from the German company network in particular, in search for or attracted by more promising opportunities. As exit began to take the place of voice, in a decentralized process of individual advantage-seeking replacing centralized collective deal-making, the capacity of as well as the need for business as a class to have its preferred institutional design imposed through politics declined, and in fact became increasingly irrelevant with declining political capacity of the national state. Just as politics was never meant to be the design and implementation of efficient institutions, the liberalization of the postwar German political economy was not an act of strategic institution-building governed by business in alliance with a competition-conscious nation-state. Rather it took place in a steady process of disorganization—quite different from the sort of grand institutional bargain from above suspected by strategy-conscious political scientists, and more in the form of a gradual decomposition of a grand political bargain from below.

Not unlike collective political capacity, economic efficiency is best conceived as a product of interested, creative improvisation and experimentation within the limits of historically given institutions that may be far from optimal for the purposes at hand but cannot easily be changed or done away with. Evasion and circumvention of social obligations may often be a more promising path to profitability than demands for political reform that the government may be unable or unwilling to concede. Other responses by inventive entrepreneurs to the social constraints under which they are forced by history or society to conduct their business include learning, in the course of which economic actors discover merit in institutions that at first glance may have appeared to them as wholly unacceptable burdens on their endeavors. A case in point is workforce codetermination in German firms (Streeck 1984a, 1997a), an institution that was originally designed to afford the interests of workers effective representation in a firm's decision-making process; limit managerial prerogative, especially with respect to the management of labor; and ensure that firms lived up to the social obligations imposed on them in the context, for example, of industrial agreements and employment policy. With time, managements realized that codetermination, unpleasant as it was and remained in many respects, also offered them an opportunity to increase the legitimacy of strategic decisions with the workforce, generally cultivate workers' good will, and turn their elected representatives into close interlocutors that were more likely than full-time trade union officials to understand and indeed share the firm's economic interests. In fact, as pointed out in our account of change in German industrial relations, as the liberalization of German capitalism proceeded, business leaders often managed to convert, in the sense of Thelen (Thelen 2002), what was intended as an institutional constraint on their right to manage into an addition to their managerial toolkit. Improvised conversion of, as it were, Durkheimian into Williamsonian institutions served them exceedingly well in an economic environment like that of the 1980s and 1990s which happened to put a premium on close cooperation at the workplace in joint pursuit of high product quality and continuous product innovation.

As suggested elsewhere (Streeck 2004a), intelligent opportunism in relation to social constraints, which is easily recognized as one specific expression of the *unruly restlessness* of the model capitalist actor, may be the very essence of entrepreneurship in the Schumpeterian sense. Capitalist bourgeois turn themselves into citizens clamoring for a redesign of inconvenient institutions by political means only under exceptional circumstances; much to the dismay of the leaders of their associations, they usually prefer to exercise their inventiveness closer to home and work with what there is, hoping to find ways to make it work for them privately and individually if it cannot be changed publicly and collectively. In the process, capitalist entrepreneurship may surprisingly manage to turn constraints into opportunities, or transform originally costly constraints into "beneficial" ones (Streeck 1997a). For example, also in Germany, it seemed to have been in part the imposition by powerful industrial unions of a flat wage structure that made employers train their workers more, to enable them actually to earn the high wages to which they had come to be entitled under the industrial agreement. This outcome was beneficial, not just to the firms and the workers concerned, but also to the economy as a whole, given that a broad supply of high skills allows for fast technological innovation and flexible structural adjustment across the board if needed.

While empirical research is likely to reveal a large number of instances of efficiency-enhancing effects of social constraints produced by capitalist creativity from below, one must not give in to the functionalist temptation to explain the constraints being turned into opportunities as intended for that purpose by those who instituted them. The point that I am trying to make is that capitalist inventiveness is capable of using institutions for economizing, for example on transaction costs, *that had originally been intended to serve very different objectives,* including not least market-breaking ones. Still, some institutions may never become economically beneficial, neither from a capitalist nor from a public policy perspective: not being meant to be used for economic benefit in the first place, they simply are not apt to be turned around for this purpose and remain economically costly, or "inefficient," forever. Nor are we interested here in institutions that are, directly or indirectly, *intended* to make economic transactions more efficient—an effect that they then may or may not have in reality. Much more revealing as to the status of economizing in capitalist political economies are the surprisingly many institutional arrangements intended for, say, redistribution or social protection that are eventually put to economic use "from below." Such secondary usage of social institutions for economizing purposes,[18] leading to second-best and sometimes even first-best competitive solutions to economic problems, can be detected *ex post* but is difficult if not impossible to predict or, for that matter, intend *ex ante*: its possibility is typically realized by *inductive discovery in practice,* rather than *deductive reasoning in theory.* In such cases, whether or not a political-economic institution will turn out to be economically beneficial depends less on its design than on the way it is enacted "on the ground." Enactment, however, is essentially unpredictable from the perspective of rule-makers, in part because it changes over time with experience: in a historical world with an open future, the theorist cannot normally see farther than the actor.[19]

A perspective like this has the advantage that it accommodates paradoxes, tensions, and conflicts that exist empirically but are denied or played down in a technocratic-functionalist worldview. To account for the observation that a certain national institutional configuration happens to "fit" a given economic environment, there is no need in a theory of *bounded economizing* in the context of Durkheimian institutions and the Polanyian double movement to show that the institutions in question had been intended collectively and designed intelligently for the purpose. Under bounded economizing, high economic performance of a social institution may come about unintendedly and, from the viewpoint of the institution in question, accidentally, as a result of interested compliance and creative enactment. Moreover, for a theory free from functionalist assumptions of equilibrium, disappearance of institutional fit and decay of economic performance would not have to be explained by changing external conditions alone. This is because such a theory provides for internal defection on the part of rule-takers in pursuit of even greater— individual—advantage, as in the case of the demise of German industrial relations, of the associations traditionally governing them, and of the German company network. Where economic efficiency of institutions may come about unintended, there is no guarantee that it will last even if external conditions remain the same, and in fact given the specific unruliness of capitalist actors always on the lookout for even better opportunities, any institutional configuration regardless of its current performance must be considered temporary and perishable.

Historical-institutionalist theory should be able to offer an action-theoretical micro-foundation for analyzing economizing within the bounds of a social order. A theory like this can work without excessively rationalist assumptions, relaxing the demands on rule-makers' foresight just as on rule-takers' compliance, by giving credit to the latter's Schumpeterian creativity. Moreover, it systematically allows for accidents, unintended effects, and good or bad luck, which are vastly underrated in today's hyper-rationalist theories of political economy. For historical institutionalism high efficiency of institutions need not be explained by their intelligent design, but may also be the result of complementary inventions by actors making the best of unchangeable constraints in the process of enacting them. A theory of this sort can account for efficiency in institutional contexts without becoming functionalist or turning into efficiency theory. It also understands that the significance of economic efficiency as a political concern may be historically contingent and may, for example, decline in a disorganizing political economy in which firms become more independent and less governable. Today we recognize the uniqueness of the now-gone period of organized capitalism when the modern democratic state was capable of deep intervention in the market, to promote both solidarity and efficiency, and when it could hope that inventive capitalists would find efficient economic uses for elements of social order created to contain the free play of market forces. This book has suggested how historical institutionalism might trace the way capitalism moved from there to here, and reconstruct the attendant changes in the structure and the mode of operation of core institutions of postwar capitalism.

Politically, the analysis of socially bounded economizing carries good as well as bad news. The good news is, or was, that political reregulation of markets could hope, with some prospect of success, for indirect effects affording capitalist actors effective ways to pursue their interests—ways that, while perhaps more demanding on them than others, fitted in a socio-political regime that provided for a modicum of social security and stability. Politics and society could aspire to reeducate the capitalist owners of the means of production, to socialize them into a social order that was not only profitable but also sustainable. In particular, given capitalist entrepreneurial inventiveness, politics was not necessarily obliged to listen to the representatives of capital protesting against social reconstruction, trusting that individual capitalists would soon know better and accommodate themselves intelligently with the inevitable. The bad news, of course, is that this effect, conditional as it is on successful efforts at innovation, cannot always be relied upon. While sometimes it simply cannot be brought about, in other cases, like the German one, it may decay over time. Constraints become beneficial if they enforce acculturation, opportunistic or not, in a social order, making private actors embed the pursuit of their interests in a normative institutional context that requires of them some sort of sacrifice (Durkheim 1964 [1893]), if only in the form of greater and more intelligent effort. Where social constraints are strong, a large part of running a business must be devoted to making the *economic* economy, as it were, compatible with a society's *moral* economy. This, however, presupposes that exit from—potentially if not yet actually beneficial—constraints is foreclosed. The ultimate bad news, perhaps, may be that this is no longer the case, making the effort of learning seem increasingly unnecessary for capitalist actors and allowing them once again to seek easier, less virtuous paths to economic success.[20]

17.5. German Capitalism: Beyond Liberalization

What about the future of "German capitalism"? As has been noted, for example in our discussion of internationalization and the decomposition of the German company network, capitalist actors, non-sentimental as they are, can reasonably be assumed to be committed not to any specific national model of capitalism, but only to their own survival and success. Their defining disposition as social actors encourages them to take an individualistic and particularistic rather than a collectivistic and universalistic view in selecting their objectives and deploying their resources to attain them. Institutions are not an end for capitalist agents, as they might be for politicians or theorists of social order, but a means to be used, circumvented, redefined, abused, or abolished instrumentally. Arising opportunities to escape from Durkheimian social obligations may be disregarded for some time, so as to not put at risk the indisputable benefits of stability and security offered by an established social regime. It is the essence of a capitalist order, however, that at one point or other the temptation will be strong enough for at least one enterprising competitor to take the first step.[21] For a time, the others may still protect themselves, for example, by defensive cartelization, but ultimately all protections are likely to erode and firms will have to follow the first mover to equalize the advantages he has achieved for himself. By then, a countermovement is likely to start, seeking reconstruction of social stability and set in motion by traditional sectors of society, or by firms that have lost, or not yet rejuvenated, their Keynesian "animal spirits." Ultimately, this will result in yet another round of growing discontent with economic stagnation among utility-maximizing agents, and in increasingly effective opposition against stability-producing but costly social constraints.

The dialectics of constraint and opportunity and of protection and competition under capitalism are illustrated by the ambivalent attraction of the Anglo-American mode of production for German capital in the 1990s. Protection from takeover allowed large German firms to operate at a low level of profitability, reflected in correspondingly low stock prices. As de Jong has shown, this pattern was common on the European Continent, where it resulted in a high share of firms' value added going to workforces

Table 17.1. Corporate performance, selected averages (2000), Germany and United Kingdom

	Germany	UK
Real returns to capital		
Price-earnings ratio	17.8	21.5
Dividend yield	2.7%	2.6%
Return on equity	18.2%	20.4%
Market valuation		
Market value (million euros)	20,754	42,337
Ratio of market value to turnover	0.51	2.14
Market value per employee (million euros)	0.14	0.97
Price-book ratio	2.5	4.6
Sales, profits, employment		
Turnover (million euros)	38,122	22,015
Return on sales (EBIT to sales)	9.4%	19.2%
Employees	138,072	60,676

Note: Averages calculated from the 19 largest British and 20 largest German industrial firms belonging to the "Europa 500."

Source: Adapted from Jackson and Höpner (2001). Handelsblatt Europa 500, Handelsblatt June 11, 2001.

and the public, as represented by the government (de Jong 1997).[22] At first glance, stock owners did not suffer, nor did firms' capacity to raise capital, as price-earnings ratios, dividend yields and return on equity were about the same as in Anglo capitalism, due to Continental firms being undervalued in the stock market.

Differences between the two modes of production as of the end of the twentieth century were highlighted by Jackson and Höpner (2001) in a comparison of the performance of the largest British and German industrial firms (Table 17.1). With roughly identical real returns to capital, German firms employed more than twice as many workers as British firms, and their turnover was a little less than double that of their British counterparts. At the same time, British profitability almost exactly doubled German profitability, and so did British firms' total market value. As a result, the ratio of market value to turnover in Britain exceeded the German ratio by a factor of four, and market value per employee was even seven times higher in Britain than in Germany. Behind this was the fact that in Germany, protection from hostile takeover and the low average profit rate it allowed for made it possible for firms to engage in activities that yielded only a low return or, perhaps, none at all, with weak sectors being cross-subsidized out of the higher returns earned in more profitable core sectors. The result was much higher sales and significantly higher employment, which may be read as a particular sort of distributive compromise between the interests of workers and share owners, made possible by national institutions that offered firms and their managements protection from potential predators who would otherwise have taken advantage of firms' inevitably low market valuation.

While each of the two systems represented in Table 17.1 might appear to be in its own kind of equilibrium, with real returns on their differently valued capital practically the same, it was the British system that became attractive to German capitalists and not vice versa. Rather than British shareholders and managers pushing for more takeover protection, a growing number of German firms began in the 1990s to discover their sympathies for a more active stock market and for more attention being paid to "shareholder value." As Deutschland AG dissolved and capital market regulation became more investor-friendly, firms had to increase the price of their shares, which in turn gave them an excellent reason for what they may always have wanted to do but never dared to propose: increasing their rate of profit. A more realistic possibility of takeover, so strongly abhorred in the past, now became gradually recognized as an excellent tool for renegotiating the—"Durkheimian"—postwar labor settlement by privatizing it at the individual firm level. With the threat of a potential loss of corporate autonomy disciplining the representatives on the workforce, managements sought a new alliance on their terms with core workforces against workforces in divisions that were, or "had to be," cut as they did not generate the "necessary" rate of return. Moreover, as managerial pay became linked to stock prices, managers' enthusiasm for liberal, Anglo-style capitalism increased even further, and with it the resolution of executive boards to move out of less than highly profitable activities and use surplus funds no longer for paying for the employment of less productive workers but, instead, for higher payouts to investors and, of course, managers.

Clearly shareholders were also impressed as they watched the liberalization of the German system slowly becoming both a competitive necessity and a tempting opportunity. Getting rid of social obligations, for example to provide employment in exchange for protection from corporate raiders, promised significantly to increase the value of current assets. This was because social entanglements of all sorts always depress asset values. The more modern, or capitalist, the system of relevant property rights, leaving disposal of property exclusively to the owner, the higher the price at which an asset may be sold.[23] Rising capitalization of German firms was to produce equal firepower in international struggles over mergers and acquisitions, which are paid mostly by swapping stock.

Even though liberalization may not change dividend yields much in the end, the one-time jump in asset values that could have been expected from a firm's escape from the German system and its transition to the Anglo-American low-employment, high-profit regime might have been temptation enough for owners willing in principle to sell out. Indeed, dissociating themselves from German protection and exposing themselves to greater risks of competition may have appeared to more and more firms both as a promising aggressive strategy for higher profit and a necessary defense in an increasingly competitive international economy.

Unfortunately, it is impossible today, when speculating about future capitalist development, to avail oneself of a theory of modern capitalism. The subject has been neglected for too long—in favor, among other things, of functionalist equilibrium theorizing on supposedly alternative versions of what has become watered down to a "market economy." So all we can note here is that German, or European, capitalists, striving to overcome stagnation through liberalization and a move toward higher-yield modes of production, have ceased to be impeded by the *Keynesian constraint* that for products to be sold, the workers who produce them must be allowed enough purchasing power to buy them. Driving up stock prices, productivity and profitability by cutting loose from social obligations, such as to provide employment by cross-subsidizing low-profit activities, is no longer counterproductive when, as in the case of the German automobile industry, more than 70 percent of production is sold outside a firm's country of origin. It also helps that in putting pressure on labor as a *factor of production,* capital can today enlist the support of labor as a *factor of consumption*—of ever more demanding consumers who as producers have to work ever harder to operate an equally more demanding production system, in a world that is supplied better than ever before with what at the time of Adam Smith were still called the "necessaries of life" (Smith 1993 [1776], 8, 36).

Again, theoretical tools for understanding the capitalist economy of today hardly exist. What seems obvious, though, is that more than at any time in the past, capitalism has become a *culture,* or even a *cult,* in addition to and on top of a regime of production and exchange, and it is only in terms of a theory that takes this seriously that capitalism's potential futures may be realistically assessed. Two examples must suffice, one from the "demand" and the other from the "supply side." In the rich countries, secular stagnation resulting from saturation of markets for standardized, "sensible" commodities was avoided by massive efforts on the part of innovative entrepreneurial firms for strategic redesign of products in the direction of diversification and "de-maturity" (Abernathy et al. 1983), making them, more than ever, suitable for symbolic rather than just utilitarian purposes, such as gaining distinction in a supposedly more egalitarian society. German "diversified quality production," to the extent that it encompasses consumption goods, is a case in point, and no industry better illustrates the mechanism at work here than automobiles. By the late 1970s, everybody expected automobiles to become a standardized, entirely utilitarian commodity, with mature product and process technologies, produced more or less in developing countries and sold around the world to consumers using them essentially to "get from A to B" (Altshuler et al. 1984). Instead, cars became ever more diversified, technologically sophisticated, and toy-like—see the SUV's that no producer can afford not to build today. In the process, of course, cars also became expensive again and highly profitable. German engineering and German production management were instrumental in leading the way out of the trap of maturity, by switching to a new product range whose use value is far exceeded by what one could call its "dream value," which in contemporary capitalism may already have taken the place of Marx's "exchange value" at the center of what Marx called the "fetishism of the commodity."

Economics has traditionally been about the satisfaction of material needs that were obvious enough as such to appear to common sense as unproblematically given, without requiring further explanation. The closer one looks at the capitalist "economy" of today, however, the less it seems to conform to this image. "Use products," as it were, seem to make up only a declining share of what most people spend their, mostly, hard-earned income on—the growing remainder going to "dream products" or "fun products" supported by and required for a hedonistic-consumeristic mass culture. Unlike "sensible" standard products, these are not at all discredited for producers by a falling rate of profit.[24] Examples include clothing, sporting goods, tourism, wine, lotteries and, of course, automobiles.[25] Rather than rooting demand in fixed material needs unproblematically translated into preferences, an economic theory that aspires to understand contemporary capitalism must make the cultural formation of consumer habits, and indeed of consumers, one of its central subjects, *given that continued capital accumulation today depends crucially on ever-rising standards of consumption.* This, incidentally, is one reason why economic sociology, to the extent that it takes on the challenge of explaining, in short, how in the course of capitalist development *symbolic value replaces utilitarian need,* should long have become a superior alternative to an economics that considers "preferences" as exogenously given and deals with their formation essentially by neglecting it as immaterial—as might have been justified in the nineteenth century when economic growth could still be imagined[26] to serve the satisfaction of as yet unserved basic material needs.

The second example concerns the supply side, with its secular development toward both high productive flexibility and almost total subsumption of human labor under capitalist relations of production, in particular capitalist employment relations. Pulled in not least by upward-drifting standards of consumption, more people than ever entered the labor markets of advanced capitalist societies in the last three decades. Especially the exodus of women from the last remaining vestige of traditional life, the family, and their enthusiastic embrace of paid employment as liberation from the burdens of traditional status has revolutionized labor markets and employment systems. Women, just as the huge masses at the industrializing periphery to which a growing share of production became relocated from the center, discovered the cultural attractions and the liberating powers of the market just in time, when new competitive conditions and the need to restore profitability required reorganization of the productive apparatus for an unprecedented level of flexibility. Such reorganization was remarkably successful where worker solidarity and the protective safeguards for producers it had been able to gain after long struggles, especially in the years after 1945, seemed useless or even hostile to the interests of the less demanding new arrivals. In traditional language, as consumers rushed to be exploited on the demand side by producers selling them ever more expensive goods with declining relative use value, capitalism managed to enlist its customers as allies on the supply side in its effort to enforce intensification of work and ever-increasing labor market flexibility *on them in their other capacity as workers*. New "class alliances" arose, between workers as consumers and capitalists as organizers of efficient production, or between consumers as workers and capitalists as competitors for survival in increasingly contested markets threatened by overproduction and under-accumulation. But there were also new conflicts, not the least of them that between consumers and workers, who often are the same people, with the former interested in competitive product markets and the latter, perhaps, in protection from progressive intensification of work and growing flexibility of employment.[27]

Here, too, culture seems to have become the decisive factor. Liberalization today involves not just enhanced freedom for entrepreneurial risk-taking but a profound reeducation of workers and their families, not only regarding their economic needs but also with respect to a new, allegedly freely chosen but in fact normatively obligatory way of life that is thoroughly adjusted and subservient to the functional demands of an evolving capitalism. Just as culture has to provide for symbolically induced artificial scarcity today—cultivating a desire for an SUV instead of a VW—it must make workers ready for flexible high-profit production, by making paid employment as such seem normatively desirable and even culturally obligatory; by preaching the superiority of individual achievement over collective entitlement; or by celebrating the efficient organization of private life in the service of continuous availability for just-in-time production. Today, a dominant theme in everyday mythology is how highly motivated consumers-cum-workers become cultural heroes by managing to arrange their lifeworld so that it is compatible with and indeed conducive to full and enthusiastic participation in both flexible work and advanced markets for surplus consumption. Images abound in popular culture especially of super-women combining full-time employment, as corporate executive or as street sweeper, with a cheerful life as loving mother and attractive lover; or of super-couples selling 3,500 hours or more per year in the labor market while simultaneously raising two happy children, whom they drive around in their latest-model family SUV for short but intensive "quality time" family vacations.

Will today's rising pressures to reorganize society in line with the ever more demanding requirements of continued capital accumulation after almost three centuries of Western capitalism not at some point have to provoke a new Polanyian countermovement, one that tries again to set a limit to the penetration of capitalist relations into the fabric of human life? How much modernization-cum-rationalization can a society sustain, and how much will it take without resistance? I believe this to be the crucial question as we observe the gradual dissolution of the stabilizing institutions of the postwar era in a new wave of global liberalization and market expansion. Today, the politics of liberalization involve above all a more or less gradual deconstruction of traditional protections against markets, and a recalibration of social policies from de- to re-commodification: emphasizing investment in employability, equality of opportunity, individual responsibility, etc. Still, one would expect sooner or later that new demands for protection from competition and for limitations on the pace of an ever more breathless "rat race" will be saddled upon the primarily market-enhancing social policies that dominated the beginning of the twenty-first century. Polanyi's account of the form and the origins of the "collectivistic" countermovement against liberalism in nineteenth century England appears astonishingly familiar and perfectly fits the modern picture of a mélange of redistributive and regulatory political interventions in the market, "spontaneous, undirected by opinion, and actuated by a purely pragmatic spirit": "Laissez-faire was planned, planning was not" (Polanyi 1957 [1944], 141).

Social policy under capitalism was always characterized by a deep ambivalence, being market-making and market-breaking at the same time, and it is not surprising that today this is most visible where so-called "work and life" issues, and in particular the question of the compatibility of "work and family," are being addressed. In the nineteenth century, Marx explained the British factory legislation, whose passage under capitalism he had at first found nothing short of puzzling, as a defense of society, including capitalists, against the very real danger at the time of the capitalist modernization of production destroying its own foundations—by killing off the working class, and in particular its children. Today it appears that it is again the reproduction of society that is at stake, in the sense of children, instead of being consumed by factories, not being born in the first place, due to their potential parents being too busy earning the income they need to be able to consume as expected. This is why demographic and family policy seem to have taken the place factory legislation occupied in the nineteenth century: responding once again to the challenge to devise methods of social intervention that organize work, and perhaps consumption as well, in ways making it possible for society to bring up a new generation and have a future, capitalist or not.

Again, a warning is in place against functionalist misunderstandings. *That something is needed does not mean that it will be delivered.* Things can go wrong; there are deadly events; and the cultural attractions of a life devoted to individual achievement and advanced consumption are many. The plasticity of human ways of life is amazingly high. Capitalist markets are not corrected or contained unless sufficient political and cultural resources can be mobilized for the purpose. In an era of declining nation-states and a loss of social grip of national politics, such resources would largely have to be newly invented and created, without a guarantee that they will. As in the past, the historical task will be to set limits to capitalist markets and capitalist modernization, allowing for the modicum of social stability human actors need to produce and reproduce a sustainable social life. Whether what will be possible in the new world of endlessly and relentlessly competitive capitalism will be sufficient for humanity is an entirely open question. Obviously, the old solutions that worked in the decades after 1945 have become obsolete. That they cannot be restored does not mean, however, that solutions are no longer needed, but neither does the fact that they are needed mean that they will be found. Every new generation seems to have to devise its own answers to the puzzles posed by the fundamental tension between the inherent dynamism of capitalism and the need for stability in human affairs. Nobody knows how long the interplay between market expansion and social reconstruction can continue, and one may well be pessimistic and see the time coming when society will run out of answers. But then, it is true that humans specialize in the unexpected; that people have achieved the most astonishing things; and that there always is a fighting chance.

Notes

1. " 'The economy, stupid' was a phrase in American politics widely used during Bill Clinton's successful 1992 presidential campaign against George H.W. Bush...The phrase, coined by Clinton campaign strategist James Carville, refers to the notion that Clinton was a better choice because Bush had not adequately addressed the economy, which was undergoing a recession at the time...The phrase is repeated often in American political culture, usually preceded by the word 'it's', and with commentators sometimes substituting a different word in place of 'economy'. e.g., 'It's the deficit, stupid!', 'It's the corporation, stupid!', 'It's the math, stupid!' " (Wikipedia).
2. *Nota bene* that these are not intended to be anything but a selection from a much broader catalogue. For example, another subject that might have been included is the tension between a regime of private property and the communism of knowledge production, which is of course particularly relevant in an emerging "knowledge economy." See also the complex "cultural" factors related to the commodification of labor and the regulation of consumption, as touched upon in the final section of this chapter.
3. See Chapter 9 on "Endogenous Change".
4. With Etzioni, who was among the first explicitly to break away from the Parsonian consensus of the 1950s, we took leave of the assumption that compliance with an institution occurs always and necessarily out of normative commitment. In fact, we explicitly left open the possibility of less than perfect socialization of actors, with compliance motivated exclusively or mainly by expediency, in the pursuit of material gain or to avoid physical violence. In the present context, contingently deficitarian socialization allows for compliance as well as noncompliance "with guile," that is, for cunning evasion of the "meaning" of an institution in line with one's material interests.

5. I avoid speaking of "capitalists" here since the reference is to actors in a market where maximization of returns on invested capital is legitimate, and perhaps necessary for social survival. Most capitalist actors will, however, in fact be capitalists, in particular capitalist organizations, just as capitalists will as a rule be more capitalist than other capitalist actors.

6. I leave aside here the possibility for less endowed actors to pool resources for collective lobbying and rule contestation. While this possibility exists and indeed is far from unimportant politically, to realize it groups must cross the difficult threshold of organization while still remaining unlikely to match the resources available especially to large firms. I also disregard the pressure on national rule-makers to take notice of the interests of rule-takers who control mobile resources on which the collective prosperity of the community depends. I merely confine myself to an ideal-typical description of core aspects of the interaction between rule-makers and rule-takers under stylized capitalist conditions.

7. Reducing Oliver Williamson's general anthropology (Williamson et al. 1975) to a class-specific actor disposition.

8. Those who find this character portrait polemical or even politically radical must be reminded that economic theory, including the "rational choice" school in sociology and political science, applies the same, admittedly unflattering, image to the human actor in general, presumably to make the modern capitalist maximizer appear less monstrous by identifying him with modern man as such. The difference between rational choice and the present treatment is that I insist that the modern disposition is roughly as unevenly distributed as capitalist economic resources are, making some of us as social actors less "rational," cold, sharp, entrepreneurial, greedy, etc. than others, and as a result both less rich and easier to exploit.

9. Easily the most bizarre among the many bizarre passages in Williamson's anthropological excursions into human motivation is his explanation why workers tend to be shortchanged in their dealings with capitalists. In discussing how company towns come about, Williamson produces the astonishing insight, out of the blue and as far as I know never to be returned to later, that, "A chronic problem with labor market organization is that workers and their families are irrepressible optimists. They are taken in by vague assurances of good faith, by legally unenforceable promises, and by their own hopes for the good life. Tough-minded bargaining in its entirety never occurs or, if it occurs, comes too late. An objective assessment of employment hazards . . . thus comes only after disappointment" (Williamson 1985, 5.2). Workers, in other words, are for inexplicable reasons too human— and thus too stupid—for this world. If they were more hard-boiled, like their capitalist employers, microeconomic theory would work, and things would be in equilibrium.

10. "Improvements, we said, are, as a rule, bought at the price of social dislocation. If the rate of dislocation is too great, the community must succumb in the process" (Polanyi 1957 [1944], 76). I emphasize change, instability, unpredictability rather than, as does Polanyi in his historical treatment, impoverishment and starvation, given that in the advanced industrial societies of today it mostly is the former rather than the latter that strains social cohesion.

11. In economic theory, which worries about the *functioning* of markets, not their containment, the Polanyian defense of society against commodification is reflected in subjects such as the immobility of labor and the downward rigidity of wages. Polanyi believed that however much progress market-making policies might achieve, the result would never be more than a temporary compromise between markets and the lifeworld, at best. Cf. Hayek, who more or less openly expressed his dismay with workers being unwilling to be persuaded to organize their lives in the steady pursuit of market signals and move instantly to where the (better-paying) jobs happen to be, thereby recklessly upsetting the miraculous working of the market economy: humanity as friction in an otherwise perfect system (see, for instance, Hayek 1950, Chapter 19).

12. While Polanyi clearly was a conservative in his defense of labor, land, and money against commodification in the course of the "frivolous experiment" of a "market society," he was obviously not a reactionary as he sided with the labor movement rather than the preindustrial elites of his time. Today's libertarian Left may, however, feel a little perplexed sometimes by Polanyi's strong advocacy of social stability and traditional values (Polanyi 1957 [1944], Chapter 21).

13. More on this in the next section.

14. "For a century the dynamics of modern society was governed by a double movement: the market expanded continuously but this movement was met by a countermovement checking the expansion in definite directions. Vital though such a countermovement was for the protection of society, in the last analysis it was incompatible with the self-regulation of the market, and thus with the market system itself" (Polanyi 1957 [1944], 130). In 1944 Polanyi believed that the double movement had come to an end, in line with similar expectations famously held by Schumpeter and others about the secular demise of modern capitalism. With the benefit of hindsight, I disregard this prediction and assume that movement and countermovement have continued and will continue until further notice.

15. Incompatibility in Polanyi contrasts starkly with the key concept of "varieties of capitalism," complementarity.

16. Another example of a destructive response to market expansion is, of course, fascism—which Polanyi considered an attempt to insure against the uncertainties of international markets by national means.

17. A further aspect of the Polanyian approach that appears enormously useful is that his political economy of capitalism is only weakly linked to a class theory.

While historically it was the working class that could be counted on as the mainstay of the countermovement against commodification, there is nothing in Polanyi's work to preclude the possibility that parts of the working class may be drawn into the movement for market expansion, and may even become its active proponents. In this case, the line of conflict between capitalist dynamism and the need for social stability would run through individuals as well as, and in addition to, running through society as a whole. See the final section of this chapter.

18. The logic is the same as in certain instances of biological evolution pointed out by Gould and Lewontin (1979).

19. Here more than anywhere else, the classical American putdown of the scholar by the practitioner applies: "If you're so smart, why ain't you rich?"

20. See Chapter 14, on "Internationalization."

21. Alternatively, as pointed out, public policy may need to have recourse to enforcing competition as an antidote to rent-seeking exploitation of social stability by inherently "immodest," "insatiable," "unscrupulous" utility-maximizing actors.

22. See also Beyer and Hassel (2005).

23. Reforms of legal property rights may thus make real money. A similar mechanism seems to be at work when publicly traded firms are taken private, extricating them from financial supervision, or when family firms are acquired by hedge funds that run them from afar without "sentimental" social attachment to the surrounding local community. Finally, as mentioned above, it appears that large German firms and their associations campaigned for the abolishment of workforce codetermination on supervisory boards in 2004 and subsequent years in part because they expected it to result in higher asset prices.

24. Technological advance being used not to make products simpler and cheaper, but to make them more complex, diversified, and expensive. Of course the theme is familiar since the time when Veblen applied his "institutional economics," where institutions really were cultural habits and vanities, to the phenomenon of fashion (Veblen 1994 [1899]).

25. On clothing Aspers (2005), on wine and lotteries Beckert (Beckert 2007a, 2007). As to automobiles, SUV means "sports utility vehicle." The name is revealing in its brazen combination of "sports" and "utility," and in fact in the way it suggests that such vehicles should have any utility at all for city dwellers who do not happen to own a horse ranch. Reference to "utility" in this context is purely ideological: it calls up the memory of a long-gone economy organized around use values, for the purpose of cultural legitimation of enormous consumption expenditures on high-technology toys. At the same time, it is clear that by only mentioning what is obvious—that purchase of an SUV cannot possibly be justified with reference to a supposed use value—one steps outside a cultural consensus that considers as a spoilsport everyone who

insists on utility being taken seriously as a criterion for limiting work effort and allocating consumption expenditure.

26. Only by the naive, of course, as Marx had already shown that capitalist "extended" accumulation was not about use value but rather about exchange value.

27. The conflict between workers as workers and workers as investors in pension or mutual funds is of the same sort. In the latter capacity workers prefer, and must prefer, the stock of firms who are more ruthless than their competition in firing them in their former capacity. See Schimank (2007).

Bibliography

Abelshauser, Werner, 2006: Der "Rheinische Kapitalismus" im Kampf der Wirtschaftskulturen. In: Berghahn, Volker and Sigurt Vitols (eds.), *Gibt es einen deutschen Kapitalismus? Tradition und globale Perspektiven der sozialen Marktwirtschaft*. Frankfurt a.M.: Campus, 186–99.

Abernathy, William J. et al. 1983: *Industrial Renaissance*. New York: Basic Books.

Altshuler, Alan et al. 1984: *The Future of the Automobile: The Report of MIT's International Automobile Program*. London: Allen & Unwin.

Amable, Bruno, 2003: *The Diversity of Modern Capitalism*. Oxford: Oxford University Press.

Apeldoorn, Bastiaan van, 2002: *Transnational Capitalism and the Struggle over European Integration*. London: Routledge.

——and Laura Horn, 2007: The Marketisation of European Corporate Control: A Critical Political Economy Perspective. *New Political Economy*. Vol. 12, No. 2, 211–35.

Artus, Ingrid, 2001: *Krise des deutschen Tarifsystems: Die Erosion des Flächentarifvertrags in Ost und West*. Wiesbaden: Westdeutscher Verlag.

Aspers, Patrick, 2005: Status Markets and Standard Markets in the Global Garment Industry. MPIfG Discussion Paper 05/10. Cologne: Max Planck Institute for the Study of Societies.

Barnard, Catherine, 2004: *The Substantive Law of the European Union: The Four Freedoms*. Oxford: Oxford University Press.

Batt, Rosemary and Hiroatsu Nohara, 2007: How Institutions and Business Strategies Affect Wages: A Cross-National Study of Call Centers. Unpublished Manuscript.

Beckert, Jens, 1996: What is Sociological about Economic Sociology? Uncertainty and the Embeddedness of Economic Action. *Theory and Society*. Vol. 25, 803–40.

——2002: *Beyond the Market: The Social Foundations of Economic Efficiency*. Princeton: Princeton University Press.

——2003: Economic Sociology and Embeddedness: How Shall We Conceptualize Economic Action? *Journal of Economic Issues*. Vol. 37, 769–87.

——2007a: Die soziale Ordnung von Märkten. In: Beckert, Jens et al. (eds.), *Märkte als soziale Strukturen*. Frankfurt a.M.: Campus, 43–62.

Beckert, Jens, 2007*b*: The Great Transformation of Embeddedness: Karl Polanyi and the New Economic Sociology. MPIfG Discussion Paper 07/1. Cologne: Max Planck Institute for the Study of Societies.

—— 2008: The Social Order of Markets. MPIfG Working Paper 08/1. Cologne: Max Planck Institute for the Study of Societies.

—— and Mark Lutter, 2007: Wer spielt, hat schon verloren? Zur Erklärung des Nachfrageverhaltens auf dem Lottomarkt. *Kölner Zeitschrift für Soziologie und Sozialpsychologie.* Vol. 59, No. 2, 240–70.

Beyer, Jürgen, 2001: "One Best Way" oder Varietät? Strategischer und organisatorischer Wandel im Prozess der Internationalisierung. MPIfG Discussion Paper 02/1. Cologne: Max Planck Institute for the Study of Societies.

—— 2003: Deutschland AG a.D.: Deutsche Bank, Allianz und das Verflechtungszentrum des deutschen Kapitalismus. In: Streeck, Wolfgang and Martin Höpner (eds.), *Alle Macht dem Markt? Fallstudien zur Abwicklung der Deutschland AG.* Frankfurt a.M.: Campus, 118–46.

—— 2005: Vom Netzwerk zum Markt? Zur Kontrolle der Managementelite in Deutschland. In: Münkler, Herfried et al. (eds.), *Deutschlands Eliten im Wandel.* Frankfurt a.M.: Campus, 177–98.

—— 2006: *Pfadabhängigkeit: Über institutionelle Kontinuität, anfällige Stabilität und fundamentalen Wandel.* Frankfurt a.M.: Campus.

—— and Anke Hassel, 2005: The Effects of Convergence: Internationalization and the Changing Distribution of Net Value Added in Large German Firms. In: Clarke, Thomas (ed.), *European Corporate Governance: Critical Perspectives on Business and Management.* London: Routledge, 170–94.

—— and Martin Höpner, 2003: The Disintegration of Organised Capitalism: German Corporate Governance in the 1990s. *West European Politics.* Vol. 26, No. 4, 179–98.

Bispinck, Reinhard, 2001: Betriebliche Interessenvertretung, Entgelt und Tarifpolitik. *WSI-Mitteilungen.* Vol. 54, No. 2, 124–32.

—— 2005: Betriebsräte, Arbeitsbeziehungen und Tarifpolitik. WSI-Mitteilungen. Vol. 58, No. 6, 301–7.

—— and Thorsten Schulten, 2003: Verbetrieblichung der Tarifpolitik? Aktuelle Tendenzen und Einschätzungen aus Sicht von Betriebs- und Personalräten. WSI-Mitteilungen. Vol. 56, No. 3, 157–66.

Blyth, Mark, 2003: Same as It Never Was: Temporality and Typology in the Varieties of Capitalism. *Comparative European Politics.* Vol. 1, No. 2, 215–25.

Bode, Ingo, 2004: *Disorganisierter Wohlfahrtskapitalismus: Die Reorganisation des Sozialsektors in Deutschland, Frankreich und Großbritannien.* Wiesbaden: VS Verlag für Sozialwissenschaften.

Bosch, Gerhard, 1986: The Dispute over the Reduction of the Working Week in West Germany. *Cambridge Journal of Economics.* Vol. 10, No. 3, 271–91.

—— and Claudia Weinkopf (eds.), 2008: *Low-Wage Work in Germany.* New York: Russell Sage Foundation.

Boyer, Robert and Ives Saillard (eds.), 2002: *Regulation Theory: The State of the Art.* London: Routledge.

Bundesministerium der Finanzen, 2006: *Finanzbericht 2006: Stand und voraussichtliche Entwicklung der Finanzwirtschaft im gesamtwirtschaftlichen Zusammenhang.* Berlin: Bundesministerium der Finanzen.

Busch, Andreas, 2005: Globalisation and National Varieties of Capitalism: The Contested Viability of the "German Model". *German Politics.* Vol. 14, No. 2, 125–39.

Büthe, Tim, 2002: Taking Temporality Seriously: Modeling History and the Use of Narratives as Evidence. *American Political Science Review.* Vol. 96, 481–93.

Campbell, John, 2004: *Institutional Change and Globalization.* Princeton: Princeton University Press.

Carruthers, Bruce G. and Terence C. Halliday, 1998: *Rescuing Business.* Oxford: Clarendon Press.

Cioffi, John W. and Martin Höpner, 2006: The Political Paradox of Finance Capitalism: Interests, Preferences, and Center-Left Party Politics in Corporate Governance Reform. *Politics and Society.* Vol. 34, No. 4, 463–502.

Commons, John R., 1924: *Legal Foundations of Capitalism.* New York: Macmillan.

Crouch, Colin and Wolfgang Streeck, 1997a: Introduction: The Future of Capitalist Diversity. In: Crouch, Colin and Wolfgang Streeck (eds.), *Political Economy of Modern Capitalism: Mapping Convergence and Diversity.* London: Sage, 1–18.

——and Wolfgang Streeck (eds.), 1997b: *Political Economy of Modern Capitalism: Mapping Convergence and Diversity.* London: Sage.

——et al. 2005: Dialogue on Institutional Complementarity and Political Economy. *Socio-Economic Review.* Vol. 3, No. 2, 359–82.

Darwin, Charles, 2004 [1859]: *The Origin of Species.* London: CRW Publishing Limited.

de Jong, Henk Wouter, 1997: The Governance Structure and Performance of Large European Corporations. *Journal of Management and Governance.* Vol. 1, No. 1, 5–27.

Deeg, Richard, 2005: Change from within: German and Italian Finance in the 1990s. In: Streeck, Wolfgang and Kathleen Thelen (eds.), *Beyond Continuity: Institutional Change in Advanced Political Economies.* Oxford: Oxford University Press, 169–202.

Dertouzos, Michael L., Richard K. Lester, and Robert M. Solow, 1989: *Made in America: Regaining the Productive Edge.* Cambridge, MA: The MIT Press.

DiMaggio, Paul and Walter W. Powell, 1983: The Iron Cage Revisited: Institutional Isomorphism and Collective Rationality in Organizational Fields. *American Sociological Review.* Vol. 48, No. 2, 147–60.

Duesenberry, James S., 1960: Comment on Gary Backer, An Economic Analysis of Fertility. In: Universities-National Bureau Committee for Economic Research Conference (ed.), *Demographic and Economic Change in Developed Countries.* Princeton: Princeton University Press, 231–40.

Durkheim, Emile, 1964 [1893]: *The Division of Labor in Society*. New York: The Free Press.

——1968 [1894]: *Les règles de la méthode sociologique*. Paris: Presses Universitaire de France.

Dustmann, Christian, Johannes Ludsteck, and Uta Schönberg, 2007: *Revisiting the German Wage Structure*. IZA DP No. 2685. Bonn: IZA Forschungsinstitut zur Zukunft der Arbeit.

Dyson, Kenneth, 2001: The German Model Revisited: From Schmidt to Schröder. *German Politics*. Vol. 10, No. 2, 135–54.

Ebbinghaus, Bernhard, 2002: Dinosaurier der Dienstleistungsgesellschaft? Der Mitgliederschwund deutscher Gewerkschaften im historischen und internationalen Vergleich. MPIfG Working Paper 02/3. Cologne: Max Planck Institute for the Study of Societies.

——2003: Ever Larger Unions: Organisational Restructuring and Its Impact on Union Confederations. *Industrial Relations Journal*. Vol. 34, No. 5, 446–60.

——2006: *Reforming Early Retirement and Social Partnership in Europe, Japan and the USA*. Oxford: Oxford University Press.

——and Philip Manow (eds.), 2001: *Comparing Welfare Capitalism: Social Policy and Political Economy in Europe, Japan and the USA*. London: Routledge.

Edelman, Lauren B., 2004: Rivers of Law and Contested Terrain: A Law and Society Approach to Economic Rationality. *Law & Society Review*. Vol. 38, No. 2, 181–98.

Eichhorst, Werner, 2000: *Europäische Sozialpolitik zwischen nationaler Autonomie und Marktfreiheit: Die Entsendung von Arbeitnehmern in der EU*. Frankfurt a.M.: Campus.

Eldredge, Niles and Stephen Jay Gould, 1972: Punctuated Equilibria: An Alternative to Phyletic Gradualism. In: Schopf, Thomas J. M. (ed.), *Models in Paleobiology*. San Francisco: Freeman Cooper.

Ellguth, Peter, 2007: Betriebliche und überbetriebliche Interessenvertretung: Ergebnisse aus dem IAB-Betriebspanel 2005. *WSI-Mitteilungen*. Vol. 60, No. 3, 155–7.

Esping-Andersen, Gøsta, 1985: *Politics Against Markets: The Social-Democratic Road to Power*. Princeton: Princeton University Press.

Etzioni, Amitai, 1961: *A Comparative Analysis of Complex Organizations: On Power, Involvement, and Their Correlates*. New York: The Free Press.

——1968: *The Active Society*. New York: The Free Press.

Fellner, William et al. 1961: *The Problem of Rising Prices*. Paris: OECD.

Fichter, Michael, 1993: A House Divided: German Unification and Organised Labour. *German Politics*. Vol. 2, No. 1, 21–39.

——1997: Unions in the New Länder: Evidence for the Urgency of Reform. In: Turner, Lowell (ed.), *Negotiating the New Germany: Can Social Partnership Survive?* Ithaca, NY: Cornell University Press, 87–112.

——and Maria Kurbjuhn, 1992: Die Gewerkschaften im Einigungsprozeß: Ausdehnung mit alten Organisationsstrukturen und neuen Integrationsproblemen. In: Eichener, Volker (ed.), *Organisierte Interessen in Ostdeutschland*. Marburg: Metropolis, 159–74.

Freud, Sigmund, 2004 [1929]: *Civilization and Its Discontents*. London: Penguin.

Freye, Saskia, 2007: Führungswechsel in der Deutschland AG: Die Wirtschaftselite im Wandel, 1960–2005. Doctoral thesis. Köln: Max-Planck-Institut für Gesellschaftsforschung.

Friedman, Milton, 1983 [1973]: The Social Responsibility of Business Is to Increase Its Profits. In: Snoeyenbos, Milton H. et al. (eds.), *Business Ethics: Corporate Values and Society*. New York: Prometheus Books.

Gernandt, Johannes and Friedhelm Pfeiffer, 2007: Rising Wage Inequality in Germany. Discussion Paper No. 06-019. Mannheim: ZEW Zentrum für Europäische Wirtschaftsforschung.

Gerschenkron, Alexander, 1968: *Continuity in History, and Other Essays*. Cambridge, MA: Belknap Press of Harvard University Press.

Glyn, Andrew, 2006: *Capitalism Unleashed: Finance Globalization and Welfare*. Oxford: Oxford University Press.

Gould, Stephen Jay, 1997: Darwinian Fundamentalism. *The New York Review of Books*. Vol. 44, No. 10, June 12. <http://www.nybooks.com/articles/1151>.

——2002: *The Structure of Evolutionary Theory*. Cambridge, MA: Belknap Press of Harvard University Press.

——and Richard C. Lewontin, 1979: The Spandrels of San Marco and the Panglossian Paradigm: A Critique of the Adaptationist Programme. *Proceedings of the Royal Society of London. Series B, Biological Sciences*. Vol. 205, No. 1161, 581–98.

Granovetter, Mark, 1991: Economic Action and Social Structure: The Problem of Embeddedness. *American Journal of Sociology*. Vol. 91, No. 3, 481–510.

Grant, Wyn, 1984: Large Firms and Public Policy in Britain. *Journal of Public Policy*. Vol. 4, 1–17.

Greif, Avner, 2006: *Institutions and the Path to the Modern Economy*. Cambridge: Cambridge University Press.

——and David A. Laitin, 2004: A Theory of Endogenous Institutional Change. *American Political Science Review*. Vol. 98, No. 4, 633–52.

Grossmann, Henryk, 1929: *Das Akkumulations- und Zusammenbruchsgesetz des kapitalistischen Systems*. Leipzig: Hirschfeld.

Hacker, Jacob, 2004: Privatizing Risk without Privatizing the Welfare State: The Hidden Politics of Social Policy Retrenchment in the United States. *American Political Science Review*. Vol. 98, No. 2, 243–60.

Haipeter, Thomas and Gabi Schilling, 2005: Tarifbindung und Organisationsentwicklung: OT-Verbände als Organisationsstrategie der metallindustriellen Arbeitgeberverbände. In: Institut Arbeit und Technik im Wissenschaftszentrum Nordrhein-Westfalen (ed.), *Jahrbuch 2005*. Gelsenkirchen: IAT, 169–84.

Hall, Peter, 2007: The Dilemmas of Contemporary Social Science. *Boundary 2*. Vol. 34, No. 3, 121–41.

——and D. W. Gingerich, 2004: Varieties of Capitalism and Institutional Complementarities in the Macroeconomy. MPIfG Discussion Paper 04/5. Cologne: Max Planck Institute for the Study of Societies.

Hall, Peter A. and David Soskice, 2001*a*: An Introduction to Varieties of Capitalism. In: Hall, Peter A. and David Soskice (eds.), *Varieties of Capitalism: The Institutional Foundations of Comparative Advantage.* Oxford: Oxford University Press, 1–68.

Hall, Peter A. and David Soskice, (eds.), 2001*b*: *Varieties of Capitalism: The Institutional Foundations of Comparative Advantage.* Oxford: Oxford University Press.

——and —— 2003: Varieties of Capitalism and Institutional Change: A Response to Three Critics. *Comparative European Politics.* Vol. 1, No. 2, 241–50.

——and Rosemary Taylor, 1996: Political Science and the Three New Institutionalisms. *Political Studies.* Vol. 44, 936–57.

Harding, Rebecca, 1999: Standort Deutschland in the Globalising Economy: An End to the Economic Miracle? *German Politics.* Vol. 8, No. 1, 66–88.

Hassel, Anke, 1999: The Erosion of the German System of Industrial Relations. *British Journal of Industrial Relations.* Vol. 37, No. 3, 483–505.

——et al. 2003: Two Dimensions of the Internationalization of Firms. *Journal of Management Studies.* Vol. 40, No. 3, 705–23.

Hay, Colin, 2005: Two Can Play at that Game . . . or Can They? In: Coates, David (ed.), *Varieties of Capitalism, Varieties of Approaches.* Houndmills: Palgrave, 106–21.

Hayek, Friedrich A., 1950: *Studies in Philosophy, Politics, and Economics.* Chicago: The University of Chicago Press.

Heemskerk, Eelke M., 2007: *Decline of the Corporate Community: Network Dynamics of the Dutch Business Elite.* Amsterdam: Amsterdam University Press.

Heidenheimer, Arnold, 1980: *Unions and Welfare State Development in Britain and Germany: An Interpretation of Metamorphoses in the Period 1901–1950. Publication Series of the International Institute for Comparative Social Research Berlin.* Berlin: Wissenschaftszentrum Berlin für Sozialforschung.

Herrmann, Andrea, 2006: Alternative Pathways to Competitiveness within Developed Capitalism: A Comparative Study of the Pharmaceutical Sector in Germany, Italy and the UK. PhD thesis. Florence: Department of Political and Social Sciences. European University Institute.

Hickel, Rudolf, 2004: Sind die Manager ihr Geld wert? *Blätter für deutsche und internationale Politik.* Vol. 54, No. 10, 1197–204.

Hilferding, Rudolf, 1981 [1910]: *Finance Capital: A Study of the Latest Phase of Capitalist Development. Edited with an Introduction by Tom Bottomore.* London: Routledge & Kegan Paul.

Hirsch, Fred and John Goldthorpe (eds.), 1978: *The Political Economy of Inflation.* London: Martin Robertson.

Hirschman, Albert O., 1992: *Rival Views of Market Society and Other Recent Essays.* Cambridge, MA: Harvard University Press.

Höpner, Martin, 2004: Was bewegt die Führungskräfte? Von der Agency-Theorie zur Soziologie des Managements. *Soziale Welt.* Vol. 55, No. 3, 263–82.

——2005a: Sozialdemokratie, Gewerkschaften und organisierter Kapitalismus, 1880–2002. *Kölner Zeitschrift für Soziologie und Sozialpsychologie.* Vol. 45, Sonderheft, 196–221.

——2005b: What Connects Industrial Relations and Corporate Governance? Explaining Institutional Complementarity. *Socio-Economic Review.* Vol. 3, No. 2, 331–58.

——2007a: Coordination and Organization: The Two Dimensions of Nonliberal Capitalism. MPIfG Working Paper 07/12. Cologne: Max Planck Institute for the Study of Societies.

——2007b: Einleitung: Organisierter Kapitalismus in Deutschland. In: Höpner, Martin (ed.), *Organisierter Kapitalismus in Deutschland: Komplementarität, Politik, Niedergang.* Habilitation thesis. Köln: Universität zu Köln, Wirtschafts- und Sozialwissenschaftliche Fakultät.

——and Armin Schäfer, 2007: A New Phase of European Integration: Organized Capitalisms in Post-Ricardian Europe. MPIfG Discussion Paper 07/4. Cologne: Max Planck Institute for the Study of Societies.

——and Gregory Jackson, 2006: Revisiting the Mannesmann Takeover: How Markets for Corporate Control Emerge. *European Management Review.* Vol. 3, No. 3, 142–55.

——and Lothar Krempel, 2004: The Politics of the German Company Network. *Competition and Change.* Vol. 8, No. 4, 339–56.

Howell, Chris, 2003: Varieties of Capitalism: And Then There Was One? *Comparative Politics.* Vol. 36, No. 3, 103–24.

Ibn, Khaldûn, 1950 [1377]: *An Arab Philosophy of History: Selections from the Prolegomena of Ibn Khaldûn.* London: Murray.

Jackson, Gregory and Hideaki Miyajima, 2007: Varieties of Capitalism, Varieties of Markets: Mergers and Acquisitions in Japan, Germany, France, the UK and USA. RIETI Discussion Paper Series 07-E-054. Tokyo: RIETI.

——and Martin Höpner, 2001: An Emerging Market for Corporate Control? The Mannesmann Takeover and German Corporate Governance. MPIfG Discussion Paper 01/4. Cologne: Max Planck Institute for the Study of Societies.

Jackson, Gregory and Richard Deeg, 2006: *How Many Varieties of Capitalism?* MPIfG Discussion Paper 06/2. Cologne: Max Planck Institute for the Study of Societies.

——Martin Höpner, and Antje Kurdelbusch, 2005: Corporate Governance and Employees in Germany: Changing Linkages, Complementarities, and Tensions. In: Gospel, Howard and Howard Pendleton (eds.), *Corporate Governance and Labor Management: An International Comparison.* Oxford: Oxford University Press, 84–121.

Jaehrling, Karen, 2008: The Polarization of Working Conditions: Cleaners and Nursing Assistants in Hospitals. In: Bosch, Gerhard and Claudia Weinkopf (eds.), *Low-Wage Work in Germany.* New York: Russell Sage Foundation, 177–213.

Jay, Martin, 1973: *Dialektische Phantasie: Die Geschichte der Frankfurter Schule und des Instituts für Sozialforschung 1923–1950*. Frankfurt a.M.: Fischer.

Jürgens, Ulrich and Martin Krzywdzinski, 2007: Zur Zukunftsfähigkeit des deutschen Produktionsmodells. In: Kocka, Jürgen (ed.), *Zukunftsfähigkeit Deutschlands: Sozialwissenschaftliche Essays. WZB-Jahrbuch 2007*. Berlin: edition sigma, 203–27.

Katz, Harry C. and Owen Darbishire, 2000: *Converging Divergences: Worldwide Changes in Employment Systems*. Ithaca, NY: Cornell University Press.

Katzenstein, Peter J., 1985: *Small States in World Markets*. Ithaca, NY: Cornell University Press.

—— 1987: *Policy and Politics in West Germany: The Growth of a Semisovereign State*. Philadelphia: Temple University Press.

Kay, Adrian, 2006: *The Dynamics of Public Policy: Theory and Evidence*. Cheltenham: Edward Elgar.

Keller, Bernd, 2006: Aktuelle Entwicklungen der Beschäftigungsbeziehungen im öffentlichen Dienst. *Die Verwaltung: Zeitschrift für Verwaltungsrecht und Verwaltungswissenschaften*. Vol. 39, No. 1, 79–99.

—— 2007a: Arbeitgeberverbände des öffentlichen Sektors. In: Schroeder, Wolfgang and Bernhard Weßels (eds.), *Die Wirtschafts- und Arbeitgeberverbände in Politik und Gesellschaft der Bundesrepublik Deutschland*. Wiesbaden: VS Verlag für Sozialwissenschaften.

—— 2007b: Wandel der Arbeitsbeziehungen im öffentlichen Dienst: Entwicklungen und Perspektiven. *Die Verwaltung. Zeitschrift für Verwaltungsrecht und Verwaltungswissenschaften*. Vol. 40, No. 2, 173–202.

Kenworthy, Lane, 2001: Wage Setting Measures: A Survey and Assessment. *World Politics*. Vol. 54, No. 1, 57–98.

Kerr, Clark, Frederick H. Harbison, and Charles A. Myers, 1960: *Industrialism and Industrial Man: The Problems of Labor and Management in Economic Growth*. Cambridge, MA: Harvard University Press.

Kindermann, Daniel, 2005: Pressure from without, Subversion from within: The Two-Pronged German Employer Offensive. *Comparative European Politics*. Vol. 3, 432–63.

Kitschelt, Herbert and Wolfgang Streeck, 2003: From Stability to Stagnation: Germany at the Beginning of the Twenty-First Century. *West European Politics*. Vol. 26, No. 4, 1–34.

Kittel, Bernhard and Hannes Winner, 2002: How Reliable is Pooled Analysis in Political Economy? The Globalization-Welfare State Nexus Revisited. MPIfG Discussion Paper 02/3. Cologne: Max Planck Institute for the Study of Societies.

Klages, Philipp, 2006: Zwischen institutioneller Innovation und Reproduktion. Zum Wandel des deutschen Corporate-Governance-Systems in den 1990ern. *Berliner Journal für Soziologie*. Vol. 15, No. 1, 37–54.

Kocka, Jürgen, 1974: Organisierter Kapitalismus oder Staatsmonopolistischer Kapitalismus. In: Winkler, Heinrich August and Gerald D. Feldmann (eds.),

Organisierter Kapitalismus: Voraussetzungen und Anfänge. Göttingen: Vandenhoeck & Ruprecht, 19–35.

Kohaut, Susanne, 2007: Tarifbindung und tarifliche Öffnungsklauseln: Ergebnisse aus dem IAB-Betriebspanel 2005. *WSI-Mitteilungen.* Vol. 60, No. 2, 94–7.

—— and Claus Schnabel, 2006: Tarifliche Öffnungsklauseln: Verbreitung, Inanspruchnahme und Bedeutung. Discussion Paper No. 41. Erlangen-Nürnberg: Friedrich-Alexander-Universität, Lehrstuhl für Volkswirtschaftslehre.

Kohn, Karsten, 2006: Rising Wage Dispersion, After All! The German Wage Structure at the Turn of the Century. Discussion Paper No. 06-031. Mannheim: ZEW Zentrum für Europäische Wirtschaftsforschung.

Krasner, Stephen D., 1988: Sovereignty: An Institutional Perspective. *Comparative Political Studies.* Vol. 21, 66–94.

Krippner, Greta, 2001: The Elusive Market: Embeddedness and the Paradigm of Economic Sociology. *Theory and Society.* Vol. 30, 775–810.

Kuhn, Thomas, 1970: *The Structure of Scientific Revolutions.* Chicago: Chicago University Press.

Lane, Christel, 2000: Globalization and the German Model of Capitalism: Erosion or Survival? *British Journal of Sociology.* Vol. 51, No. 2, 207–34.

Lash, Scott and John Urry, 1987: *The End of Organized Capitalism.* Oxford: Polity Press.

Lehmbruch, Gerhard, 1991: Die deutsche Vereinigung: Strukturen und Strategien. *Politische Vierteljahresschrift.* Vol. 32, No. 4, 585–604.

—— 1993: Institutionentransfer: Zur politischen Logik der Verwaltungsreform in Deutschland. In: Seibel, Wolfgang et al. (eds.), *Verwaltungsreform und Verwaltungspolitik im Prozess der deutschen Einigung.* Baden-Baden: Nomos, 41–66.

—— 1994: The Process of Regime Change in East Germany: An Institutionalist Scenario for German Unification. *Journal of European Public Policy.* Vol. 1, No. 1, 115–42.

—— 1995: Sektorale Variationen in der Transformationsdynamik der politischen Ökonomie Ostdeutschlands. In: Seibel, Wolfgang and Arthur Benz (eds.), *Regierungssystem und Verwaltungspolitik.* Opladen: Westdeutscher Verlag, 118–215.

—— 1996: Die Rolle der Spitzenverbände im Transformationsprozeß: Eine neo-institutionalistische Perspektive. In: Kollmorgen, Raj et al. (eds.), *Sozialer Wandel und Akteure in Ostdeutschland.* Opladen: Leske + Budrich, 117–45.

Leibfried, Stephan and Herbert Obinger, 2003: The State of the Welfare State: German Social Policy between Macroeconomic Retrenchment and Microeconomic Recalibration. *West European Politics.* Vol. 26, No. 4, 199–218.

Liebert, Nicola, 2004: *Globalisierung, Steuervermeidung und Steuersenkungswettlauf: Die zunehmende Umverteilung von unten nach oben.* WEED Arbeitspapier Berlin: Weltwirtschaft, Ökologie und Entwicklung.

Lütz, Susanne, 2002: *Der Staat und die Globalisierung von Finanzmärkten.* Frankfurt a.M.: Campus.

Luxemburg, Rosa, 1913: *Die Akkumulation des Kapitals: Ein Beitrag zur ökonomischen Erklärung des Imperialismus*. Berlin: Buchhandlung Vorwärts Paul Singer GmbH.

Machiavelli, Niccolo, 1976: *The Prince. New Translation, Introduction, and Annotation by James B. Atkinson*. Indianapolis: Bobbs-Merrill.

Manow, Philip, 2001: Business Coordination, Collective Wage Bargaining and the Welfare State: Germany and Japan in Historical-Comparative Perspective. In: Ebbinghaus, Bernhard and Philip Manow (eds.), *Comparing Welfare Capitalism*. London: Routledge, 27–51.

—— 2007: *Social Protection and Capitalist Production: The Bismarckian Welfare State and the German Political Economy, 1880–1990*. Amsterdam: Amsterdam University Press.

—— and Eric Seils, 2000: Adjusting Badly: The German Welfare State, Structural Change, and the Open Economy. In: Scharpf, Fritz W. and Vivien A. Schmidt (eds.), *Welfare and Work in the Open Economy. Volume II: Diverse Responses to Common Challenges*. Oxford: Oxford University Press, 264–307.

Mares, Isabela, 2003: *The Politics of Social Risk: Business and Welfare State Development*. Cambridge: Cambridge University Press.

Marx, Karl, 1966 [1894]: *Das Kapital. Kritik der Politischen Ökonomie. Dritter Band*. Berlin: Dietz Verlag.

—— and Friedrich Engels, 1972 [1848]: Manifest der Kommunistischen Partei. In: Marx, Karl Friedrich Engels (eds.), *Werke* Vol. 4. Berlin: Dietz Verlag, 459–93.

Massa-Wirth, Heiko, 2007: *Zugeständnisse für Arbeitsplätze? Konzessionäre Beschäftigungsvereinbarungen im Vergleich Deutschland-USA*. Berlin: edition sigma.

—— and Hartmut Seifert, 2004: Betriebliche Bündnisse für Arbeit nur mit begrenzter Reichweite? *WSI-Mitteilungen*. Vol. 57, No. 4, 246–54.

Mayntz, Renate, 2004: Mechanisms in the Analysis of Social Macro-Phenomena. *Philosophy of the Social Sciences*. Vol. 34, No. 2, 237–59.

—— and Fritz W. Scharpf, 1995a: Der Ansatz des akteurzentrierten Institutionalismus. In: Mayntz, Renate and Fritz W. Scharpf (eds.), *Gesellschaftliche Selbstregulierung und politische Steuerung*. Frankfurt a.M.: Campus, 39–72.

—— and —— (eds.), 1995b: *Gesellschaftliche Selbstregelung und politische Steuerung*. Frankfurt a.M.: Campus.

Mayr, Ernst, 1988: *Towards a New Philosophy of Biology: Observations of an Evolutionist*. Cambridge, MA: The Belknap Press of Harvard University Press.

—— 2001: *What Evolution Is*. New York: Basic Books.

Merton, Robert K., 1957: *Social Theory and Social Structure*. Glencoe, Ill.: The Free Press.

Möller, Joachim, 2005: *Lohnungleichheit in West- und Ostdeutschland im Vergleich zu den USA*. Regensburg: Universität Regensburg, Wirtschaftswissenschaftliche Fakultät, Institut für Vokswirtschaftslehre.

Moore, Barrington, 1966: *Social Origins of Dictatorship and Democracy: Lord and Peasant in the Making of the Modern World*. Boston: Beacon Press.

Moravcsik, Andrew, 1998: *The Choice for Europe: Social Purpose and State Power from Messina to Maastricht*. Ithaca, NY: Cornell University Press.

Müller-Jentsch, Walter, 1993: *Konfliktpartnerschaft: Akteure und Institutionen der industriellen Beziehungen*. München: Hampp.

Müller-Jentsch, Walther, 1995: Germany: From Collective Voice to Co-Management. In: Rogers, Joel and Wolfgang Streeck (eds.), *Works Councils: Consultation, Representation, and Cooperation in Industrial Relations*. Chicago: Chicago University Press, 53–87.

Müller, Hans-Peter and Manfred Wilke, 2003: Gewerkschaftsfusionen: Der Weg zu modernen Multibranchengewerkschaften. In: Schröder, Wolfgang and Bernhard Weßels (eds.), *Die Gewerkschaften in Politik und Gesellschaft der Bundesrepublik Deutschland*. Wiesbaden: Westdeutscher Verlag, 122–43.

Naphtali, Fritz (ed.), 1984 [1928]: *Wirtschaftsdemokratie: Ihr Wesen, Weg und Ziel*. Köln: Bund-Verlag.

North, Douglass C., 1990: Institutions and Their Consequences for Economic Performance. In: Cook, Karen and Margaret Levi (eds.), *The Limits of Rationality*. Chicago: Chicago University Press, 383–401.

—— 1997: Economic Performance through Time. 1993 Nobel Prize Lecture. In: Persson, Torsten (ed.), *Nobel Lectures, Economics 1991–1995*. Singapore: World Scientific Publishing Co.

O'Sullivan, Mary, 2007: Acting Out Institutional Change: Understanding the Recent Transformation of the French Financial System. *Socio-Economic Review*. Vol. 5, No. 3, 398–436.

Obinger, Herbert, 2007: Sozialpolitische Nettoausgaben im internationalen Vergleich. *ZES Report*. Vol. 12, No. 2, 1–5.

Offe, Claus, 2006: *Reflections on America: Tocqueville, Weber & Adorno in the United States*. Cambridge: Polity.

Olson, Mancur, 1971: *The Logic of Collective Action: Public Goods and the Theory of Groups*. Cambridge, MA: Harvard University Press.

—— 1982: *The Rise and Decline of Nations*. New Haven, CT: Yale University Press.

Pestoff, Victor A., 2006: Globalization and Swedish Business Interest Associations in the Twenty-First Century. In: Streeck, Wolfgang et al. (eds.), *Governing Interests: Business Associations Facing Internationalization*. London: Routledge.

Pierson, Paul, 2000: Increasing Returns, Path Dependence, and the Study of Politics. *American Political Science Review*. Vol. 94, No. 2, 251–68.

—— 2001: From Expansion to Austerity: The New Politics of Taxing and Spending. In: Levin, Martin A. et al. (eds.), *Seeking the Center: Politics and Policymaking at the New Century*. Washington, D.C.: Georgetown University Press, 54–80.

—— 2004: *Politics in Time: History, Institutions, and Social Analysis*. Princeton: Princeton University Press.

Polanyi, Karl, 1957 [1944]: *The Great Transformation: The Political and Economic Origins of Our Time*. Boston: Beacon Press.

Polanyi, Karl, 1992 [1957]: The Economy as Instituted Process. In: Granovetter, Mark and Richard Swedberg (eds.), *The Sociology of Economic Life*. Boulder, CO: Westview Press, 29–51.

Pontusson, Jonas, 2005: Varieties and Commonalities of Capitalism. In: Coates, David (ed.), *Varieties of Capitalism, Varieties of Approaches*. Houndmills: Palgrave MacMillan, 163–88.

Rehder, Britta, 2003: *Betriebliche Bündnisse für Arbeit in Deutschland: Mitbestimmung und Flächentarif im Wandel*. Frankfurt a.M.: Campus.

——2006: Legitimitätsdefizite des Co-Managements. Betriebliche Bündnisse als Konfliktfeld zwischen Arbeitnehmern und betrieblicher Interessenvertretung. *Zeitschrift für Soziologie*. Vol. 35, No. 3, 227–42.

Ritter, Gerhard A., 2006: *Der Preis der deutschen Einheit: Die Wiedervereinigung und die Krise des Sozialstaats*. München: Beck.

Robinson, Joan, 1962: *Economic Philosophy*. London: Watts.

Rostow, Walt W., 1990 [1960]: *The Stages of Economic Growth: A Non-Communist Manifesto*. Cambridge: Cambridge University Press.

Roth, Guenther, 1976: History and Sociology in the Work of Max Weber. *British Journal of Sociology*. Vol. 27, No. 3, 306–18.

Rudolph, Wolfgang and Wolfram Wassermann, 2007: *Trendreport Betriebsräte-wahlen 2006: Ergebnisse der erweiterten Analyse*. Kassel: Büro für Sozialforschung Kassel.

Ruggie, John Gerard, 1982: International Regimes, Transactions and Change: Embedded Liberalism in the Postwar Economic Order. *International Organization*. Vol. 36, No. 2, 379–99.

——1998: Globalization and the Embedded Liberalism Compromise: The End of an Era? In: Streeck, Wolfgang (ed.), *Internationale Wirtschaft, nationale Demokratie: Herausforderungen für die Demokratietheorie*. Frankfurt a.M.: Campus, 79–97.

Sachverständigenrat zur Begutachtung der gesamtwirtschaftlichen Entwicklung, 2006: *Jahresgutachten 2006/07: Widerstreitende Interessen: Ungenutzte Chancen*. Wiesbaden: Statistisches Bundesamt.

Scharpf, Fritz W., 1991: *Crisis and Choice in European Social Democracy*. Ithaca, NY: Cornell University Press.

——1996: Negative and Positive Integration in the Political Economy of European Welfare States. In: Marks, Gary et al. (eds.), *Governance in the European Union*. London: Sage, 15–39.

——1998a: Balancing Positive and Negative Integration: The Regulatory Options for Germany. In: Dettke, Dieter (ed.), *The Challenge of Globalization for Germany's Social Democracy*. New York: Berghahn Books, 29–60.

——1998b: Negative and Positive Integration in the Political Economy of Euro-pean Welfare States. In: Rhodes, Martin and I Meny (eds.), *The Future of European Welfare*. Houndmills: Macmillan, 155–77.

——2007: Reflections on Multilevel Legitimacy. MPIfG Working Paper 07/3. Cologne: Max Planck Institute for the Study of Societies.

——and Viven A. Schmidt (eds.), 2000: Welfare and Work in the Open Economy. *Volume II: Diverse Responses to Common Challenges.* Oxford: Oxford University Press.

Schettkat, Ronald, 2006: *Lohnspreizung: Mythen und Fakten.* Düsseldorf: Hans-Böckler-Stiftung.

Schickler, Eric, 2001: *Disjointed Pluralism: Institutional Innovation and the Development of the U.S. Congress.* Princeton: Princeton University Press.

Schimank, Uwe, 2007: Die Anlagefonds und der Mittelstand: Paul Windolfs und Christoph Deutschmanns Studien über den "Finanzmarkt-Kapitalismus". *Leviathan.* Vol. 35, No. 1, 47–61.

Schmid, Frank A., 1997: Vorstandsbezüge, Aufsichtsratsvergütung und Aktionärsstruktur. *Zeitschrift für Betriebswirtschaft.* Vol. 67, No. 1, 67–83.

Schmitter, Philippe C., 1974: Still the Century of Corporatism? *Review of Politics.* Vol. 36, 85–131.

——and Wolfgang Streeck, 1999: The Organization of Business Interests: Studying the Associative Action of Business in Advanced Industrial Societies. MPIfG Discussion Paper 99/1. Cologne: Max Planck Institute for the Study of Societies.

Schnabel, Claus, 2005: Gewerkschaften und Arbeitgeberverbände: Organisationsgrade, Tarifbindung und Einflüsse auf Löhne und Beschäftigung. Discussion Paper No. 34. Erlangen-Nürnberg: Friedrich-Alexander-Universität.

Schröder, Wolfgang and Hartmut Ruppert, 1996: Austritte aus Arbeitgeberverbänden: Motive, Ursachen, Ausmaß. *WSI-Mitteilungen.* Vol. 49, No. 5, 316–28.

Schumpeter, Joseph A., 1975 [1942]: *Capitalism, Socialism, and Democracy.* New York: Harper.

——1991 [1918]: The Crisis of the Tax State. In: Swedberg, Richard (ed.), *The Economics and Sociology of Capitalism.* Princeton: Princeton University Press, 99–141.

——2006 [1912]: *Theorie der wirtschaftlichen Entwicklung.* Berlin: Duncker & Humblot.

Seifert, Hartmut, 2002: *Betriebliche Bündnisse für Arbeit: Rahmenbedingungen, Praxiserfahrungen, Zukunftsperspektiven.* Berlin: edition sigma.

Sewell, William H., Jr., 2005: *Logics of History: Social Theory and Social Transformation.* Chicago: Chicago University Press.

——2008: The Temporalities of Capitalism. *Socio-Economic Review.* Vol. 6. <doi:10.1093/ser/mwn007>.

Shonfield, Andrew, 1965: *Modern Capitalism: The Changing Balance of Public and Private Power.* London: Oxford University Press.

Skocpol, Theda, 1979: *States and Social Revolutions: A Comparative Analysis of France, Russia, and China.* Cambridge: Cambridge University Press.

Smith, Adam, 1993 [1776]: *An Inquiry into the Nature and Causes of the Wealth of Nations*. Oxford: Oxford University Press.

Soskice, David, 1990: Wage Determination: The Changing Role of Institutions in Advanced Industrialized Countries. *Oxford Review of Economic Policy*. Vol. 6, 36–61.

—— 1999: Divergent Production Regimes: Coordinated and Uncoordinated Market Economies in the 1980s and 1990s. In: Kitschelt, Herbert et al. (eds.), *Continuity and Change in Contemporary Capitalism*. Cambridge: Cambridge University Press, 101–34.

Steinmetz, George, 1991: Workers and the Welfare State in Germany. *International Labor and Working Class History*. Vol. 40, No. 1, 18–46.

Streeck, Wolfgang, 1979: Gewerkschaftsorganisation und industrielle Beziehungen: Einige Stabilitätsprobleme industriegewerkschaftlicher Interessenvertretung und ihre Lösung im System der industriellen Beziehungen der Bundesrepublik Deutschland. In: Matthes, Joachim (ed.), *Sozialer Wandel in Westeuropa. Verhandlungen des 19. Deutschen Soziologentages*. Frankfurt a.M.: Campus, 206–26.

—— 1982: Organizational Consequences of Corporatist Cooperation in West German Labor Unions: A Case Study. In: Lehmbruch, Gerhard and Philippe C. Schmitter (eds.), *Patterns of Corporatist Policy-Making*. London: Sage, 29–81.

—— 1984a: Co-Determination: The Fourth Decade. In: Wilpert, Bernhard and Arndt Sorge (eds.), *International Perspectives on Organizational Democracy. International Yearbook of Organizational Democracy*. London: John Wiley & Sons, 391–422.

—— 1984b: Neo-Corporatist Industrial Relations and the Economic Crisis in West Germany. In: Goldthorpe, John H. (ed.), *Order and Conflict in Contemporary Capitalism: Studies in the Political Economy of West European Nations*. Oxford: Clarendon Press, 291–314.

—— 1987: Industrial Relations and Industrial Change: The Restructuring of the World Automobile Industry in the 1970s. *Economic and Industrial Democracy*. Vol. 8, 437–62.

—— 1989a: Successful Adjustment to Turbulent Markets: The Automobile Industry. In: Katzenstein, Peter J. (ed.), *Industry and Politics in West Germany: Toward the Third Republic*. Ithaca, NY: Cornell University Press, 113–56.

—— 1989b: The Territorial Organization of Interests and the Logics of Associative Action: The Case of Handwerk Organization in West Germany. In: Coleman, William D. and Henry J. Jacek (eds.), *Regionalism, Business Interests and Public Policy*. London: Sage, 59–94.

—— 1991: On the Institutional Conditions of Diversified Quality Production. In: Matzner, Egon and Wolfgang Streeck (eds.), *Beyond Keynesianism: The Socio-Economics of Production and Employment*. London: Edward Elgar, 21–61.

—— 1994: Pay Restraint without Incomes Policy: Constitutionalized Monetarism and Industrial Unionism in Germany. In: Boyer, Robert et al. (eds.), *The Return to Incomes Policy*. London: Francis Pinter, 114–40.

—— 1997*a*: Beneficial Constraints: On the Economic Limits of Rational Voluntarism. In: Hollingsworth, J. Rogers and Robert Boyer (eds.), *Contemporary Capitalism: The Embeddedness of Institutions*. Cambridge: Cambridge University Press, 197–219.

—— 1997*b*: German Capitalism: Does It Exist? Can It Survive? *New Political Economy*. Vol. 2, No. 2, 237–56.

—— 2001*a*: High Equality, Low Activity: The Contribution of the Social Welfare System to the Stability of the German Divergences: Worldwide Changes in Employment Systems. *Industrial and Labor Relations Review*. Vol. 54, No. 3, 698–706.

—— 2001*b*: Introduction: Explorations into the Origins of Nonliberal Capitalism in Germany and Japan. In: Streeck, Wolfgang and Kozo Yamamura (eds.), *The Origins of Nonliberal Capitalism: Germany and Japan*. Ithaca, NY: Cornell University Press, 1–38.

—— 2001*c*: Tarifautonomie und Politik: Von der Konzertierten Aktion zum Bündnis für Arbeit. In: Arbeitgeberverbände, Gesamtverband der metallindustriellen Arbeitgeberverbände (ed.), *Die deutschen Arbeitsbeziehungen am Anfang des 21. Jahrhunderts: Eine Bestandsaufnahme. Wissenschaftliches Kolloquium aus Anlass des Ausscheidens von Dr. Werner Stumpfe als Präsident von Gesamtmetall*. Köln: Deutscher Institutsverlag, 76–102.

—— 2003: *No Longer the Century of Corporatism: Das Ende des "Bündnisses für Arbeit"*. MPIfG Discussion Paper 03/4. Cologne: Max Planck Institute for the Study of Societies.

—— 2004*a*: Educating Capitalists: A Rejoinder to Wright and Tsakalatos. *Socio-Economic Review*. Vol. 2, No. 3, 425–83.

—— 2004*b*: *Taking Uncertainty Seriously: Complementarity as a Moving Target*. Proceedings of OeNB Workshops No. 1. Wien: Österreichische Nationalbank.

—— 2005: From State Weakness as Strength to State Weakness as Weakness: Welfare Corporatism and the Private Use of the Public Interest. In: Green, Simon and William E. Paterson (eds.), *Governance in Contemporary Germany: The Semisovereign State Revisited*. Cambridge: Cambridge University Press.

—— 2006*a*: Nach dem Korporatismus: Neue Eliten, neue Konflikte. In: Münkler, Herfried et al. (eds.), *Deutschlands Eliten im Wandel*. Frankfurt a.M.: Campus, 149–75.

—— 2006*b*: The Study of Interest Groups: Before "The Century" and after. In: Crouch, Colin and Wolfgang Streeck (eds.), *The Diversity of Democracy: Corporatism, Social Order and Political Conflict*. London: Edward Elgar, 3–45.

—— 2007: Endgame? The Fiscal Crisis of the German State. MPIfG Discussion Paper 07/7. Cologne: Max Planck Institute for the Study of Societies.

Streeck, Wolfgang, and Anke Hassel, 2004: The Crumbling Pillars of Social Partnership. In: Kitschelt, Herbert and Wolfgang Streeck (eds.), *Germany: Beyond the Stable State*. London: Frank Cass, 101–24.

—— and Britta Rehder, 2003: Der Flächentarifvertrag: Krise, Stabilität und Wandel. *Industrielle Beziehungen*. Vol. 10, No. 3, 341–62.

—— and —— 2005: Institutionen im Wandel: Hat die Tarifautonomie eine Zukunft? In: Busch, Hans-Werner et al. (eds.), *Tarifpolitik im Umbruch*. Köln: Deutscher Institutsverlag, 49–82.

—— and Christine Trampusch, 2005: Economic Reform and the Political Economy of the German Welfare State. *German Politics*. Vol. 14, No. 2, 174–95.

Streeck, Wolfgang, and Jelle Visser, 2005: Conclusions: Organized Business Facing Internationalization. In: Streeck, Wolfgang et al. (eds.), *Governing Interests: Business Associations Facing Internationalization*. London: Routledge, 242–72.

—— and Kathleen Thelen, 2005: Introduction: Institutional Change in Advanced Political Economies. In: Streeck, Wolfgang and Kathleen Thelen (eds.), *Beyond Continuity: Institutional Change in Advanced Political Economies*. Oxford: Oxford University Press, 1–39.

—— and Kozo Yamamura (eds.), 2001: *The Origins of Nonliberal Capitalism: Germany and Japan*. Ithaca, NY: Cornell University Press.

—— and Martin Höpner, 2003: Einleitung: Alle Macht dem Markt? Fallstudien zur Abwicklung der Deutschland AG. In: Streeck, Wolfgang and Martin Höpner (eds.), *Alle Macht dem Markt?* Frankfurt a.M.: Campus, 11–59.

—— and Philippe C. Schmitter, 1984: Community, Market, State and Associations? The Prospective Contribution of Interest Governance to Social Order. *European Sociological Review*. Vol. 1, 119–38.

—— and Wyn Grant, 1985: Large Firms and the Representation of Business in the UK and West German Construction Industries. In: Cawson, Alan (ed.), *Organized Interests and the State: Studies in Mesocorporatism*. London: Sage, 145–73.

—— Peter Seglow, and Pat Wallace, 1981: Competition and Monopoly in Interest Representation: A Comparative Analysis of Trade Union Structure in the Railway Industries of Great Britain and West Germany. *Organization Studies*. Vol. 2, 307–29.

Stryker, Robin, 1994: Rules, Resources, and Legitimacy Processes: Some Implications for Social Conflict, Order, and Change. *American Journal of Sociology*. Vol. 99, No. 4, 847–910.

—— 2003: Mind the Gap: Law, Institutional Analysis, and Socioeconomics. *Socio-Economic Review*. Vol. 1, No. 3, 335–67.

Thelen, Kathleen, 1999: Historical Institutionalism in Comparative Politics. *Annual Review of Political Science*. Vol. 2, 369–404.

—— 2000: Why German Employers Cannot Bring Themselves to Dismantle the German Model. In: Iversen, Thorben et al. (eds.), *Unions, Employers and Central Banks: Macroeconomic Coordination and Institutional Change in Social Market Economies*. Cambridge: Cambridge University Press, 138–72.

—— 2002: How Institutions Evolve: Insights from Comparative-Historical Analysis. In: Mahoney, James and Dietrich Rueschemeyer (eds.), *Comparative Historical Analysis in the Social Sciences*. New York: Cambridge University Press.

—— 2004: *How Institutions Evolve: The Political Economy of Skills in Germany, Britain, the United States, and Japan*. Cambridge, MA: Cambridge University Press.

Tocqueville, Alexis de, 1983: *The Old Regime and the French Revolution*. New York: Anchor Books.

—— 1988 [1835–40]: *Democracy in America*. New York: Harper Perennial.

Trampusch, Christine, 2005*a*: From Interest Groups to Parties: The Change in the Career Patterns of the Legislative Elite in German Social Policy. *German Politics*. Vol. 14, No. 1, 14–32.

—— 2005*b*: Institutional Resettlement: The Case of Early Retirement in Germany. In: Streeck, Wolfgang and Kathleen Thelen (eds.), *Beyond Continuity: Institutional Change in Advanced Political Economies*. Oxford: Oxford University Press, 203–28.

—— 2006*a*: Postkorporatismus in der Sozialpolitik: Folgen für die Gewerkschaften. *WSI-Mitteilungen*. Vol. 59, No. 6, 347–52.

—— 2006*b*: Status quo vadis? Die Pluralisierung und Liberalisierung der "Social-Politik" als Herausforderung für die politikwissenschaftliche und soziologische Sozialpolitikforschung. *Zeitschrift für Sozialreform*. Vol. 52, No. 3, 299–323.

Turner, Lowell, 1998: *Fighting for Partnership: Labor and Politics in Unified Germany*. Ithaca, NY: Cornell University Press.

Veblen, Thorstein, 1994 [1899]: *The Theory of the Leisure Class*. New York: Penguin.

Vitols, Sigurt, 2006: Das "deutsche Modell" in der politischen Ökonomie. In: Berghahn, Volker and Sigurt Vitols (eds.), *Gibt es einen deutschen Kapitalismus? Tradition und globale Perspektiven der sozialen Marktwirtschaft*. Frankfurt a.M.: Campus, 44–59.

Weber, Max, 1988 [1903–6]: Roscher und Knies und die logischen Probleme der historischen Nationalökonomie. In: Winckelmann, Johannes (ed.), *Gesammelte Aufsätze zur Wissenschaftslehre*. Tübingen: Mohr, 1–145.

Wiesenthal, Helmut, 2003: German Unification and "Model Germany": An Adventure of Institutional Conservatism. *West European Politics*. Vol. 26, No. 4, 37–58.

Wilke, Manfred and Hans-Peter Müller, 1991: *Die Gewerkschaften des DGB im deutschen Vereinigungsprozeß*. Konrad-Adenauer-Stiftung: Forschungsberichte No. 68. Melle: Knoth.

Williamson, Oliver E., Michael L. Wachter, and Jeffrey Harris, 1975: Understanding the Employment Relation: The Analysis of Idiosyncratic Exchange. *The Bell Journal of Economics*. Vol. 6, 250–78.

—— 1985: *The Economic Institutions of Capitalism: Firms, Markets, Relational Contracting*. New York: The Free Press.

—— 1987: The Economics of Governance: Framework and Implications. In: Langlois, Richard N. (ed.), *Economics as a Process*. Cambridge: Cambridge University Press.

Williamson, Oliver E. and William G. Ouchi, 1981: The Markets and Hierarchies Program of Research. In: Vandeven, Andrew (ed.), *Perspectives on Organization Design and Behavior*. New York: Wiley, 347–70.

Windolf, Paul and Jürgen Beyer, 1995: Kooperativer Kapitalismus: Unternehmensverflechtungen im internationalen Vergleich. *Kölner Zeitschrift für Soziologie und Sozialpsychologie*. Vol. 47, No. 1, 1–36.

Winkler, Heinrich August and Gerald D. Feldmann (eds.), 1974: *Organisierter Kapitalismus: Voraussetzungen und Anfänge*. Göttingen: Vandenhoeck & Ruprecht.

Wrong, Dennis, 1961: The Oversocialized Conception of Man in Modern Sociology. *American Sociological Review*. Vol. 26, No. 2, 183–93.

Zysman, John, 1983: *Governments, Markets, and Growth: Financial Systems and the Politics of Industrial Change*. Ithaca, NY: Cornell University Press.

Index

Italic numbers denote reference to illustrations.